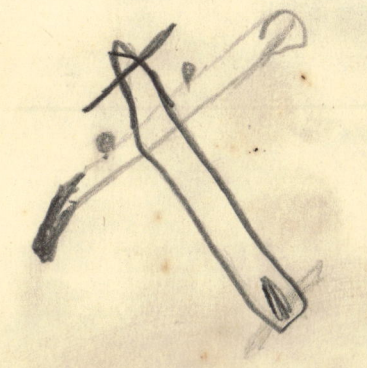

Harold Brenneman

Harold Brenneman

Harold Brenneman

My Grad book

Harold Brenneman
Wakarusa, Indiana
Box 274

HEALTH AND GROWTH SERIES

THE BODY'S NEEDS

*****
******

W. W. CHARTERS, Ph.D.
Bureau of Educational Research, College of Education,
Ohio State University

DEAN F. SMILEY, M.D.
Medical Adviser and Professor of Hygiene,
Cornell University

RUTH M. STRANG, Ph.D.
Assistant Professor of Education,
Teachers College, Columbia University

Illustrated with Drawings by
A. GLADYS PECK
and Photographs by
DORIS DAY

NEW YORK
THE MACMILLAN COMPANY
1936

COPYRIGHT, 1935,
BY THE MACMILLAN COMPANY.

All rights reserved—no part of this book may be reproduced in any form without permission in writing from the publisher, except by a reviewer who wishes to quote brief passages in connection with a review written for inclusion in magazine or newspaper.

Set up and electrotyped. Published January, 1935.
Reprinted June, October, 1935; January, June, 1936.

PRINTED IN THE UNITED STATES OF AMERICA

FOREWORD TO THE TEACHER

The major objectives of the authors in preparing the *Health and Growth* series were initially defined with clarity and kept in mind with consistency in the preparation of the texts.

In order to bring to the construction of the series the best thought concerning what should go into the books and how they should be organized, exhaustive basic studies of a wide variety were carried on over an extended period of time:

Statistics concerning the incidence of children's diseases and accidents were collected and interpreted to provide an indication of the school age at which materials upon these subjects should be most appropriately taught. Health columns in newspapers and health bulletins for laymen were analyzed to discover the vocabulary children should be taught to enable them to continue to read intelligently popular health articles after graduation and in adult life. The difficulty of words was ascertained for each grade to enable the authors to use words known by eighty per cent of the class, except necessary technical terms which would be carefully explained. A complete list of such preliminary studies made is given in the *Teachers' Manual*.

The initial purpose of this series, as it should be of any series of textbooks, is to lead the child to like the subject — to make its mastery so interesting that it becomes a favorite subject of study. The primary method of creating this interest is to teach a unit when the learner sees a good reason for its introduction — precautions when colds are in season, safety in the "accident years" of childhood. Supplementary methods are legion. They include, of course, illustrations that depict real health situations.

A second objective that has special significance in this field is to establish habits of health. To that end what one *does* is of more importance than what one *knows*. Good health is maintained by actions and not by knowledge alone. To acquire habits of right living, no time is so opportune as the period of childhood. All methods of habit building should be used — interest in the activity, an understanding of its physiological purpose, repetition until habituation occurs, use in varied situations, and satisfaction in the outcome.

A third objective of major importance is to furnish the child with the latest scientific information about health and disease. Much misinformation is still prevalent in the homes of the nation. This can be eradicated in the next generation only provided the child learns proved facts in the schoolroom. Much can be eradicated in the homes of this generation by the practice of having the child read his texts with his parents.

For their co-operation in the preparation of the posed photographs, the authors' indebtedness is gratefully acknowledged to Supervising Principal Charles A. Philhower, Principal B. D. Stuart of the Franklin School, and Principal G. D. Smith of the Roosevelt Junior High School of Westfield, New Jersey.

The Authors

CONTENTS

Part One

Planning and Eating Meals	3
Digesting Food	40
Water, Safe and Satisfying	58
Milk in Your Daily Meals	71
Meat in Your Daily Meals	87
Sweets in Your Daily Food	96
Fruits and Vegetables in Your Daily Food	104
Somebody Hurt or in Pain?	122
Preventing Illness	142
Using — Not Abusing — the Eyes	157
Making Vacations Pleasant and Worth While	169

Part Two

Unseen Worlds	195
How to Make and Keep Milk Safe	204
Aiding Digestion	214
A Healthful School Lunch	221
Keeping House	229
Facts about Smoking	244
Facts about Alcohol and Drugs	256

CONTENTS

Preventing Tooth Decay 264
Battling with Bacteria 273
Protection from Bacteria 284
Chemical War on Bacteria 301
Protecting Others from Bacteria . . . 319
Insects That Carry Disease 333
Safety for More and Better Adventures . . 344
Buying Your Own Clothes and Shoes . . 356
Buying and Cooking Food 367
Planning Your Day 378

    APPENDIX: Height-Weight Tables . . 395
    GLOSSARY 399
    INDEX 419

PART ONE

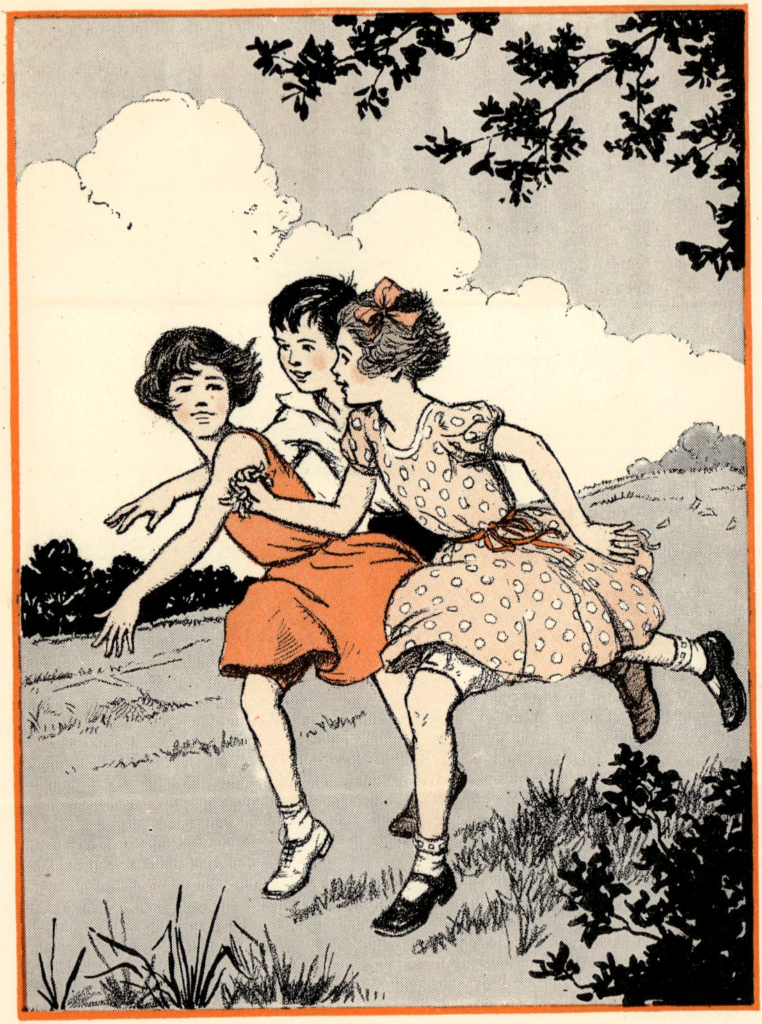

PLANNING AND EATING MEALS

The Need of Food

Have you ever thought that food makes play possible? Without food you could not go fishing, run races, or play handball, baseball, volley ball, basket ball, dodge ball, hare and hounds, and the other games you like. You could not dance or do stunts.

During one month teachers kept a record of the questions which boys and girls asked about health. A great many of these questions were about food. It is not strange that people are interested in food. Just think how much time is spent in buying, cooking, and eating food. Last year, you probably ate three meals every one of the 365 days of the year — a total of more than a thousand meals. If you live to be sixty years old and eat three meals every day, how many more meals will you eat during your lifetime?

We can "eat ourselves sick" or "eat ourselves well." Studying how to plan healthful meals, how to buy fresh foods cheaply, and how to cook them in the best way is very worth while.

Facts about food which you already know. Can you answer the following questions? If you do not know the answer to any question, look it up at the end of this chapter. Do not guess.

1. What are the best foods to eat at recess or after school if you need a lunch?
2. Why should you not eat between meals unless you really need extra food?
3. When is candy bad for you?
4. Why is milk good for children?
5. What foods are made from milk?
6. What is better for breakfast than hot breads, such as biscuit, buns, and pancakes?
7. What is graham*[1] bread?
8. What drinks are healthful?
9. What drinks are unhealthful?
10. How much time is needed for each meal?

Why do you need food? Food has three chief uses: to help you grow, to give you power to work and play, and to keep the body in good working order.

Food is needed for growth. A baby weighing eight pounds may grow into a man or woman weighing

---

[1] Starred words are defined in the Glossary at the end of the book.

twenty times that amount. Food helps to make children grow. It is possible to make children and

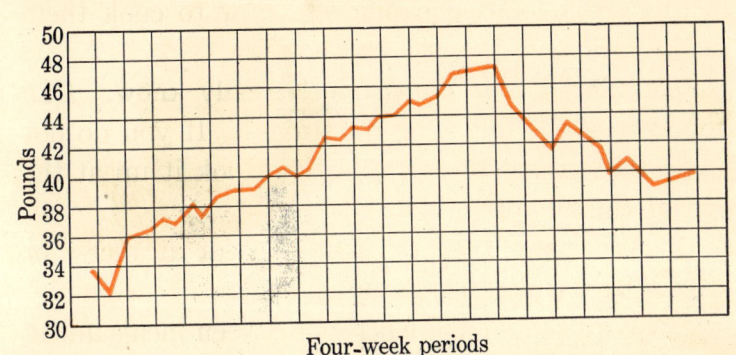

A quart of milk was taken away from the diet in the thirteenth period.

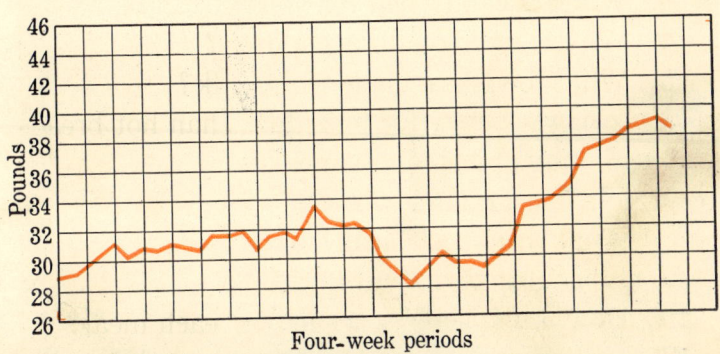

A quart of milk was added to the diet in the thirteenth period.

Growth curves of children

animals stop growing just by changing their food. Look at the weight records on this page. A line going upward means gain in weight. A line going downward means loss in weight. See how the lines go up when the children are given milk. See how the lines go down when the milk is taken away.

Food for growth

Photo by J. C. Allen & Son

A child becomes taller and heavier as his body cells* grow in size and number. Body cells are the smallest parts of the body. They are the

KINDS OF BODY CELLS

building blocks. Look at the pictures of cells on this page.

Cells are of many different kinds. There are muscle* cells. Muscles are made of muscle cells. There are bone cells. Bones are made of bone cells. There are nerve* cells and blood cells. The skin is

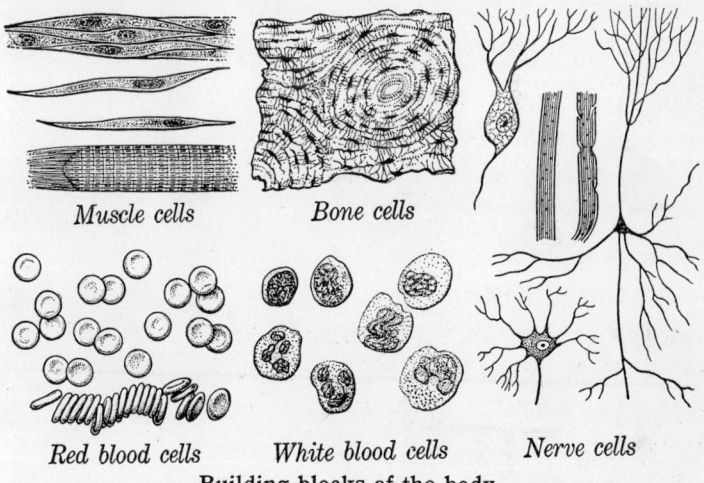

Muscle cells   *Bone cells*

Red blood cells   *White blood cells*   *Nerve cells*
Building blocks of the body

built of millions of tiny skin cells. Cells of the same kind grouped together are called tissues.* There are muscle tissues, bone tissues, nerve tissues, and other kinds of tissue. The cells are surrounded by water. One might say cells are water animals. They need water and food all the time.

Food is needed for power. Food gives energy,* or power to work and play. A person who, for some time, has been too sick to eat becomes weak. He can hardly walk when he first tries to get out of bed. The players on a football team are careful to have the right kind and amount of food. They need power. A general once said that an army marches on its stomach. What do you think he meant?

How does food furnish power? How does gasoline in the automobile engine make the automobile go? Gasoline is fuel. It is burned in the engine. Food is fuel. It is burned in the body. As it burns, energy is let loose. This energy moves the muscles in somewhat the same way that the energy from gasoline makes an automobile engine run.

At the same time heat is given off. As the food burns, it gives off heat, just as coal gives off heat when it is burned. You have noticed how warm a room becomes when there are a great many people in it. Some of the heat which makes the room warm is given off from people's bodies. The heat is produced by food burning in body cells.

Food is needed to keep the body in good working order. Certain substances in food help to keep the body running. The very life of every cell depends upon the right amount of iron. Without the right amount of calcium* the heart would not beat. Without calcium the muscles of the arms and legs would not move. Without calcium and other sub-

OTHER USES OF FOOD

stances in food you could not think or feel; food would not digest; wastes would not be removed. These substances in food make growth possible. They also help the body to use its fuel to the best advantage. Milk, leafy vegetables, and raw

Food is needed for power.

vegetables and fruits are *not merely fuel* and growth material. They are three of the most important kinds of food to keep the body working smoothly.

Planning Healthful Meals

How can you judge whether a breakfast is healthful? A healthful breakfast is one which contains foods from the first four of the following groups:

Breakfast foods

1. Milk in some form: a glass of milk to drink; milk on cereal;* milk toast; or hot milk with a little cocoa or other flavor.

2. Cereal or bread in some form: hot cooked cereal, such as oatmeal, cream of wheat, or cornmeal; ready-to-eat cereal, such as rice flakes, corn flakes, or puffed

wheat; toast — crisp and dry; or hard rolls. Butter, cream, or other food furnishing fat is, of course, eaten with the bread or cereal.

3. Fruit, if possible: an orange or orange juice; fresh fruit and berries in season; cooked fruit, such as applesauce; or dried or canned fruit.

4. An egg, if your mother can afford it: soft boiled, poached, or scrambled.

5. No foods which are very rich, or sweet, or soggy. Foods of this kind are sirups and cake, and soft hot biscuit, rolls, and pancakes.

6. No overstimulating* drinks, such as coffee.

Do boys and girls eat healthful breakfasts? Now judge the following breakfasts which some boys and girls ate one Saturday morning. Which of the menus do you think are healthful for a boy or girl? Which do you think can be improved? Write the good breakfasts on a piece of paper. Change the poorly planned breakfasts into good ones. Then write them also. Show the good menus to your mother.

1. Corn flakes and milk
    Soft-boiled egg and toast
    Cup of hot milk
2. Cup of coffee
    Rolls and butter
3. Fruit
    Pancakes with sirup
    Cup of coffee
4. Oatmeal and milk
    Roll and butter
    Glass of milk

5. An orange or tomato juice
   A cup of cream of wheat with ½ cup of top milk

   A slice of toast and an egg
   Glass of milk

Why are some of the above breakfasts better than others? Breakfast No. 1 is a good breakfast. It has milk with the cereal and hot milk to drink. It has toast and an egg. Does it lack anything?

Breakfast No. 2 has only one of the essentials* of a good breakfast. What is it? It has coffee, which crowds out good food. Coffee is too stimulating. It furnishes no power for work or play.

Breakfast No. 3 is a poor breakfast in spite of the fruit. It has no milk. The pancakes and sirup are not so good as hard toast and butter, and coffee has stolen in again.

Breakfast No. 4 is cheap and healthful. There is plenty of milk and cereal and bread in this breakfast. Some raisins or dates in the oatmeal would make it taste still better. An orange or other fresh fruit would be an excellent addition.

No. 5 contains all the essentials of a good breakfast. It includes milk, cereal and bread, fruit, and an egg. There are no sweet, rich, or overstimulating foods in this breakfast.

MAKING A GOOD BREAKFAST BETTER

Can a well-planned breakfast be spoiled? It is not the food alone that makes a good breakfast. At least two other things are important: time to eat it and pleasant company. The best breakfast, like No. 5, may

What makes this a good breakfast?

be spoiled by eating it in a hurry, by not chewing it well, or by worrying about being late to school.

A boy and girl with the help of their wise mother have the following plan: They go to bed at eight or half past eight so that they can get up at seven o'clock the next morning. This gives them time to bathe, dress, and eat an orange or other fruit. They come in to breakfast at a quarter to eight.

14   PLANNING AND EATING MEALS

They sit down at a clean table set with pretty dishes and often having flowers or fruit in the center. They have half an hour to laugh and talk and eat a good,

1. Milk in different forms. (Compare page 18.)

MAKING MEALS PLEASANT 15

hot cereal with creamy milk on it, crisp brown toast, scrambled eggs, and a glass of milk. Then they

2. Fruits and vegetables. (Compare page 18.)

16 PLANNING AND EATING MEALS

quickly clear the table, wash the breakfast dishes, and pack their books for school. They walk to school slowly and safely in about fifteen minutes.

3. Cheese, beans, and eggs. (Compare page 18.)

Which foods make a healthful lunch or supper? You will find in a healthful lunch or supper many of

GOOD FOODS FOR LUNCH AND SUPPER 17

your good breakfast foods. Test your lunches and suppers by the following rule: A good lunch or supper is one which includes some food from each of the following four groups:

4. Bread, cereal, and starchy vegetable. (Compare page 18.)

1. Milk in some form: a glass of milk to drink; milk soup; milk toast; a simple pudding made of milk, such as custard,* junket,* or rice pudding.

2. Vegetables and fruit, one of them served raw: carrots, peas, beets, corn, and the like; lettuce, celery, cabbage, beet greens, asparagus, dandelion greens, string beans, spinach, Swiss chard,* or other greens; oranges, tomatoes, apples, pears, peaches, grapes, bananas, berries, or other fruit.

3. Cheese, eggs, peanut butter, or baked beans.

4. Bread, cereal, or starchy vegetable: bread, toast, or rolls; wheat cereal, rice, macaroni; potatoes.

No foods should be included that are over-stimulating to children or difficult to digest: coffee, tea; sweet, rich foods, such as cakes and rich pies; fat meats in large amounts.

No meat is necessary if meat is served in another meal during the day. Butter, cream, or other fat is, of course, eaten with the bread, vegetables, and other foods. Many people like a salad dressing made of three tablespoonfuls of oil, one tablespoonful of lemon juice, and salt and pepper.

Judge other children's lunches and suppers by your rule. Now, having a pattern by which to judge lunches and suppers, choose the most healthful ones from the following luncheons and suppers which boys and girls actually ate one day. Write the best lunches and suppers. Which of the meals do you think could be made better? Change the poorly planned meals into good ones. Then write them also and show them to your mother.

1. Cocoa and buns
   Chocolate cake
2. Vegetable salad
   Bread and butter
3. Roast beef
   Potatoes
   Apple pie
4. Meat sandwiches
   A cup of coffee
5. Egg sandwiches
   Fruit
6. Cereal and milk
   Applesauce
7. Baked potato, carrots, and spinach
   Lettuce and tomato salad
   Cup custard

Why some of the lunches and suppers are better than others. Lunch No. 1 lacks vegetables and fruit. There is too much chocolate, which, like coffee, is overstimulating. A fruit salad, cocoa, and bread would have been a better choice.

Lunch No. 2 is good as far as it goes. A glass of milk or cup of junket would complete it. On cold days a thick vegetable soup instead of the salad would be excellent.

No. 3 is really a dinner. You do not need two dinners in one day.

No. 4 is another poor lunch in the group. Don't you think so? It has no milk, no vegetables, no fruit, no cheese, no eggs. Instead of these healthful foods, you find coffee, which is not a food at all.

No. 5 is a school lunch which almost any boy or girl might have. It is very easy to scramble the eggs and spread them between slices of buttered bread, to wash the fruit, and to put the sandwiches and fruit wrapped in waxed paper in the lunch box. A handful of raisins and nuts is a good sweet to add.

No. 6 is a simple, healthful supper. A big bowl of corn flakes or rice or other cereal with at least a cup of creamy milk and a dish of applesauce is a lunch or supper fit for a king.

In No. 7 you find excellent foods for either lunch or supper: milk and egg in the custard, both cooked and raw vegetables, and no food that is too sweet, or too rich, or overstimulating.

The eating of a meal should also be well planned. Sometimes a good lunch is spoiled by eating it in a hurry, by quarreling with a brother or sister, or by being scolded by one's father or mother. Sometimes a well-planned lunch is spoiled by being served on dirty dishes on a table or in a room that is not clean.

Tom does not spoil the good lunch which his mother has ready for him when he comes home from school. He leaves school promptly at twelve o'clock, because the safety patrol is on duty then. Tom walks

WISE LUNCHEON PLANS 21

home briskly in ten minutes, washes his hands and face, and has a half-hour to sit down and eat the lunch which his mother has ready for him. While he is eating, he has time to talk with his mother about interesting things which have happened. He has

fifteen minutes to walk back to school. He does not have to hurry.

Jane lives a mile from the school and would have to eat in a hurry if she went home at noon. So she takes her lunch to school. On sunny days she and her friends eat their lunches out of doors. It is like having a picnic every day. They spend the entire noon hour out of doors playing games like Still Pond No More Moving, Steps, and Blindman's Buff.

Sometimes they take a walk after they have eaten. Sometimes they give a play.

Angelina lives four blocks from the school, and since her mother works during the day she has to come home at noon and get lunch for her little brothers and sisters. They have a very simple lunch of buttered graham crackers and milk, or cereal and milk, or hot milk toast. It takes only five minutes to prepare a lunch of this kind and they have a half-hour in which to eat it. Angelina's mother usually also gives them some fruit — apples, peaches, pears, grapes, or stewed prunes or other dried fruit. When they have eaten lunch, the children wash their own bowls and spoons and help put the dishes away.

Use the following guide in choosing your dinners. Dinner is usually the meal which all the family eat together. In some places it is served at noon; in other places people have their dinner at night.

A well-planned dinner includes: (1) meat, fish, eggs, cheese, or milk; (2) potatoes, bread, or cereal; (3) a green leafy vegetable; (4) some raw vegetable or fruit; (5) no tea or coffee; (6) no very rich or sweet foods which irritate* the stomach or are hard to digest. Butter, fat of meat, or other kinds of fat are, of course, included in the meal.

Some boys and girls eat much better dinners than others. The following are dinners which some children have eaten. Which meals do you think are well planned? Which do you think could be improved? Write the best dinners. Change the

1. Dinner foods. (Compare pages 25-27.)

24   PLANNING AND EATING MEALS

poorly planned dinners into good ones. Then write a list of the foods which they contain.

2. Dinner foods. (Compare pages 25–27.)

FOODS FROM WHICH TO BUILD DINNERS 25

1. Meat
    Mashed potatoes,
    string beans
    A glass of milk
2. Frankfurters
    A glass of milk
    Chocolate cake
3. Potatoes, beets, spinach, raw celery
    Milk and cake

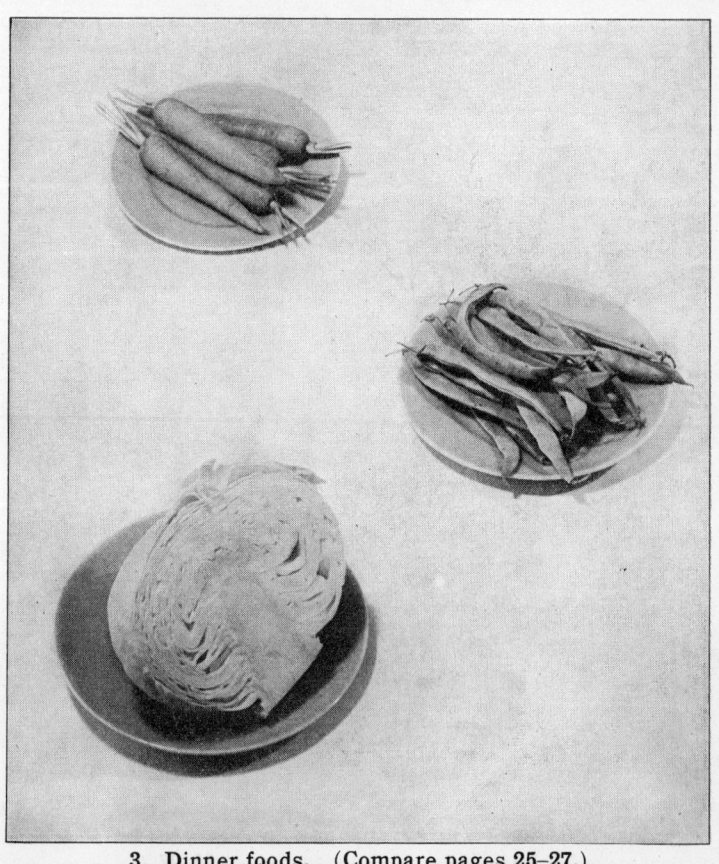

3. Dinner foods. (Compare pages 25-27.)

26 PLANNING AND EATING MEALS

4. Meat
   Potatoes and gravy

5. Fish
   Potatoes, string beans

4. Dinner foods. (Compare pages 25-27.)

BUILDING BETTER DINNERS

Lettuce salad with
French dressing
Bread pudding

6. Meat and bread
Macaroni* and cheese
Cake and tea

Why are some of these dinners better than others?
The first dinner is a good one which many people eat. A peach, pear, apple, piece of celery, or other raw fruit or vegetable in season would make this dinner better. Of course, butter or other fat will be included.

The second does not meet the requirements of a good dinner, does it? Frankfurters frequently have too much pepper and other seasoning in them. Chocolate cake is a very rich and sweet dessert. There are no vegetables or fruit in this meal.

No. 3 is a vegetable dinner which many people like. They frequently have a poached egg on the spinach. Milk with cake, such as sponge cake, molasses cake, or cookies, is a good dessert.

Dinner No. 4 is common in the United States. But is it a healthful meal? No, it is lacking in cooked green vegetables and in salad or raw fruit. A cooked green vegetable, such as spinach, cabbage, or Swiss chard, and a dessert of sliced oranges and bananas or other raw fruit would make this dinner of meat and potatoes more healthful.

No. 5 is a well-planned dinner. Fish may well be served instead of meat several times a week.

No. 6 is a poorly planned meal because three of its foods — bread, macaroni, and cake — are in one group. They are all starchy foods. A dinner of macaroni and cheese and a fruit salad would be a much better meal. What are you going to put in place of the tea?

Dinner is often the pleasantest meal of the day. If it is in the evening, the day's work is over. The family is together. Some people have fruit or flowers and lighted candles on the table. Dinner can be a jolly meal, with well-cooked food served cleanly and neatly.

Should summer meals be different from winter meals? If winter meals are simple and well planned, you will not need to change them much in summer. The chief changes you may wish to make are: (1) to include less meat in warm weather, (2) to serve more vegetables and fruits and less fatty foods, and (3) to have all the foods cooked still more simply.

In warm weather, food spoils quickly if it is not kept cold. People who have iceboxes keep milk, butter, and cooked foods in the coldest part of the icebox. The electric refrigerator* is now very commonly used. It keeps all the foods placed in it about equally cold. People who have no iceboxes try to cook just enough food for one meal. They try not to have "left-overs."

CHOICE AND CARE OF FOODS

Spoiled food may cause sickness. You cannot always tell whether food is fit to eat by its taste. In one town a number of people suddenly became sick. Some people thought it was meat that had caused

How should the inside of the icebox be kept?

the trouble. Then someone examined the meat. He said it was good to eat because it did not look spoiled or smell spoiled. He was so sure it was safe that he ate several pieces of it himself. He too soon became ill.

If cooked food has been standing uncovered in a warm place from one meal to the next, it is safer not to use it. Why should food be kept covered? How can you keep flies away from your food in the summer?

In cold weather you should try to have some hot food in every meal. By eating warm food, you are bringing heat into the body. If you eat cold food, you are using body heat to warm the food.

Other questions about meals. *Should we change our meals when we change our work and play?* Do you eat the same kind and amount of food at camp that you eat when you are studying hard at school? If your father were chopping down trees in the northern woods, would he eat the same meals that he eats when sitting at a desk most of the day?

When you change your work and play, you should change the amount of food in your meals. You do not often need to change the kind of food. At camp you should have the same kind of simple, well-planned meals that you have at home. The breakfasts, dinners, and suppers you have planned are good for both winter and summer and for school days and vacations.

Your habits should not change greatly during the year. When you are at school, you should play or work out of doors in the afternoons and on Saturdays.

When you are having your vacation, you should spend part of the day resting and reading.

How many meals a day should we eat? Savages have had to eat whenever they could get food. Two thousand years ago certain people were thought greedy because they had two meals a day. In the days when knights rode to battle, few of the English people had more than two meals a day. At the present time some people in Europe sit down to eat four or five times a day.

In the United States, three meals daily is the rule. There are two good reasons for having three meals a day: (1) The day's food can be comfortably eaten in three parts. There is little danger of filling the stomach too full. (2) The appetite for each meal may be better if most of the last meal has left the stomach.

Some very thin children gain weight when they have crackers and milk or orange juice in the middle of the morning or in the middle of the afternoon. But it is not a good plan to eat at these times unless the doctor says you need more than three regular meals.

QUESTIONS ANSWERED

Answers to the questions asked on page 4. 1. The best foods to eat at recess or after school if the doctor says that you really need them are: plain crackers and milk, orange juice, or other fruit. Just a drink of water is the best choice for children who are well fed.

2. One reason why we should not eat much food between meals is that it takes away our appetite for the three regular meals.

3. Candy is bad for us: (*a*) when it is eaten between meals; (*b*) when it is eaten at the beginning of a meal; (*c*) when it crowds out vegetables, cereals, and fruits; (*d*) when it is left sticking to the teeth after meals; (*e*) when more than two pieces about the size of a walnut are eaten at one time.

4. Milk is good for children because: (*a*) it helps them to grow; (*b*) it helps to build strong teeth and bones; (*c*) it helps to keep children well.

5. Butter, cream, cheese, and buttermilk are made from milk.

6. Hot cereal is better than hot breads for breakfast.

7. Graham bread is made from the whole-wheat grain. It was named for Sylvester Graham, who told people how healthful bread made from the whole wheat is.

8. Healthful beverages* are water, milk, orange juice, and other fresh-fruit juices.

9. Unhealthful beverages are tea, coffee, most "soft" drinks, beer, wine, and other drinks with alcohol in them.

10. You should allow at least fifteen minutes for breakfast and half an hour for the other two meals.

OTHER CHILDREN'S QUESTIONS

The following are questions which children have asked about food. First try to answer each question yourself. If you are sure you know the right answer, write it on a piece of paper. Then find the answer among the answers given. Compare it with your answer. You will have to hunt for the right answer, because the answers are not in the same order as the questions. If you do not know the answer to a question, look it up among the answers given. Do not guess.

1. Why do so many grown-ups drink coffee?
2. Why does coffee keep some people awake at night?
3. Why shouldn't we drink coffee?
4. What does *food value** mean?
5. How can we help our muscles to grow?
6. What kinds of food do lumberjacks eat? Why?
7. Why did sailors formerly die from scurvy?*
8. What is a menu?*

Answers. Coffee keeps some people awake at night because it contains a stimulant* called *caffeine*.* A stimulant says "Hurry up! Keep going!"

Muscles grow when you use them and when you eat the right kind and amount of food. Big muscles, however, are not always a sign of health. It is better to develop all the muscles in the body through many kinds of exercise than to overdevelop* certain muscles through a single kind of exercise.

Lumberjacks who work hard out of doors all day in cold weather need a large amount of food to give them power to work. They usually eat more meat, fat, baked beans, jam, and bread than do people who are sitting at a desk all day.

A *menu* is the list of foods served in a meal. Breakfast menus are given on page 11; luncheon menus, on page 19; dinner menus, on page 25. Write a good menu for your mother.

Grown-ups drink coffee because they have formed the "coffee habit." Some people have formed the habit because everybody else in their families drank coffee, or because coffee made them feel less tired for a short time, or because they were not eating the right kind and amount of food. Many grown people enjoy a cup of coffee and it does not seem to be harmful to them.

You should not drink coffee because: (*a*) Coffee crowds out milk. (*b*) Coffee keeps you wide awake and active when you need rest. (*c*) Coffee makes you more tired than ever when its stimulating* effect has worn off. (*d*) Coffee furnishes nothing the body needs for growth.

Sailors used to die from scurvy because they could

Why are sailors healthier today than they were fifty years ago?

not get any fresh vegetables or fruit. When they had been on the high seas for about six weeks with nothing to eat but salted meats and bread, scurvy was likely to appear. A very small amount of raw potato, lemon juice, or orange juice will prevent scurvy. Why do sailors today seldom have scurvy when it was so common in early days?

Food has value, or as we say, *food value*, when it contains the things which you need to make you grow, to give you power to work and play, and to help to keep you well.

THINGS TO DO

1. Take stock of your good food habits just as a storekeeper takes stock of all the things in his store. To how many of the following questions can you truly answer, "Always"? To how many would you answer, "Often"? To how many, "Seldom," or "Never"?

a. When you have money to spend at recess or after school, do you buy fruit or something to play with instead of candy?

b. Do you choose fruit instead of candy whenever choice is offered?

c. Do you eat at a time only one piece, or at the most two pieces, of candy about the size of a walnut?

d. Do you drink orange juice, grape juice, or other pure fresh-fruit juices instead of bright-colored drinks and other kinds of "soft" drinks?

e. Do you refuse alcoholic drinks of all kinds and, unless a doctor advises it, every kind of drug?

TAKING STOCK OF YOUR FOOD HABITS

f. Do you wash fruit before eating it raw?

g. Do you refuse to eat food from which another person has taken bites?

h. Do you say "no" to tea and coffee?

i. Do you use at least three cups of milk a day?

j. Do you eat a cooked, green leafy vegetable every day?

k. Do you eat two raw vegetables or fruits every day?

l. Do you eat whole-wheat or graham bread instead of white bread part of the time?

m. Do you eat a good breakfast of cereal or bread and milk and fruit, if possible, every day?

Why wash fruit?

n. Do you eat a good dinner of green leafy vegetables, raw vegetables or fruit, milk, bread and butter, and a small piece of meat, fish, or an egg every day?

o. Do you eat a healthful lunch or supper of bread or cereal and milk and vegetables or fruit every day?

PLANNING AND EATING MEALS

p. Do you eat willingly the food set before you?

q. Do you make mealtime a happy time by talking about pleasant things, by eating neatly, and by having other good table manners?

Can you make this breakfast still better?

r. Do you always wash your hands before eating?

s. Do you rest a while after eating?

t. Do you have a natural bowel movement* at a regular time every day?

u. Do you spend at least fifteen minutes for

SUMMER AND WINTER MENUS

breakfast and half an hour for each of the other two meals? Do you chew your food well?

If you do all these things, you have good food habits.

2. Here are menus for two days. Three are well suited to summer; the others, to winter. Which are the summer and which are the winter menus?

BREAKFAST	DINNER	SUPPER OR LUNCH
Fresh fruit	Omelet with asparagus tips	Vegetable salad
Corn flakes with cream		Toast
Toast	Creamed potatoes	Ice cream
Milk	Graham toast	
	Fruit cup	
	Milk	

BREAKFAST	DINNER	SUPPER OR LUNCH
Oranges	Potato soup	Macaroni and cheese
Oatmeal with cream	Beef with vegetables	Applesauce
Egg	Raw cabbage	Baked Indian pudding
Toast	Pumpkin pie	
Cocoa		

3. Try to find out what people in other lands eat, how they eat, and when they eat. Your geography books may tell you. If your father and mother or grandfather and grandmother came from other

countries, they can tell you about the food habits of those countries. People who have traveled will also give you the facts. Share what you have learned with your classmates.

4. Talk over this chapter in class with your teacher. Make a list of the facts you have learned. Make a list of the new health habits mentioned in the chapter. Write these lists. Put a star after each habit you have already formed. Try to form the other good habits as soon as possible. Do these things with each chapter in this book. 5. Make a class scrapbook of the new or important words in each chapter and write the meanings of each. Use each in a sentence. Find a picture about each, if possible. Such words are followed by a (*) the first time they appear in this book, and the meaning of each is given in the Glossary.

DIGESTING FOOD

Why is it important to chew food well? Why should you eat at regular times? How is digestion* helped by outdoor work and play? Why should you wash your hands and face before eating? Why should mealtime be a happy time? Why should you rest after eating? How does the body get rid of wastes?

THE CHANGES IN FOOD AS IT DIGESTS

What happens to the food you eat? Before you can answer the questions on page 40, it is necessary to know the answer to another question: "What happens to the food you eat?" The shortest answer is: "It is digested."* What takes place in digestion? In digestion foods are changed into a liquid which the body can use.

Foods like bread and meat in their solid form cannot give you energy for work and play. These solid foods must first be dissolved.* When you put salt in water, what happens? The salt disappears. It has been dissolved. When you put sugar in water, what happens? The sugar disappears in the water. It, too, has been dissolved. In a similar way all food must be changed to liquid form before the body can use it. That is, it must be dissolved.

Other changes take place, too, which you may sometime learn about. The process of changing food so that the body can use it is called *digestion*. The parts of the body where these changes take place are called the *digestive tract** (or the *digestive system**). You will find a picture of it on page 42.

Where does digestion begin? What happens to food in the mouth? The teeth cut off pieces of food and grind them into smaller pieces. Chewing

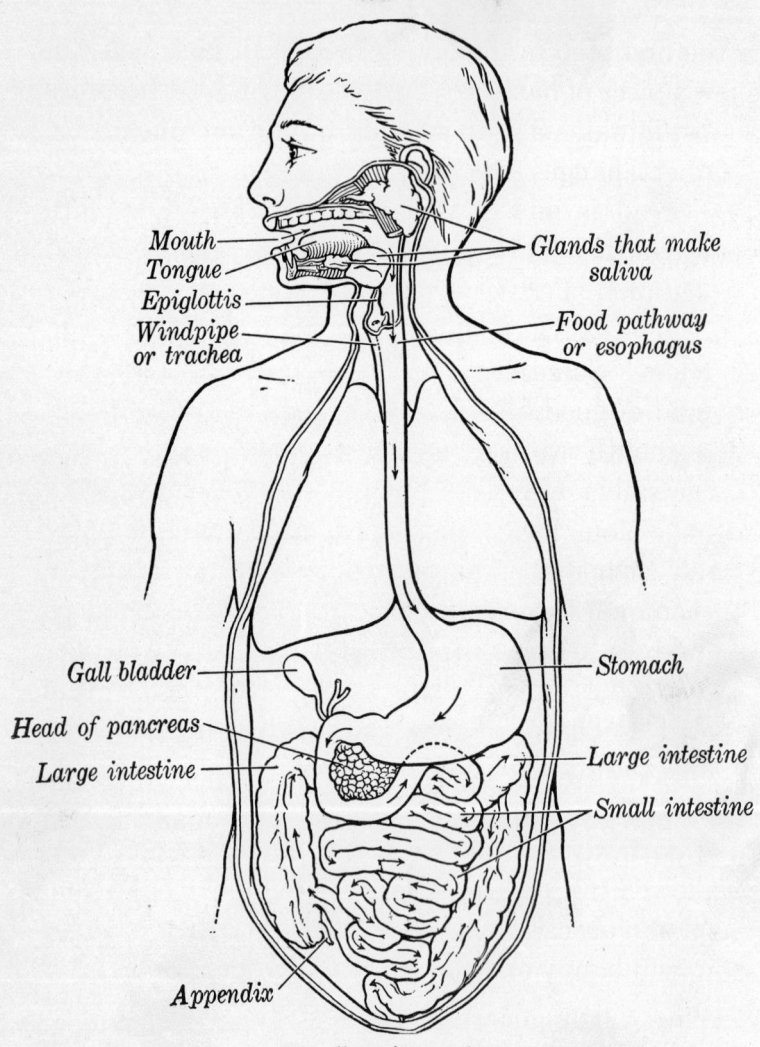

The digestive system

DIGESTION IN THE MOUTH

is the first step in dissolving food. In fact, you can chew a piece of hard, dry bread so long that it becomes almost liquid. Try to do this at your next meal.

Other changes are taking place while you chew. The bread is mixed with a liquid that flows into your mouth. This liquid is a digestive juice called the *saliva*.* Perhaps you have heard saliva called *spit*. The saliva begins to flow when the teeth begin to chew. Sometimes just the smell or even the thought of good food makes the saliva flow — makes "the mouth water," as some people say.

The saliva begins to change starch to a kind of sugar. You have seen cornstarch and laundry starch at home. They are pure starch. Many of our common foods contain starch. There is starch in potatoes. Bread contains starch. Have you ever noticed that bread tastes sweeter the longer you chew it? That is because the saliva is beginning to change the starch to sugar.

When food is swallowed, it goes down a tube — a food pathway — into the stomach. After you have swallowed the food, the changes are hidden from you. All that you can do to help digestion then is to be calm and happy and to rest or play quiet games after eating.

The stomach is a bag made of muscles, which stretches when food is put into it. On page 44 you will see a picture of the stomach when it is empty and when it is full. A person's stomach can hold only a certain amount of food at one time. All the food eaten in one meal may not entirely disappear from the stomach for six or seven hours.

The stomach has a lining very much like the lining of the mouth and throat. This lining can be made

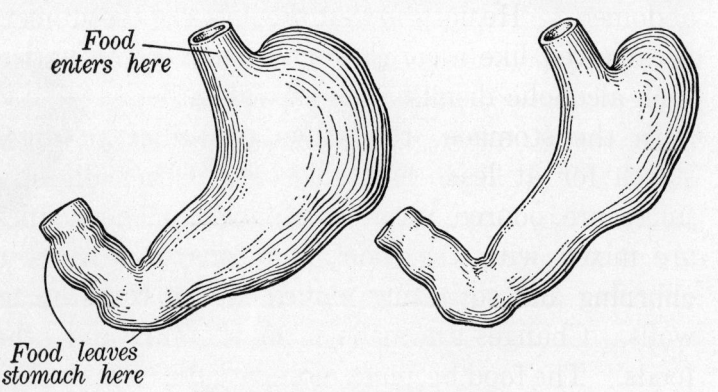

Food enters here

Food leaves stomach here

The stomach, full and empty

sore, or be irritated, by certain foods. Have you ever noticed any foods which made the lining of your mouth sore or hurt your throat? Candy, sweet syrups, pickles, pepper, spiced cakes, and other very sweet, very sour, or very spicy foods sometimes irritate the stomach lining. Lemonade, which is made from sour lemons and sugar, may irritate a sensitive stomach. Fresh, unsweetened orange juice is better.

Do you see that bran — the outside coat of the wheat seed or grain — might irritate the lining of the stomach? Why? Some people cannot eat bran muffins and bran bread for this reason.

Alcoholic* drinks also irritate the lining of the stomach. One doctor was able to look into the stomach of a patient who had been wounded in the abdomen.* He noticed that the lining of the stomach became red like a sore throat whenever the patient took alcoholic drinks, such as whisky.*

In the stomach, the saliva continues to digest starch for at least half an hour. Other digestive juices are poured into the stomach. These juices are mixed with the food by means of a series of churning and squeezing movements of the stomach walls. Changes are made in meat, milk, and other foods. The food becomes more liquid as it is churned in the stomach with the digestive juices.

As soon as the food in the stomach has become like smooth, thin soup, it is passed on into a tube about twenty feet long. This part of the digestive system is called the small *intestine*.* Find the small intestine in the picture on page 42. Here more digestive juices are mixed with the food. These digestive juices make the final changes in the food. It is now ready to be taken into the blood. The digested food finds its way into the little blood vessels in the lining of the small intestine. It is then carried by the blood to all the cells of the body.

There is some food that cannot be changed into a form which the body can use. Certain parts of fruits and vegetables, such as the tough threads you find in celery, cannot be dissolved by the digestive juices. The coarse pieces of bran from the outside of grains cannot be made liquid.

This left-over food may leave the body after a day or more. There are left-over digestive juices, too, and bodies of bacteria.* All of this waste material passes from the small intestine to another tube called the *large intestine* which you can see in the picture on page 42. What a long journey the food has had before the part which is not used in furnishing energy and building cells leaves the body!

The waste material stays in the large intestine until you have a bowel movement. That is the only way it can be got rid of. Waste which piles up in the large intestine may cause headaches or a tired feeling. This delay of bowel movement is called *constipation*.*

Good Habits in Eating

Now that you have followed the food along the digestive tract, it will be easier to answer the questions (page 40) at the beginning of this chapter.

Why chew well? Chewing breaks up the food into small pieces so that the digestive juices can make the changes more quickly. Look at the pictures of the large lump of food and the same lump broken into many pieces. Imagine digestive juices all around them. In which case is the food touched more often by digestive juices?

Another reason for chewing food well is that chewing brings out the flavor. You never know how delicious whole-wheat bread and butter tastes until you have chewed it well. Almost every food has its own delicious taste. Why not enjoy it? You enjoy your food more when you chew it thoroughly.

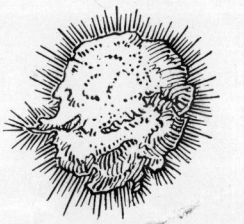

In order to chew well, you need strong teeth. Drinking milk, eating oranges, lettuce, and other fresh fruits and vegetables, and chewing some hard food in every meal help to build strong teeth and keep them from decaying.* Brushing the teeth after each meal whenever possible and going to the dentist twice a year also help. Have you formed all of these habits? You are probably getting more of your second teeth — your permanent* teeth — this

48 DIGESTING FOOD

year. Now is your chance to take good care of them when they first appear. You will not get any more in their places if you lose them by neglecting to do the simple things that help to prevent decay. Sound teeth are needed for the first step in digestion.

When are the best times to brush the teeth?

Why eat at regular times? When your mother plans your mealtimes, she chooses the best time for each meal. Supper or dinner should not be later than half past six. When you have meals earlier or later than the regular times, you are taking a second-best

REASONS FOR REGULARITY OF MEALS

choice of hours. Another reason for having your meals on time is that you are likely to feel hungry when your regular mealtime comes around. The

Why play out of doors?

digestive system seems to be more ready to digest food at regular mealtimes. You should be prompt for meals and you should not ask your mother for something to eat before the regular mealtime.

Why play and work out of doors between meals?
Appetite* is improved by being out of doors. Have you heard people say they were "working up an appetite" when they had spent the morning or afternoon

Why wash the hands before eating?

out of doors? When the appetite is good, digestive juices flow more freely and food digests better.

Why wash the hands and face before eating? Although we eat with knives and forks, we touch some foods such as bread with our hands. Bacteria from our hands and lips may be carried by the food into the mouth. Washing the hands and face thoroughly before eating helps to keep bacteria out of the body.

Why be pleasant? Food digests better when people are happy. You can spoil the best-planned meal for yourself and for the entire family by being cross, quarreling, or getting angry at mealtime.

We have proof of this. A famous scientist,* Walter B. Cannon, took pictures of a cat's stomach at work. How? He did it with an X-ray* machine, after he had first fed the cat a harmless substance which made the contents of its stomach easily seen. After eating, the contented cat began to digest its food. The stomach was working beautifully, mixing the food with the digestive juice. Then a strange dog was brought into the room. You know how excited and angry a cat often gets when it sees a dog. And what happened to the digestion which had started so well? The X-ray showed that the movements of the cat's stomach had stopped. Digestion had stopped.

Dr. Cannon found that even a cross or worried feeling caused digestive movements and the flow of digestive juices to stop. It pays to be pleasant at mealtime. Good table manners help to make a meal pleasant for everyone.

Why rest after eating? "After dinner, rest a while" is a good rule. It is natural that digestion cannot go on so well when you are working hard or playing an exciting game as when you are sitting or lying down. The effects of excitement on digestion last for some time. It is better also to rest a while before eating than to rush to meals directly from an exciting game.

Sometimes cramps* are caused by going swimming too soon after eating. During cramps certain muscles contract* against a person's will. Cramping muscles are painful. Why are cramps dangerous to a person swimming in deep water? People usually wait at least two hours after eating before they go swimming. Being too tired may also cause cramp.

How to get rid of body wastes. When the large intestine becomes so full that the indigestible waste material begins to press against its walls, certain muscles of the intestine begin to contract. They make squeezing movements. The waste material is shoved along the large intestine in much the same way that a rubber tube full of mud might be squeezed along its length until the mud is forced out at one end.

Do you see any suggestions in these facts for preventing constipation? First, develop strong muscular* walls in the intestine so that they will push the waste along with force. Second, eat some foods which will make the waste material bulky enough to press against the walls. Third, pay attention to the urge to go to the toilet whenever the signal is given.

What helps to make strong muscular walls? The same things which you have learned help to make strong muscles — exercise, good food, sunlight.

What kind of food makes a bulky waste in the intestine? Foods which have an indigestible thread-like part furnish bulk. Fruits, vegetables, and whole grains furnish this bulky part of the food. Many fruits and vegetables contain mild acids also, which encourage intestinal movement, especially if taken as soon as you get up in the morning. A glass of orange juice the first thing in the morning often helps to cause a natural bowel movement. Green leafy vegetables are very useful in getting rid of body waste and in thus preventing constipation.

A regular time for going to the toilet is also helpful in preventing constipation. If you go to the toilet every day at a certain time before or after breakfast and have a bowel movement then, it becomes easier and easier to form the daily habit.

Certain medicines help to make the muscles of the intestine move. They are called laxatives* or cathartics.* Castor oil is a cathartic which has been used a great deal. But when these medicines are used often, the muscles of the intestinal walls become weaker and weaker. They get the habit of expecting the medicine to help them and they become less and less able to send the waste material out of the body by their own strength. The lining of the intestine may become irritated by certain medicines. Therefore it is a good plan not to take laxatives or cathartics unless there is a real need for them.

Can you make some rules for getting rid of waste material in the body — five *do's* and three *don'ts*? What you have just read should help you.

OTHER CHILDREN'S QUESTIONS

Answer as many of the following questions as you can. Find the answers to the others.

1. Is it unhealthful to eat before going to bed?
2. Why do the natives of some countries eat with their fingers?
3. What foods are good for the teeth?
4. Why do gums bleed when the teeth are brushed?
5. How often ought you to clean your teeth?
6. What effect does putting oil of cloves in a tooth have on a toothache?

Answers. It is a good plan to clean your teeth at least twice a day. One of these times should be before you go to bed. Cleaning the teeth may help to prevent toothache. It certainly makes your mouth feel more pleasant.

Many people enjoy an apple or orange before going to bed. Some people take a glass of warm milk on cold nights. But any other food before going to bed is unnecessary so soon after you have eaten a good supper or dinner. Stimulating or rich foods, such as chocolate, tea, cake, and candy, should never be eaten

Celery and carrots — two of Nature's toothbrushes

before going to bed. They overload the stomach. They often keep people awake.

Milk, orange juice, tomato juice, lettuce, raw celery, and cabbage are some of the foods which are very good for the teeth.

The gums bleed when you brush them because they are not so healthy and firm as they should be. Perhaps bacteria are causing a disease of the gums. What does your dentist think about it?

"Fingers were made before forks" is an old saying. As people became more civilized, they began to use forks instead of fingers. In some countries today people still eat with their fingers. Why should we not eat with our fingers?

Putting oil of cloves in an aching tooth may stop the pain for a while, but it does not take away the cause of the pain. You should go to the dentist even though the tooth stops aching.

Things to Do

1. Study your own weight and growth. The table in the Appendix gives the height and weight of boys and girls of different ages and of different body builds. Decide whether you are of the tall, slender type, the short, stocky type, or the average type. Then find your age in the age column and your height in the height column. Now you are ready to compare your weight with the average weight for your height and age. Talk it over with your teacher or the school nurse.

2. When you go to the dentist, ask him to tell you the names of your teeth. Which are your permanent teeth? What are the names of the teeth you are getting this year?

THE TEETH, ONE BY ONE

3. Grate a potato or apple and find the stringy part that helps make the bulk needed to start intestinal movements. **4.** Do you have a toothbrush of your own? Do you keep it in a glass by itself or hanging in direct sunlight? Do you always use your own

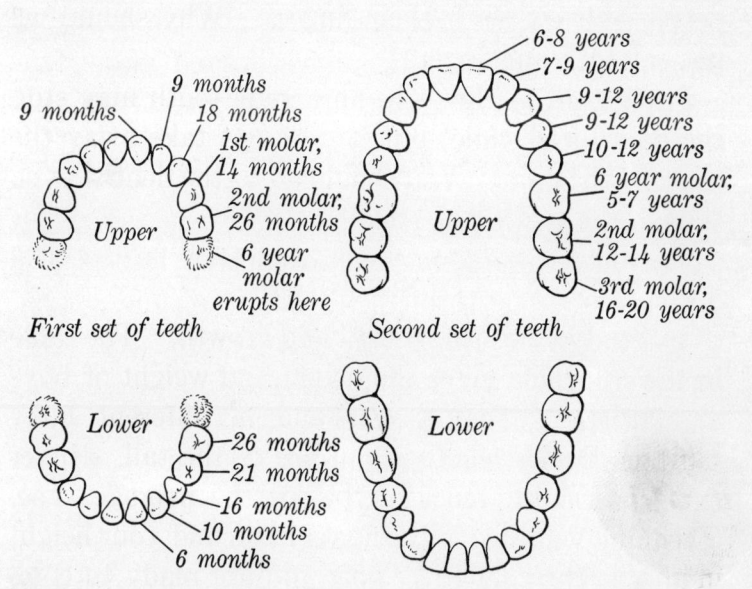

First set of teeth

Upper:
- 9 months
- 9 months
- 18 months
- 1st molar, 14 months
- 2nd molar, 26 months
- 6 year molar erupts here

Lower:
- 26 months
- 21 months
- 16 months
- 10 months
- 6 months

Second set of teeth

Upper:
- 6-8 years
- 7-9 years
- 9-12 years
- 9-12 years
- 10-12 years
- 6 year molar, 5-7 years
- 2nd molar, 12-14 years
- 3rd molar, 16-20 years

Lower

brush? What other habits regarding the care of the teeth do you think are important? **5.** Have you found any new health habits in this chapter? Add them to your list. Mark yourself on each of them, as suggested in the first chapter, page 40. **6.** Add the new words in this chapter to the class scrapbook. After each word write its meaning. If you are not sure of the meaning, look it up in the Glossary before you try to write it. Mark yourself on the new habits and learn the new words in each chapter.

WATER, SAFE AND SATISFYING

What is it that may cost little and yet is something that people at times have desired more than anything else in the world? One answer to this riddle is *water*.

OUR NEED OF WATER

You have probably read of people lost in the desert, stumbling through the hot sand and unable to get water. Perhaps you have read of sailors far out at sea, their water supply gone — "water, water, everywhere, and not a drop to drink." You yourself have surely been walking on a hot day and felt that you would give a great deal for a drink of cold, satisfying water.

People have lived as long as forty days without food; they can live only a few days without water. What happens to plants when you forget to water them? Water is necessary for all life and growth. You need water mainly for four reasons.

1. If your weight is 100 pounds, about 58 of those pounds are water. You are more than one half water; and your body is losing water all the

WATER, NECESSARY FOR LIFE 59

time. Sometimes you can see the water leaving your body in the perspiration* from the skin. Water is passing off from your skin all the time in small amounts even though you cannot see it. This

One use of water. Name other uses.

water that you cannot see is called *invisible perspiration.** Sometimes, on a cold day, you can see the water in your breath.

2. Water is needed for everyday cleanliness. How much water do you use in washing your hands and

face every day and in taking baths? How much water does your mother use in washing the dishes and in washing clothes? How much does she use in cooking? In what ways is water used in your town

Another use of water

or city? Is it used in washing the streets, putting out fires, and watering lawns? In some cities about a hundred gallons of water per person are used every day. Water is needed to keep the body clean inside as well as outside. It helps to carry away waste from the body.

USES OF WATER

3. Water also helps to digest your food. You remember that all the food you eat must be dissolved before it can be used to furnish power for work or play. Food is finally dissolved in water. The digestive juices, such as the saliva in the mouth, are largely water. Water makes up a part of all the juices which help to digest food.

4. You remember that the blood flowing round and round through the body helps to keep it the same temperature all over. The blood is chiefly water. Thus water helps to keep the body temperature just right in somewhat the same way that water in an automobile or motorboat engine prevents the engine from becoming overheated. How does the water in the perspiration help to cool the body?

How much water do you need every day? It is said that about three quarts of water are needed every day. Must we, then, drink twelve glasses of water a day? No, because there is a good deal of water in all our food. Potatoes are about three fourths water. Apples are slightly more than four fifths water. Tomatoes and oranges are still more watery. Even a loaf of bread is about one third water. We get almost four glasses of water in the quart of milk we drink daily.

A good rule is to drink a glass of water as soon as you get up, a second glass in the middle of the morning, and a third glass in the middle of the afternoon. You may have a glass of water at meals if you do not have soup or other liquid food and if you do not use the water to wash down the food. Take a drink of water at other times when you feel thirsty. In

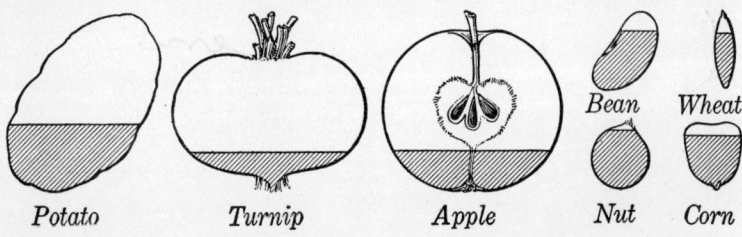

Potato   Turnip   Apple   Bean Nut   Wheat Corn
The white parts show how much water there is in common foods.

all these ways, the body is supplied with the water it needs.

OUR WATER SUPPLY

Is water ever dangerous? Water which contains bacteria that cause disease is dangerous. Water may look clear and sparkling and still contain dangerous bacteria. Many people have died of *typhoid fever** because the water they drank contained the bacteria which cause typhoid fever.

Where do people obtain their drinking water? If you had lived in far-off times, you would have got your water from brooks and rivers and springs. If you had lived in New York City more than one hundred years ago, you might have gone to the Chatham Street Tea-water Pump with your pail or jug to get water for your mother. There is a drawing of this old pump on page 64. You would have waited your turn while children and housewives, in

dresses and aprons which look queer to us now, filled their pails with water. You might have gone there on a certain day and found a crowd of people standing about the pump with empty pitchers.

"What is the matter?" you might have asked. And someone would have told you: "You cannot get any more water here. The water is not safe. The doctor says it has made many people sick." Then you would have gone away with your pail to get safe water somewhere else.

Well water is easily contaminated,* that is, made dangerous by bacteria. Have you ever seen an old

Chatham Street Tea-water Pump

well? In what ways might bacteria get into a well? Sometimes you pass old wells when you walk in the country. Never take a drink from them, no matter how thirsty you are. Never drink from any brooks, springs, or wells which you do not know to be safe. If you have any doubt about safety of the water, boil it ten minutes. Boiling kills bacteria.

DANGER FROM OLD WELLS

If you live in a big city, you turn the faucet and fill your glass with safe water from the city water supply. Cities spend many millions of dollars to secure safe water. But it is money well spent. The people in New York City drink water which comes to them from the Catskill Mountains ninety miles

A country water supply

from the city. It has been gathered from hills and woods where few people live. It is held behind a great dam. There it forms a beautiful lake. It has been thrown by fountains into the sunlight. It has

66   WATER, SAFE AND SATISFYING

traveled many miles in pipes so large that an elephant could walk through some of them and have room to swing his trunk from side to side. It has

Courtesy New York Board of Water Supply
Giving the city water supply a sun bath

been filtered* and treated with chlorine.* Filtering strains out bits of dirt, many bacteria, and other substances. Chlorine is a gas which kills the remaining bacteria. Finally the water reaches the people in the city. The cost of building this great water system was $193,000,000. More money is

CITY WATER SUPPLIES TODAY

spent daily to keep safe water flowing night and day to the city.

Los Angeles brings water from mountains 250 miles

Courtesy Department of Water and Power, Los Angeles

Convict Lake, one source of water for Los Angeles

away from the city. No other city brings its water from such a long distance. This water is needed for plants as well as for people.

San Francisco, like Los Angeles, brings water from high and far-away mountains. Before reaching the city it passes through one of the longest tunnels in the world.

The use of water. After so much care has been taken to make the water safe, people should keep it safe. They should never use cups or glasses from which other people have been drinking. They should keep the drinking fountains in schools and in parks clean, and they should not press their lips against the bulbs of the fountains.

Cool water is better than ice water because it does not chill the stomach. It is seldom wise to put ice in drinking water. Even though most of the ice we buy is frozen from safe drinking water, there are many chances for the ice to become contaminated. Some bacteria can live for months in ice. If you put contaminated ice in your drinking water, you have made the water unsafe.

"Drink four to six glasses of water a day" is a good rule. But be sure the water is safe.

OTHER CHILDREN'S QUESTIONS

If you do not know the answer to a question, look it up among the answers given. Do not guess.

1. What is the answer to this question, which I read in a paper: If you were shipwrecked on an island, which would you rather have, a loaf of bread, a barrel of water, or a $10 bill? Why?

ANSWERS TO QUESTIONS ABOUT WATER

2. Why is it necessary to drink plenty of water?
3. How do you know when water is safe?
4. How does Chicago keep its water supply safe?

Answers. You know that water is safe: (1) if it comes directly from a big city water supply; (2) if it bubbles up from a spring in the mountains far away from the houses and camps of people; (3) if it has been boiled and kept in a covered jar or pail which has also been carefully washed with boiling water; (4) if it comes from a tested well.

If there were no drinking water on the desert island, the barrel of water would be the most important thing to choose. People can live only a few days without water. They might be rescued before they starved to death. The $10 bill, of course, would be of no use.

Chicago keeps its water supply safe by pumping it from far out in Lake Michigan, filtering it, and treating it with chlorine which kills the germs.

It is necessary to drink plenty of water to help the body to get rid of its wastes, to digest food, and to keep an even temperature in hot and in cold weather.

THINGS TO DO

1. As a class, study the water supply of your school. Is there any chance for bacteria to get into the water you drink in school? Do all the boys

and girls drink only from their own cups? Or do you have paper cups so that each child can have a fresh one each time he drinks? If you do not have paper cups, plan to earn money to buy cups or a drinking fountain for the school. Try to make it easy and safe to drink water in your school.

2. Where does the water supply in your home come from? Is there any chance for bacteria to get into the water you drink at home? Make a list of all the things you can do to make sure that the water you drink is healthful.

3. Make a poster showing ways in which bacteria may get into drinking water. 4. Make a poster reminding people to drink at least four glasses of water a day. 5. Start a health library in your class. Bring all the books, magazines, and newspaper clippings about health which you can find. Paste the clippings neatly in small scrapbooks. Make one book of food clippings. In another put pictures and facts about exercise. Use a separate book for each of the main health problems. You can make the scrapbooks yourself by sewing pieces of wrapping paper together. 6. What has water to do with health? What has water to do with sickness? What has water to do with your personal appearance?

7. Write a story about the travels of a drop of water from the time it falls as rain until it reaches

your glass on the table. Name the different people who help to make it safe to drink. What do they do? 8. Discuss these questions in class: Is water from a cold spring in the country safe? How do country people make sure that their water is safe?

MILK IN YOUR DAILY MEALS

How much milk should I have every day? Is it true that milk is a perfect food? Is canned milk as good as fresh milk? How can we use all the milk we have on the farm? Have you ever asked these questions? This chapter will help you to answer some of the questions about milk.

You can easily separate milk into its different parts. If you let the cream rise to the top and beat it or churn it long enough, you will get butter. Butter fat is better than lard (the fat of pork) and better than the fat of other meats. We need some fat every day. Fat helps to keep us from getting hungry between meals and is a good source of energy.

If you let the skimmed milk (the milk from which the cream has been taken) become sour, you can separate it into two parts — the curds* and the whey.* The curds are the solid white part from which cottage cheese or pot cheese is made. The whey is the watery part. Even the watery part has food value. It contains milk sugar and other substances needed for health and growth. Farmers feed both whey and skimmed milk to hogs to fatten them.

Is milk necessary for health and growth? Many people make milk their chief food. Certain Arab

Curds and whey

tribes, noted for their health and strength, live largely on the milk of goats, sheep, and camels. The milk quickly sours and is eaten as curds or cheese.

The Chinese, however, have very little milk. But they eat the green leaves of many plants. We also

USE OF MILK IN OTHER LANDS

eat green leaves — lettuce, spinach, and other leafy vegetables. The Chinese eat these, too. But they eat more of such food than we do. They also eat

Growing up on milk

many leaves which we do not eat, such as sweet-potato leaves and even the leaves of trees. Green leafy vegetables help to keep them well. It is very important for us to have either milk or green leafy vegetables. It is best to have both.

Babies live almost entirely on milk during their first year. They grow faster in the first year than at any other time of their lives.

In a children's home there were 84 children, almost all of whom were in poor health. This seemed queer, because they had clean, pleasant rooms and lovely woods and fields in which to play. They had cereal for breakfast, and beef soup and cereals and vegetables, such as potatoes, carrots, onions, beets, and cabbage, for the other meals. They had all the bread they wanted to eat. Sometimes they had apples and bananas. A scientist decided to find out why these children were sickly. He studied the food they ate — their diet.* He saw at once that they were getting practically no milk.

To find out whether or not milk would make a difference, he divided the children into two groups that were alike in many ways. One group ate the same foods they had been having. Each of the children in the other group had a quart of milk a day.

Did milk make a difference? A record of the growth of these children was kept. Their weight increased when a quart of milk was added to their diet; but their weight decreased when the milk was taken away from their diet. One child of five years who had a quart of milk a day almost doubled his weight in a year. At the beginning he weighed only 28 pounds; at the end of the year he weighed about 53 pounds. Several children who did not gain at all on the cereal, vegetable, and meat diet made very large gains when the quart of milk was added to their other food. Not only did the children who were given a quart of milk a day gain in weight, but they also became more lively. Those of the other group did not seem to care about anything.

The same thing happened with a group of English boys. These boys, living together in the same school, usually ate the same food. But as an experiment,* each boy in one group was given a pint of milk in addition to his regular food. Another group had an extra piece of butter; a third group had a serving of water cress. The boys who had only their regular food gained, on the average, almost four pounds in weight during the year. But the boys who had the pint of milk in addition gained seven pounds; those who had the extra butter gained six and a half pounds; and those who had the water cress in addition to the regular food gained about five and a half pounds. What does this experiment show?

Even a small amount of milk makes a difference. This difference is most clearly shown in experiments with white rats. One family of rats had a diet of one sixth whole-milk powder and five sixths ground whole wheat. That would be like a diet of bread and milk for you — a great deal of bread and a small amount of milk. The other family of the same age had more milk. Their diet consisted of one third whole-milk powder and two thirds ground whole wheat. Both families had a little common salt. The only difference between the two diets was in the amount of milk. The first family grew very well. Their children and grandchildren and great-grandchildren grew as big as white rats usually do. They had healthy children. They lived as long as white rats usually live. But the family which had twice as much milk grew bigger, lived longer, and had more children. They were superior in every way. The larger amount of milk made the difference. Boys and girls should have a quart of milk a day. How many quarts should your mother buy for your family if she can afford it?

Milk also helps to build strong bones. What are bones made of? A large part of the bone is calcium. Milk and cheese are rich in calcium. A quart of milk furnishes as much calcium as a small child needs in a day.

Have you ever thought how important bones are and how many different kinds have to be built? Feel the bones in your hand. Suppose it had no bones. Would it be of any use to you? Feel the top part of your head. The scalp* is stretched over a

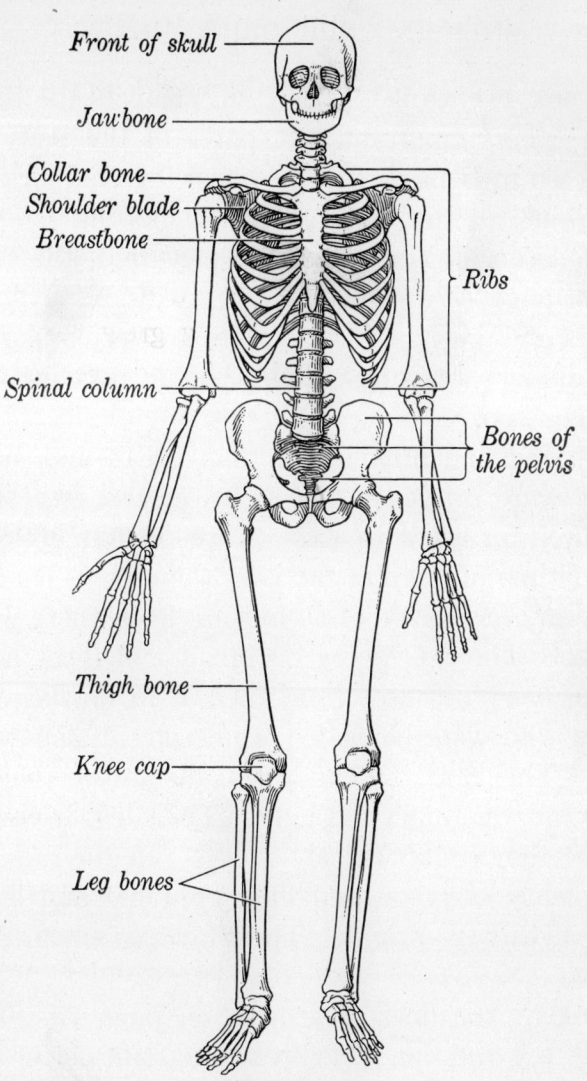

The skeleton

bony box, the skull.* The skull protects the brain. What other important soft parts of the body are protected by bones? All the bones together form the framework of the body. This framework is called the skeleton.* You will find a picture of the skeleton on page 77.

Milk and green leafy vegetables are very important in building bones. Sunlight has a part in bone building, too.

Is bread and milk better than bread and meat? Some white rats on a diet of bread and meat grew very well for a few weeks. (Three or four weeks in the lifetime of a white rat is in some ways equal to two years in the life of a child.) Then there was a change. The rats living on bread and meat began to look very different from their twin brothers and sisters who were being fed whole wheat and whole milk. The rats on the meat diet were smaller. Their fur was rough and ugly. Their legs were bent so that they could scarcely walk. But the rats that had plenty of bread and milk grew big and lively. Their eyes were bright. Their fur was smooth and glossy.

Look at the lines of growth on page 79. Then answer the question: "Is bread and milk better than bread and meat?"

Which rat grew best?

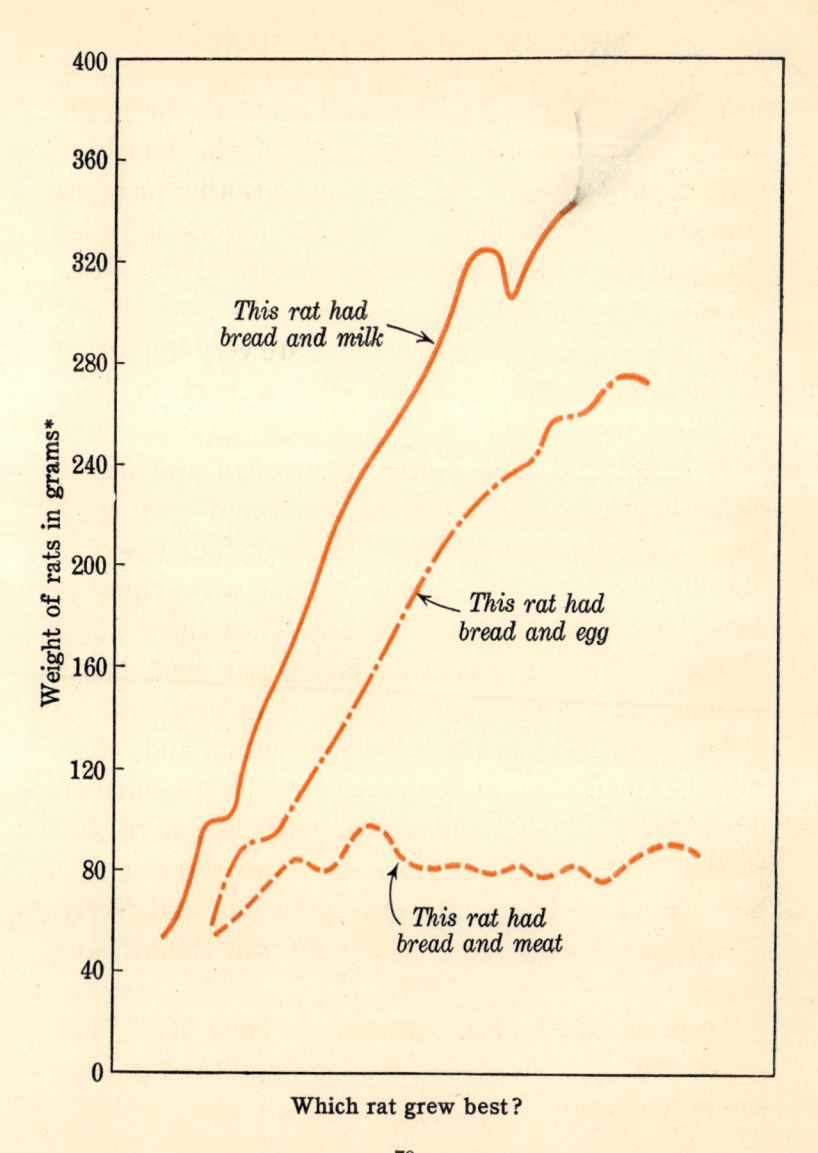

Other Children's Questions

The following are questions which children have asked about milk. If you are sure you know the right answers, write them. If you are not sure you know the answer to a question, find it among the answers given below.

1. Are the people on dairy farms healthy because they have plenty of milk?
2. Will children who drink milk grow taller than those who do not?
3. Why does milk make us gain in weight?
4. Could a person live on milk alone?
5. Is milk flavored with chocolate as good as plain milk?
6. Is goat's milk the same as cow's milk?
7. Is evaporated milk as healthful as fresh milk?
8. Why is cheese a good food?
9. May we serve the children with tea at our Japanese party?
10. What does calcium do for the body?

Answers. Milk flavored with chocolate furnishes more energy than plain whole milk. It is good if you are taking a long walk or playing games all day. It is not so good as the plain milk if you are in school. It is stimulating and is sweetened with sugar, while plain fresh milk is mild and naturally sweet.

What makes this a healthful place for cows?

Photo by J. C. Allen & Son

People on dairy farms have a good chance to be healthy; but sometimes, although there is plenty of milk, the children do not drink a bit of it. Perhaps you know children who seldom drink milk even though their fathers sell gallons and gallons of milk for other people's children. People on dairy farms should be healthy because they have milk and fresh vegetables to eat, outdoor work to do, clean, fresh air to breathe, plenty of clear sunlight, and a quiet place in which to sleep.

A little baby lives entirely on milk for the first few months. But very soon other foods are added. First orange juice, prune juice, or spinach juice, and egg yolk; then gruel* is added to the baby's diet to give him more power to kick and creep. Then a hard piece of bread gives exercise to his jaws and helps his teeth to push through. Then, as the child grows older, more of these same foods — vegetables, fruit, cereal, and bread — are added to the milk. A grown person could hardly live on milk alone; but all through life meals can be built of the "Big Three" — milk, cereal, and green leafy vegetables.

Milk helps us to gain in weight because it gives us fat and sugar of a kind which is easy to digest. Milk also contains other substances which are necessary for growth.

ANSWERS TO QUESTIONS ABOUT MILK

Cheese is a good food because it is made from milk and contains many of the food values of milk. Cheese should be eaten with bread, butter, and fruit

Milk at dinner

or vegetables. It should not be eaten alone or in large amounts because then it is difficult to digest.

Goat's milk is richer than cow's milk. The curd is somewhat harder to digest. For this reason it is not so good for babies. Ghandi, the great leader in India, lives largely on goat's milk and dried fruits. In Italy almost every family has its own goat.

Evaporated milk is almost as healthful as fresh milk, and it is cheap and easy to keep. If you have plenty of orange juice or tomato juice and green leafy vegetables in your diet, it does not make much

Milk at recess

difference whether you use fresh or evaporated milk.

Calcium is necessary to build bones and teeth. It is also necessary to keep the entire body in good working order. Milk is an excellent food to supply calcium.

MILK AND GROWTH

No, it will be better to serve the children with milk rather than with tea at your Japanese party.

Your height depends most on how tall your father and mother are and how tall your grandfathers and

Milk at supper

grandmothers were. But children and animals have grown more nearly as tall as they should be when they have been given better food. The Japanese children in America, for example, are in general taller and heavier than those of the same class in Japan. This may be because the Japanese children in America have better food in childhood than those in Japan.

Things to Do

1. Read this chapter to your family. **2.** Make an exhibit of milk and milk products: whole milk in bottles, loose milk, dried milk, condensed* milk, evaporated milk, buttermilk, sweet butter, salt

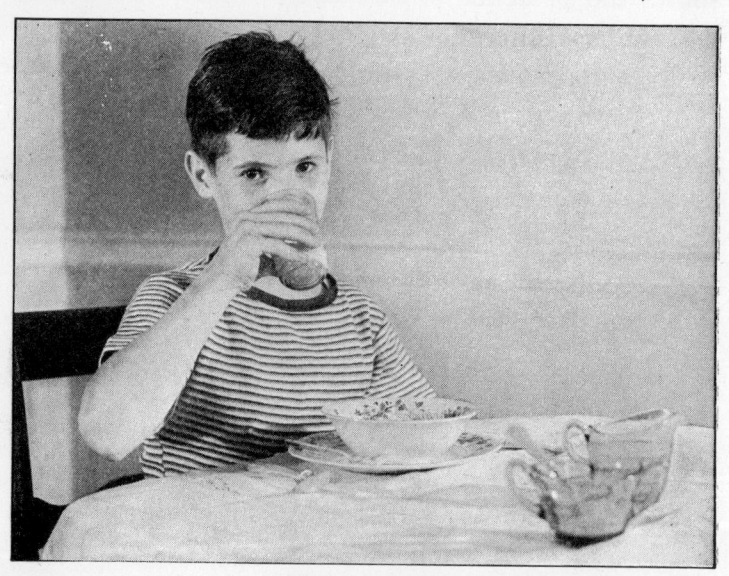

Milk at breakfast

butter, American cheese, cottage cheese, cream cheese and other kinds of cheese, milk sugar (bought at the drug store), and cream. Add also as many dishes made with milk as you can — junket, custard, ice cream, milk toast, milk soup, macaroni and cheese, and others which you have at home. Let each child in the class bring one food. If it is not possible to bring the real food, find a picture of it. **3.** Test for clean handling the milk you drink. Tie a layer of absorbent cotton over a glass. Pour a little milk through the cotton. A dark stain on the cotton shows the presence of dirt in the milk. Test milk from several different places in this way. Use a clean piece of absorbent cotton for each test.

4. Plan a day's menus for your family in which each child gets a quart of milk in some form, and no tea or coffee. **5.** Give proofs that milk makes a difference in health and growth. **6.** Where does the milk you get every day come from?

MEAT IN YOUR DAILY MEALS

Shall I choose meat in the school lunchroom today? Shall I make meat sandwiches for the lunch I take to school? Should I give my small brothers and sisters meat when they ask for it? Have you ever asked these questions?

Shall I buy meat today? Or shall I buy milk, cheese, fish, eggs, peas, or beans instead of meat? Have you ever heard your mother ask these questions? They are questions which you would ask too if your mother went away for a few days and left you to keep house.

Is meat necessary for health? Many strong, healthy people in other lands eat little or no meat. In China most of the people eat meat only a few times a year. Their diet is largely of vegetable foods. They have the strength to do hard work. There are many healthy people in Japan who eat only about one and one-half pounds of beef a year. Austrian farmers, as a rule, eat meat only on holidays. Many Italian farmers live almost entirely on vegetable soup made of beets, broccoli,* or potatoes to which onions, parsley, and tomato paste are added. When they serve the soup, they sprinkle ground, dry cheese over it. They eat meat only at Christmas time and in the haying season.

Most people in the United States have meat for dinner. They like it and feel that a meal is not complete without it. But some people in our own country do not eat any food obtained from animals. These people are called vegetarians.* Many people in good health eat milk and eggs but no meat. They are near-vegetarians. Do you know any people who are vegetarians? People can grow and keep healthy without meat.

Three scientists fed white rats on a vegetarian diet of corn, green leaves, and cooked dried peas. The rats grew as fast and as big as similar rats that had meat in addition to these vegetables. The vegetarian rats also had many healthy children. Certain animals can grow and keep healthy without meat if they have milk.

There are people who live on meat, just as there are people who live without meat. Some tribes of Eskimos live on meat. Their food and clothing come almost entirely from sea birds and other sea animals. They eat all parts of the animals, not chiefly the muscle meat as we do. These Eskimos have strong bodies. They have excellent teeth. They are healthy.

Now, how would you answer the question: Is meat necessary? Give reasons for your answer. One woman said: "I must buy meat for my husband. He needs a large amount of meat because he does so much hard work." How would you answer her?

Is meat better than eggs or fish? In one experiment children who had an egg every day grew a little better than those who ate similar foods without the egg. The mother who buys milk and eggs for her children can be sure she is giving them foods they need for health and growth. She should not worry because she cannot afford to buy meat.

Perhaps you have heard people say that brown eggs are better than white eggs. The color of the shell really makes no difference in the food value of the egg. It is the food the chickens eat and the way they live that makes a difference in the food value of the eggs. The best eggs are from chickens that eat green grass and live out in the sunlight.

Fish and meat are much alike in food value. Fish can be used in place of meat. Fish furnishes more iodine* than meat. The iodine in sea fish is important for health. In high mountain regions and in other parts of the country far away from the ocean there is little iodine in the water and in the home-grown vegetables. A lack of iodine may lead to a disease called *goiter** which is common in some parts of our country.

Fish is much cheaper than meat in many places. Some boys and girls catch fish for their families. When you have fish, you need not buy meat.

What are the advantages and disadvantages of meat? Meat has four good points:

1. Chewing meat exercises the teeth and gums. Tough meat requires vigorous chewing.

2. Meat furnishes iron. Liver is a very valuable source of iron.

3. Meat is appetizing. Just the smell of meat cooking over an open fire makes one hungry.

4. Meat increases the heat of the body. For this reason, meat is valuable for people who live in cold countries.

Fresh fish for dinner — if they have good luck

The chief disadvantages of meat are:

1. It tends to crowd out the milder-flavored milk and eggs and vegetables. These foods furnish substances which meat lacks and are more important for health and growth than is meat. Eggs and green vegetables are good sources of iron.

2. Meat, in general, costs more than other muscle-building foods.

3. Large amounts of meat and eggs are likely to cause excessive gas in the large intestine. This often disappears when milk takes the place of meat.

4. Meat is a disadvantage to people in warm countries or to people who live in warm rooms in cold countries, because it increases the heat produced in the body. Meat is a heating food.

How much meat should we eat? Some doctors say that school boys and girls may have two ounces of meat a day. Do you know how large a piece that is? When you go to the butcher's, ask him to show you a piece of meat that weighs two ounces. A piece of steak $4 \times 1 \times \frac{1}{2}$ inches weighs about one ounce. Take out your ruler and see just how large a piece this is. A piece twice as big would weigh two ounces. Other doctors say one ounce of meat is enough for children.

There will be days when you will have fish, peas or beans, or eggs in place of meat. A quart of milk a day makes more than two ounces of meat unnecessary. You can eat too much meat, too many sweets, too many vegetables even. You can have too much of any good thing. "Nothing in excess"* is best.

Other Children's Questions

Try to answer these questions which children have asked about meat. Look up the answers to those which you cannot answer. Do not guess.

1. Why is more meat eaten by the Eskimos than by people in the tropics?
2. Why do people in Norway eat so much fish?
3. What is the best way to cook fish?
4. Why do some people say that eggs are not good for you?

Answers. Three of the best ways to cook fish are boiling, baking, and broiling. A baked fish stuffed like a chicken with a bread dressing tastes very good. You can bake potatoes while the fish is baking. Have you ever broiled fish over a fire out of doors? If you have, you know how good broiled fish tastes.

In the far North people eat more meat than do people in the tropics because they can get meat more easily than fruit, vegetables, and cereals, and because it helps to keep them warm.

People who say eggs are not good for you are probably thinking of persons who ate too many eggs at one time. Too much of any food is not wholesome. An egg a day is healthful for almost everyone.

The people in Norway can catch fish from the

A holiday dinner

sea more easily than they can raise animals for meat. They are wise to use fish instead of meat part of the time.

THINGS TO DO

1. Tell your father and mother the reasons why milk is more important than meat in the diet of school children. 2. Prepare a two-minute talk on each of the following subjects:

Why children should not have meat oftener than once a day.

Milk makes a difference in the growth and health of children.

Eggs as food for children.

Ways in which peas, beans, or fish may be used in place of meat in a meal.

Why fish is an important food.

Do men who work hard have to have meat to give them strength?

Advantages of eggs as a food for all the year around.

3. Make a poster showing the advantages and disadvantages of meat. On one side, print the advantages; on the other side, the disadvantages.

4. Work out these problems in an arithmetic class:
(*a*) Which is cheaper — to kill a hen and eat the meat or to eat the eggs the hen lays during the year?
(*b*) Which is cheaper — to kill a cow and eat the beef or to let the cow give milk during the year and eat the milk, butter, cheese, and cream?

5. Find the cost in your neighborhood of one pound each of milk, eggs, bread, oranges, beefsteak, butter, apples, and potatoes. (A pint of milk weighs about a pound.) **6.** Where does the meat in the butcher shops come from? Follow its journey step by step from the farm or range where the animals were raised to the butcher shop. Your geography books might help you to find this information. Your father or the butcher might help you, too.

7. Suppose you had all the bread and milk you needed for your family and had 30 cents more to spend for the day's food. What would you buy? Write your breakfast, dinner, and supper menus. Read pages 10–28 to see whether you have planned three meals that include all the foods necessary for health. If you had more money to spend, what other foods would you buy?

8. Answer the questions at the beginning of this chapter.

SWEETS IN YOUR DAILY FOOD

How shall I spend the five cents father gave me? What shall I buy when I go to an ice-cream store with my friends? What kind of desserts shall I ask mother to make? What kind of dessert shall I choose in the school lunchroom? What sweets shall I put in my lunch box? What sweets shall we take on our picnic? What shall we have to eat at my birthday party? Have you ever asked these questions? This chapter will help you to answer them.

SUGAR AND HEALTH

Is sugar necessary for health? When you go to the store and ask for a pound of sugar, you usually get

IS SUGAR NECESSARY?

white sugar. This white sugar is made from sugar cane or sugar beets. White sugar is very familiar to us, but in some parts of the world thousands of children and adults have never seen sugar, or eaten candy, cake, or desserts sweetened with white sugar. They have natural sweets, such as fresh fruits, dates, figs, and honey. The Arabs' sweets are dates and several other kinds of fruit.

Our great-great-grandmothers used cane sugar only on special occasions. Each one ate, on the average, only about 10 pounds of sugar during the entire year. Today in the United States we use sugar enough in one way or another to amount to about 100 pounds for each person each year. Before the white men came, the only sweets the Indians had were wild fruits, berries, and vegetables. Many Indian tribes had excellent health and perfect teeth.

Even if you ate no sugar at all, you would find a certain kind of sugar carried in your blood. The body makes sugar. All the starch in the bread, cereal, and potatoes which you eat is changed to one kind of sugar. Some of it is changed to sugar in the mouth. You get sugar anyway, even though you do not eat it.

People who have always had natural sweets like them better than candy, cakes, and desserts made with white sugar. Do you remember the story of

Persephone, Mother Nature's daughter, who was carried by King Pluto down to his golden palace underground? Do you remember that the king's cook made all kinds of sweet, rich cakes and pastries to tempt her appetite? Persephone had no desire for these sweet foods. She pushed them all aside. When King Pluto asked her what she wanted, she said she would like some fruit from her mother's garden better than anything else in the world.

Is sugar harmful? The Indians in our country today no longer have a simple diet of natural foods. They buy meat, white flour, sirup, molasses, and sugar. On this diet their teeth have become badly decayed.

The farmers in Italy have plenty of goat's milk, cheese, and green vegetables. Their sweets are largely natural fruits. They often have fruits for dessert. Some Italians who come to American cities soon get a taste for sweets made from white sugar. Many children of foreign parents in America are not well nourished because coffee and candy have crowded out milk and green vegetables and fruit.

The people in Iceland before 1850 were in excellent health. Decayed teeth were almost unknown. What happened in 1850? In 1850 they began to import coffee, candy, sugar, tobacco, beer, wine, and flour. Now the people of Iceland have as poor teeth as many

IS SUGAR SOMETIMES HARMFUL?   99

Americans have. The children have certain diseases, such as rickets,* which they never had when they were living on a small number of natural foods.

What are the advantages and disadvantages of

What wise choice have these boys and girls made?

sugar? Sugar has two advantages: (1) Most people like the taste of sugar, unless, like Persephone, they have been brought up on fruits and other natural sweets. (2) Sugar furnishes energy cheaply; but only a small amount of the power to work and play can safely be furnished by white sugar.

Sugar has many serious disadvantages:

1. It furnishes little which the body needs for growth.

2. Candy and cake between meals and at the beginning of a meal may spoil the appetite for other foods. Sugar tastes so good that the milk, cereal, vegetables, and fruit which are needed for health and growth are apt to taste flat if eaten directly afterwards. Without milk, fresh fruits, lettuce, and other natural foods, good teeth cannot be built. Candy and other foods made of sugar crowd out more important foods.

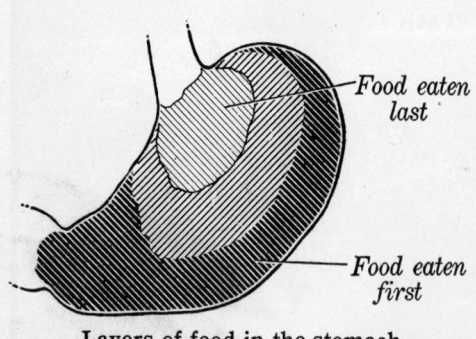

Food eaten last

Food eaten first

Layers of food in the stomach

3. If taken in large quantities, sweets are likely to ferment* instead of digesting quickly. Have you ever seen a jar of fruit that had spoiled? Bubbles form in it. It becomes sour. Sweets may ferment in the same way in the digestive tract. Some people have a "sour stomach" if they eat many sweets.

4. Candy and other very sweet foods eaten between meals or just before meals may irritate the

lining of the stomach. When you eat a piece of candy near the end of a meal, the sugar does not come directly in contact with the lining of the stomach. The other foods which have been eaten lie

Buying fresh fruit juice instead of other drinks

between the lining of the stomach and the sweet food you have eaten at the end of the meal.

How much sugar may we eat? You may have enough sugar daily to sweeten your stewed fruit, custard, cereal, bread pudding, or ice cream and in addition to give you a piece of candy at the end of a meal. You should have none of your daily supply of sugar for candy at recess or after school or for sweet drinks at the soda fountain. But you can have fruits and other natural sweets. These are better than bread and butter and sugar or bread and jelly.

Almost all candy and drug stores now serve delicious fresh-fruit drinks. They have grape juice. They have orange juice squeezed fresh while you wait. If you go with your friends to a drug store, you can order grape juice or orange juice. Even though your friends still get ice-cream sodas and other "soft" drinks, you can be original and up-to-date and buy fruit and milk drinks. Orange juice and grape juice are much better than soda water, cider, ginger ale, and other drinks like these.

Now turn back to the beginning of this chapter and answer the questions which were asked on page 96.

OTHER CHILDREN'S QUESTIONS

Can you answer them?
1. Is candy harmful?
2. Why does candy harm the stomach?
3. Why are dates an excellent food?
4. What are the values of milk chocolate?

Answers. Milk chocolate is a good food to furnish energy quickly. Mountain climbers take it with them on long climbs. Soldiers take it with them on

lining of the stomach. When you eat a piece of candy near the end of a meal, the sugar does not come directly in contact with the lining of the stomach. The other foods which have been eaten lie

Buying fresh fruit juice instead of other drinks

between the lining of the stomach and the sweet food you have eaten at the end of the meal.

How much sugar may we eat? You may have enough sugar daily to sweeten your stewed fruit, custard, cereal, bread pudding, or ice cream and in addition to give you a piece of candy at the end of a meal. You should have none of your daily supply of sugar for candy at recess or after school or for sweet drinks at the soda fountain. But you can have fruits and other natural sweets. These are better than bread and butter and sugar or bread and jelly.

Almost all candy and drug stores now serve delicious fresh-fruit drinks. They have grape juice. They have orange juice squeezed fresh while you wait. If you go with your friends to a drug store, you can order grape juice or orange juice. Even though your friends still get ice-cream sodas and other "soft" drinks, you can be original and up-to-date and buy fruit and milk drinks. Orange juice and grape juice are much better than soda water, cider, ginger ale, and other drinks like these.

Now turn back to the beginning of this chapter and answer the questions which were asked on page 96.

Other Children's Questions

Can you answer them?
1. Is candy harmful?
2. Why does candy harm the stomach?
3. Why are dates an excellent food?
4. What are the values of milk chocolate?

Answers. Milk chocolate is a good food to furnish energy quickly. Mountain climbers take it with them on long climbs. Soldiers take it with them on long marches. It is not so good for people who are indoors a large part of the day.

Dates are a natural sweet. They furnish energy.

Teach younger children to like natural sweets.

They aid growth. They are rich in iron, too.

You can find the answers to the other two questions in the chapter.

Things to Do

1. Make an exhibit of natural sweets. Bring the foods to school if you can — dates, figs, all kinds of fresh fruit, a honeycomb, a piece of sugar cane, and

some maple sirup. Put these all in little dishes or bottles on a table. Make a poster to place on the back of the table telling why natural sweets are better than sugar. If you cannot make an exhibit of real foods, cut out pictures of natural sweets and paste them neatly on colored paper. See how large a collection you can make. **2.** If you have small brothers or sisters, try to teach them to like natural sweets better than candy and rich cakes. Show them that you enjoy eating an apple or orange after school and fresh or stewed fruit for dessert.

3. Where does the white sugar you buy come from? Go to the library to find the story of sugar — how white sugar is made from the sugar beet or the sugar cane. Tell this story to the class.

FRUITS AND VEGETABLES IN YOUR DAILY FOOD

What kind of fruit shall I have for breakfast? What vegetables and fruits shall I have for dinner, lunch, and supper? What is the best fruit to put in my lunch box? What vegetables and fruits shall we plant in our garden? Why is it important for us to eat fruit and vegetables? How can we get the vegetables and fruit we need? Have you ever asked any of these questions? This chapter will help you to answer them.

The Need of Fruits and Vegetables

Are fruit and vegetables necessary for health? In the time of Columbus sailors who went on long voyages often had scurvy. This disease was so common on shipboard that it was called "the calamity

Fruit for the lunch box

of sailors." Doctors and captains of ships soon learned that a little orange or lime juice every day would prevent and cure scurvy.

Guinea pigs soon get scurvy when they have nothing but cereals or bread to eat. Their gums become sore. Their teeth become loose. They are quickly cured by a little fresh raw cabbage or carrots.

In parts of India where the diet consists largely of cereals the people are in much poorer health than in parts of the same country where the green leaves of various kinds of plants are eaten in large amounts. What green leafy vegetables do you eat? Lettuce, cabbage, celery, spinach, broccoli, beet greens, and Swiss chard are some of the green leaves commonly eaten in our country.

Although people can live on vegetable foods alone, as some vegetarians do, it is not easy to find a diet solely of vegetable foods that will be satisfactory. The best health cannot easily be secured with vegetable foods only. But if milk, eggs, and meat or fish are added to the vegetable diet and if other health rules are followed, good health and growth result.

In what ways may vegetables and fruits be misused? Even vegetables may be harmful if eaten in excess. It is not wise to overload the digestive tract with coarse vegetables and cereals. "Nothing in excess" is the best rule. The disadvantages of vegetables and fruits are due, not to the vegetables and fruits themselves, but to the wrong use of them. Overeating is one wrong use. As you have been told, you can have too much of any good thing.

Carelessness in cleaning them is another wrong use. Raw fruits and vegetables should be thoroughly washed before you eat them. You will also, of course,

PROTECTIVE FOODS

not eat an orange or apple or other fruit that has been partly eaten by someone else.

What are the advantages of vegetables and fruits?

1. Green leafy vegetables are "protective foods." They protect people from illnesses caused by a poor diet.

2. Vegetables and fruits are the best foods to start a natural bowel movement. They do this without irritating the digestive tract, as bran sometimes does.

3. Vegetables and fruits are rich in some of the food substances in which bread and cereals are poorest.

Some people say that "celery strengthens the nerves." Celery is an excellent vegetable, but it does not have a special effect on the nerves. Like other vegetables, it aids health and growth in general.

There is an old saying that "fruit is golden in the morning, silver at noon, and lead at night." It is true that fruit is "golden in the morning." But fruit is also "golden" at other times of the day for most people.

VEGETABLES AND FRUITS FOR EVERYONE

Can you get the vegetables and fruits you need every day? A good rule is: Every day eat a generous serving of some cooked green leafy vegetable; potatoes or other similar vegetable; and two servings of raw vegetables or fruit. Can you follow this rule? The green vegetable may be steamed, or boiled in a small amount of water, and served at lunch or dinner. The potatoes, carrots, onions, and other vegetable may be baked, boiled, or steamed. Raw vegetables make a delicious salad. A dish of ripe fruit from which each person can choose the kind he likes furnishes one of the best desserts. Drinking a large glass of orange juice or tomato juice the first thing in the morning is an excellent way to begin the day.

If you live in the country, you can plant vegetables in the garden and have plenty of vegetables all the year round. Can you not see them marching to your table? Here come dandelions and asparagus early in the spring. They are followed by spinach, peas, lettuce, and young tender carrots which are so good when eaten raw. The young beet plants which are pulled to thin out the growing beets furnish delicious beet greens. In the summer string beans, lettuce, Swiss chard, tomatoes, lima beans, carrots, beets, summer squash, and cabbage come marching by. In the fall more spinach and lettuce, sweet corn, beans, and other vegetables appear on your table. In the winter the vegetables keep marching along — celery, winter cabbage, parsnips, turnips, carrots, onions, dried beans, pumpkins, squash,

The march of the vegetables from spring to winter

109

and sweet potatoes. And the good white potatoes are in the line all the year round. What other vegetables do you have in your home?

You know the march of the fruits too. It is possible for most people to have some excellent fresh fruit all the year.

People in cities and towns can buy almost any kind of fruits or vegetables at any time of the year. Lettuce, spinach, and other fresh vegetables are sent from warm, sunny regions to cold, wintry towns and cities. Fruits, vegetables, and other foods are kept fresh by being stored in a cold place. They are sent in refrigerator cars or by boat in cold storage, that is, in a place which is kept so cold that fruits and vegetables will keep as fresh as possible. They are often kept in cold storage until they are sold.

Suppose you have more vegetables and fruit in the spring and summer than you can use. How can you save them for the winter? Someone has said in regard to summer fruit and vegetables: "Eat what you can, and what you can't eat, can." Do you think that is a good plan?

Fruit canned in a sirup in which there are three cups of sugar for every two cups of water is better than jellies and jams. Jellies and jams and rich preserves are too sweet for frequent use except in very small quantities. "An apple a day keeps the

CANNING AND COLD STORAGE

doctor away" is an old saying. Although apples are a valuable fruit, this saying is not the only truth, because milk and cereals and green vegetables, sunlight, sleep, exercise, and cleanliness are also needed for good health as well as for natural growth.

Summer vegetables for winter use

Canned tomatoes are one of the best winter vegetables. In the city you can buy many kinds of vegetables every day of the year. It is usually best to buy each kind of vegetable when it is most plentiful and cheap. Dried peas and beans are very cheap. They do not take the place of fresh vegetables, but they can be used in place of meat once or twice a week. It is an old saying that pea soup served by a bride to her husband as the first meal will make the husband content. Pea soup made with milk served on cold winter nights helps to make all the family content.

Can you learn to like all the healthful vegetables? Think of some of the different kinds of fruits and vegetables which are grown in the United States. How many of these vegetables are you eating?

You can learn to like all kinds of vegetables. One day the boys and girls in your grade asked why some people dislike certain foods. They gave the following reasons:

1. The food was burned or spoiled or not properly cleaned.

2. The food was served on dirty dishes.

3. Too much of the food was served at one time.

4. Other people in the family did not like the food, and the children copied them.

5. The food was eaten at a time when the person was angry or frightened or sad.

6. The child just had a notion he did not like a certain food, even though he had never tasted it.

One girl thought that she did not like carrots. One day her father said: "Try eating just the orange-colored pieces." So she picked out these pieces and before she knew it, she had eaten almost all the carrots on her plate. People who do not like vegetables can usually learn to eat them. It is only once in a while that a person really cannot eat certain foods.

OTHER CHILDREN'S QUESTIONS

Answer as many as you can. If you do not know the answer to a question, look it up among the answers given. Do not guess.

1. Why should we eat vegetables and fruit?
2. Is asparagus as good for us as spinach?
3. Are dandelions good to eat?
4. Why do farmers feed carrots and turnips to cattle?
5. Should you eat carrots raw or cooked?
6. Is it all right to eat canned vegetables?
7. Do raisins and lettuce have iron in them?

Answers. Young tender dandelions, like other green leafy vegetables, are very good for us. They are the first fresh green leaves some people can get in the spring. Many people like the bitter taste of dandelion greens.

Carrots may be eaten either raw or cooked. They may be chopped fine and served as a salad. They may be cut in cubes or slices and boiled or steamed. They may be used in vegetable soups.

Vegetables are good for "man and beast." Farmers say carrots make their horses' coats thick and shiny. This is probably true. Experiments have shown that the fur or hair of animals that eat the right kind of food is apt to be thick and smooth, while the fur or hair of those that do not have milk or vegetables is apt to be thin and rough.

Asparagus and spinach are alike in many ways. Both aid health and growth. Both are rich in iron.

Yes, raisins and lettuce both have iron in them. But raisins are not so rich in iron as are green vegetables, egg yolk, whole grains, and roast beef.

Vegetables properly canned are healthful. They have just as much iron as the fresh-cooked vegetables. They are as good as fresh-cooked vegetables in almost every way.

We should eat vegetables and fruit because: (1) they have food values that are lacking in meat and cereals; (2) they aid growth and health; (3) they are good sources of iron; (4) they help to keep the lower part of the digestive tract clean; (5) they are appetizing.

Things to Do

1. Read this chapter to your mother and talk with her about the vegetables and fruits you can have every day. **2.** All the food substances needed for health and growth are furnished by vegetables, fruit, milk, eggs, and grains. Add cereal or bread, milk, and an egg, meat, or fish to the vegetables and fruit in the following menus and thus make six excellent meals. Write the completed menus.

SUMMER MENUS	WINTER MENUS IN THE COUNTRY
Breakfast	*Breakfast*
Fresh fruit or berries	Baked apple
Dinner	*Dinner*
Potatoes	Potato
Spinach	Canned tomato
	Raw cabbage
Supper	*Supper*
Fruit salad	Cream of celery soup
	Canned peaches

3. Learn how to cook vegetables properly. Ask your mother whether you may help her. If there is a cooking teacher in your school, ask her what is the best way to cook some of the vegetables you have most frequently. Ask your teacher if she knows where you could get a little book about cooking vegetables. **4.** Look up *constipation* in the Index and read the pages referred to. What else besides a moderate amount of fruits and vegetables is useful in helping to get rid of body wastes?

5. Make posters showing: (*a*) fruits you can have for breakfast; (*b*) fruits and vegetables you can have for dinner and supper; (*c*) fruits and vegetables you can put in your lunch box.

6. Find in a cookbook recipes for five fruit salads, such as pineapple and cream cheese salad and orange

and prune salad. Tell your mother about them. She might like to have you make one for dessert some day. **7.** Make this salad. The family will like it: Chop in fine pieces two carrots, washed and scraped, a few pieces of clean celery, a few slices of cabbage, and some outside leaves of lettuce. Serve with a little salt or fruit juice for the younger children. Serve with olive oil and lemon juice, salt, and pepper for the older people.

8. If you have more vegetables in the summer and fall than you can use, ask your mother to show you how to can or dry them for the winter.

A fruit salad

9. If you live in the country and have no vegetable garden, try to plant one this spring.

First, choose a sunny spot for your garden with good soil. Soil furnishes material from which plants make their food.

Second, fertilize the soil if necessary. Your father will tell you what kind of fertilizer, if any, he wishes you to use.

Steps in making a garden
Give a title to each of the four garden pictures.

MAKING A GARDEN

Third, spade the garden deeply or ask some older person to do this for you. It is heavy work. Spading makes the soil loose so that the roots of plants

Photo by J. C. Allen & Son

can grow down into it easily and find food. After the ground is spaded, you should rake the soil smooth.

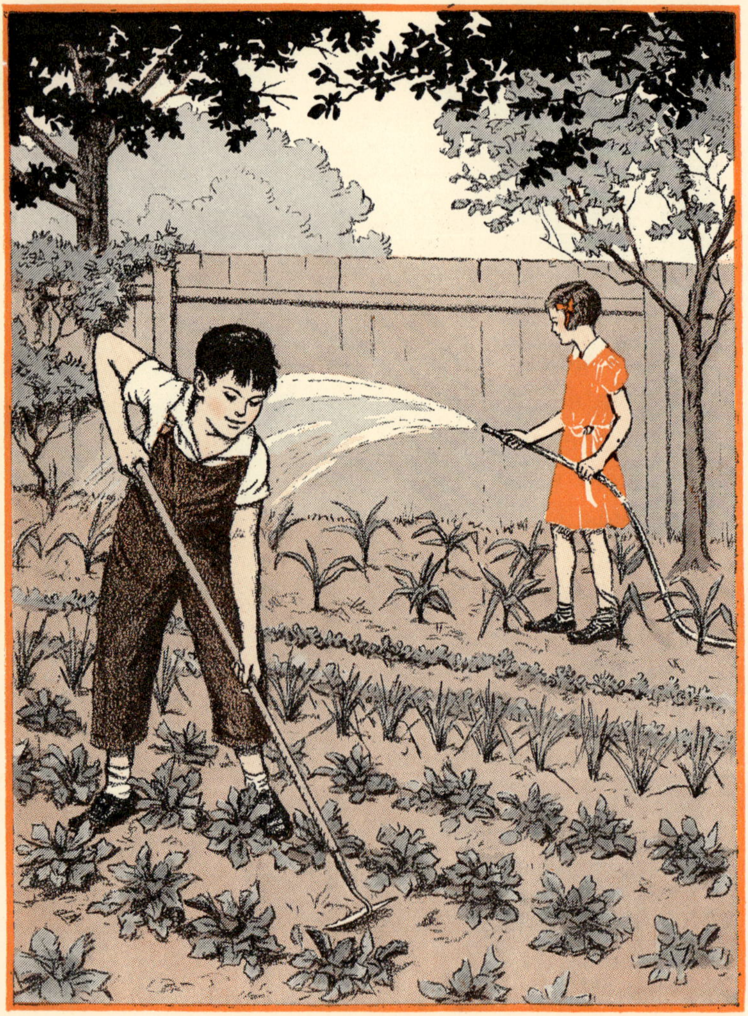

VEGETABLES FROM THE GARDEN

Fourth, plant the seeds. Be sure to choose some green leafy vegetables.

Fifth, water the plants in the evening when it is necessary.

Sixth, keep the garden free from weeds and the top soil loose.

Seventh, gather the vegetables as they get ripe and enjoy them with your meals.

10. Make a chart to show the vegetables you may have each month in the year from your own garden. If you store them properly, which vegetables may you have in the winter and early spring months of next year?

Photo by J. C. Allen & Son

11. Store the vegetables for winter in a clean, dry, cool place, but where they cannot freeze.

SOMEBODY HURT OR IN PAIN?

When a person has been hurt very badly and is not in further danger, go for help. Find a policeman, a doctor, or some other adult who knows exactly what to do. You can easily make an injury worse by moving a person when you do not know just what should be done. It is better to do nothing at all than to do the wrong thing. However, if you are very far from help, do the best you can.

Call a doctor at once if the person: (1) is seriously injured, that is, has been hurt badly; (2) is unconscious, that is, does not know what is going on about him — loses consciousness;* (3) has fits or convulsions;* (4) has severe pain in the head or abdomen. These are all cases for the doctor.

But boys and girls can learn to treat small cuts, scratches, sprains,* and bruises.* Sometimes you are on camping trips or in other places miles away from a doctor. Then, in case of an accident, it is very important to know what to do until the doctor comes. Treating such injuries is called giving *first aid*.*

First Aid for Wounds

First aid to a cut foot. Tom was chopping wood. The ax slipped and cut his foot. It was a fairly bad cut. Tom lived in a lonely part of the mountains, ten miles away from the nearest doctor. But Tom's

Name the steps in treating a cut.

mother had learned to give first aid. So she knew exactly what to do when Tom cut his foot. On a shelf she had a first-aid box. In this box was a roll of sterilized gauze,* a bottle of tincture* of iodine, and *adhesive tape.*

Sterilized gauze is very thin white cloth cut in a strip an inch or two wide. It has been treated in such a way as to kill all the bacteria on it. Heating in a hot oven, ironing with a hot iron for several minutes, or boiling will sterilize a piece of cloth. Iodine kills bacteria. Adhesive tape is a narrow strip of gummed cloth which sticks fast to anything on which it is placed. Ask your teacher to get each of these things so that you may see it and have a first-aid box in your classroom.

Tom's mother went to her first-aid box at once. Then she scrubbed her hands and nails with soap and hot water. In the meantime, Tom had cut away the shoe and stocking. With a piece of sterilized gauze, Tom's mother washed the skin all around the cut. Then she put tincture of iodine on the cut. "This iodine will make the cut sting," said his mother, "but it will kill the germs." Then she put several pieces of the sterilized gauze over the cut and fastened a bandage* skillfully round and round the ankle and the injured foot. "The bandage will keep out the germs," she said.

How to treat small cuts and scratches. The skin. It is wise to treat even a small cut or scratch or a broken blister just as Tom's mother treated his cut foot. In fact, whenever the skin is broken, there is danger that bacteria may get into the body. The skin is a germ-proof coat as long as it is not broken and not irritated. This coat has two parts — the outer part or epidermis* and the inner layer called the dermis.* The epidermis has many layers. You can see the outer layers clearly when a blister is formed. The cells of the outer layers are not sensitive.* There are no nerves in the epidermis. That is why you can prick a blister or the top layer of your skin and feel no pain.

Look at the skin on the palm of your hand. Do you see many fine lines? If the skin were perfectly clean, through a magnifying* glass you could see tiny openings on the sides of these lines. These are the pores.* The pores are the mouths or openings of the sweat glands.* The sweat glands pour a watery liquid (sweat or perspiration) out on the skin — from one to two pints a day, on the average. The perspiration helps to cleanse the skin by washing the dirt from the openings of the pores.

Cuts do not heal quickly if bacteria get into them. The very careful person will take the following four steps in treating cuts:

1. Wash the skin around the cut with boiled water. Work with clean hands and keep the wound clean.

2. Put, or apply, as the doctor says, a small amount of tincture of iodine on the cut. Your

Treat even a small cut properly.

doctor may tell you of other substances which can be used to kill germs in cuts.

3. Cover the cut with a piece of sterilized gauze, being sure nothing has touched the gauze before it is laid on the cut.

4. Keep the gauze in place by a bandage or by adhesive tape.

FIRST AID FOR DEEP WOUNDS

Your teacher, the nurse, or the Scout leader will show you the best way to bandage a finger, foot, hand, or arm. Practice bandaging until you can do it well. Cuts and scratches are very common, so be sure you know exactly how to treat these injuries.

How to treat more serious accidents. *Deep wounds.* Mary ran a nail into her foot as she was climbing down from a fence. The nail made a deep wound. In a deep wound of this kind the best things to do are: (1) To make the wound bleed by pinching it. The blood will help to wash out the dirt and bacteria. (2) Not to treat the wound yourself. Go to the doctor or to an older person who knows how to treat wounds of this kind. (3) To pour on *hydrogen peroxide** if you have it.

Serious bleeding. Accidents sometimes happen far away from any doctor or nurse. Jack cut his arm very badly when he was camping with three other boys. He was losing blood rapidly. Something had to be done. Two of the boys were very much frightened. The third boy, Bill, had studied first aid. He knew what to do to stop the bleeding.

Bill saw that the blood was coming out quickly in spurts. That showed him that a large artery* was cut. So he pressed his fingers on a certain spot above the cut. The wound began to bleed more slowly. Bill was shutting off the blood above the cut. "Bring

Best places to put pressure when an artery is cut

me a clean towel and a small, clean handkerchief," he said. The other boys got these things quickly. Bill put the folded handkerchief just above the cut. This made a pad pressing on the artery just as his fingers had pressed on it. Then he twisted the towel tightly over the pad. (See drawing on page 128.) This means of stopping bleeding is called a *tourniquet.** Every fifteen minutes he loosened the tourniquet. Finally the bleeding stopped entirely. All the boys were proud of Bill and decided to learn more about first aid.

The Blood and Blood Vessels

In order to do what Bill did, a person must know something about the blood and the *blood vessels.** Here are a few important facts:

When a person cuts his finger, blood comes out, as everyone knows. What is blood? It is chiefly water. What makes it look red? The red color is due to the red blood cells — the red *corpuscles,** they are called. Millions of these red corpuscles give the color to the blood. There are white corpuscles, too. Each kind of cell has its own work to do. The red corpuscles carry oxygen.* The white corpuscles destroy bacteria and other harmful substances. The corpuscles float in the watery part of the blood.

The blood is carried to all parts of the body by the blood vessels. In general, the blood vessels that carry blood rich in oxygen and dissolved food *to* all parts of the body are called *arteries*. The blood vessels that carry more of the wastes and less oxygen *from* the various parts of the body are called *veins.** The arteries branch into smaller and smaller tubes until they are as fine as hairs. These very small blood vessels are called *capillaries** or *capillary tubes*. The word *capillary* means *hairlike*. It is the blood in the capillaries in the skin which makes your cheeks pink.

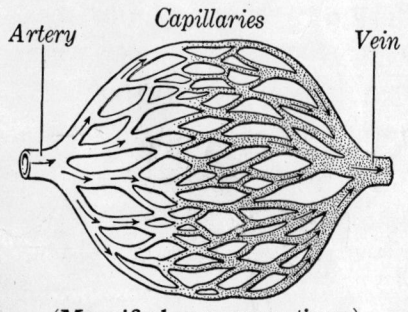

The capillaries run together like little brooks flowing together to make a river. The tubes into which the blood from the capillaries flows are the veins. The diagram on this page shows how the arteries branch into capillaries and the capillaries unite into veins.

In an injury the bleeding may be from an artery, from capillaries, or from a vein. The first aid you give depends upon the kind of blood vessel which has been cut. How can you tell which kind it is? Do you remember that Bill noticed that the blood was coming from Jack's arm in spurts? That showed him that an artery had been injured. The blood in

THE BLOOD VESSELS AND THE HEART

arteries flows in spurts as the heart pumps it through the body.

You have felt your heart on the left side of your chest beating — thump, thump, thump — very regularly. Each beat is a contraction* of the heart muscles which sends the blood out into the arteries. When you squeeze a rubber ball filled with water and send the water out in spurts, you are doing the same kind of thing that the heart is doing. The heart starts the blood leaping through the arteries. Put your fingers on the inside of your wrist where the doctor places his fingers to "feel your pulse."* Can you find the little artery there? Can you feel the blood flowing through it in regular beats?

If you wished to stop the water flowing out of a hose, you would pinch it together or perhaps put your foot on it. That would keep the water from flowing out. In the same way, Bill stopped the blood from flowing out of the artery by pressing his fingers on it.

At which side of the wound would you apply the pressure* — between the wound and the heart or on the side away from the heart? Since the blood in an artery comes from the heart, you would, of course, press your fingers on the artery between the wound and the heart. If the artery is a large one, sterilized gauze should be pressed right into the wound and held there tightly. If the bleeding does not stop, you must find some place where you can press the artery against a bone. This is what Bill did when he made the tourniquet.

The blood flows out of the little capillaries slowly. Bleeding from capillaries is easily stopped by pressing a sterilized piece of gauze over the wound.

The blood flows through the veins more slowly and smoothly than through the arteries. Bleeding from veins can often be stopped by pressing a sterilized piece of gauze over the cut. If the bleeding does not stop, you can press directly on the vein. On which side of the wound should you put the pressure? Since the blood in veins is flowing back to the heart, you should press on the side of the wound farthest from the heart.

OTHER MISHAPS

Broken bones. Sometimes a bone is broken and pushes its way through the skin. A doctor should be called at once. All you can do is to wash the skin around the wound with alcohol and lay a piece of sterilized gauze over the wound. If you have no alcohol or sterilized gauze, do not touch the injured place. Do not try to move the person unless he is in danger.

If a person with a broken bone that has not pushed through the skin must be moved, splints* can be

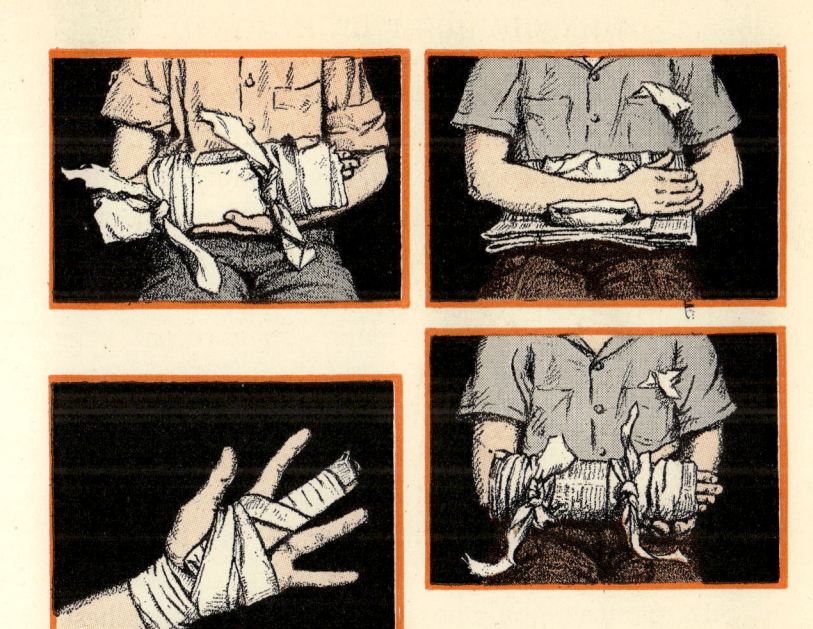

Splints to keep broken bones in place

used. Splints are pieces of wood or other stiff material that are fastened around the arm or leg as in the picture on page 133. Sometimes a pillow is used to protect the broken bone when a person is moved.

How should burns be treated? Burns are one of the most common accidents. In a recent year 6,120 people, almost one third of them children, were burned to death in the United States. That is about 17 deaths a day caused by burns. Every year the money lost through fires would pay the salary of the President of the United States for more than six thousand years.

Severe burns should be treated by a doctor. Burns in which the skin simply becomes reddened can be treated by covering the burned part with an oily substance and then with a clean cloth. When healing, burns should be kept covered and not allowed to become wet.

What should you do if a younger child gets something in his ear? Wait until you can get a doctor or an older person who knows what to do. It is a dangerous thing to work around the ear with a match, toothpick, or any other pointed object. You might make a hole in the eardrum and even cause deafness. If an insect enters the ear, you can keep it from buzzing around by putting a few drops of castor oil or sweet oil in the ear. If you do not have them, do nothing until the doctor comes.

What should you do for a person who is choking on something caught in his throat? Let the person face the light, hold down the tongue with a teaspoon, and try to see the object. You may get it out with pincers or your fingers. If not, place the person head down and slap him hard on the back. This may loosen the object in the throat so that it will fall out. Send for a doctor at once if you do not succeed.

What should you do if a person faints? When a person loses consciousness from any of the causes named below, we say he has *fainted*. He does not know what is going on about him. The doctor tries to find out the cause of the fainting and treats the patient accordingly. The patient may be suffering from nervous shock or from fainting due to serious bleeding, intense heat, electricity, or other causes. Some of the signs of shock are pale skin, lips, and nails; cold and moist body; and weak pulse. If you do not know the cause, put the person who has fainted on the floor or bed with no pillow under his head if his face is pale, and with a pillow if his face is red. Get a doctor as soon as possible. If a person *feels* faint, tell him to sit down and put his head down between his knees. This often prevents fainting.

What to do if: *a.* a person faints; *b.* feels faint

Frostbite. If your ears or hands or feet have been frostbitten, rub them with your hand but keep away from a fire or a warm room. The frozen parts should become warm again slowly, not suddenly. Do not use the old remedy of rubbing frostbitten feet, fingers, or ears with snow. That has been found to do more harm than good.

What should you do for a sprained ankle? If the pain is severe, send for a doctor, because the sprain may be a serious one or a bone may be broken. A sprained ankle may begin to swell quickly. Raise the foot higher than the rest of the body. Keep putting cold applications* — that is, cloths wrung out of very cold water — around the part for several hours. This treatment lessens the pain and the swelling. Do not let the person walk on a sprained ankle. Arrange to have him carried home. Apply a cold application to severe bruises also.

What should you do if a person is bitten by a snake? A bite from a poisonous (venomous*) snake should be treated at once. Do not delay. Apply a tourniquet lightly as in the case of bleeding from an artery so that it is between the wound and the heart. Loosen the tourniquet a very little bit every ten or fifteen minutes until it is completely loosened. What does the tourniquet do? Why do you wish to keep blood from going to the heart? What does the blood coming from the snake bite contain? If the tourniquet is loosened little by little, only very small amounts of the poison are allowed to pass to the heart. These very small amounts may do no harm. Send for a doctor. Make the tiny wound bleed by cutting with a small, clean knife. The blood helps to wash out some of the snake's poison (venom*). Suck out the poison. This may be done by putting the opening of a heated bottle over the cut. This is called the "cutting-suction method" and is described in the latest First Aid book of the American Red Cross. Scouts use this method.

What should you do for a person who has a headache? Do not give him headache medicine. The best things to do for his headache are: (1) Have him lie down in a quiet place and try to sleep. If the pain is severe, put on his forehead an ice cap or a cloth kept cold by wringing it out of ice water. (2) Have him see a doctor if his headaches are frequent or severe.

What should you do for a person who has a nosebleed? The best way to treat a nosebleed is to: (1) put the person flat on his back; (2) loosen his collar and put a cold towel at the back of his neck and over his nose and forehead; (3) if necessary, pinch the soft part of the nose and hold it until the blood clots (the thickening of the blood as it flows out is called *clotting*); (4) call a doctor if the bleeding does not stop.

What should you do for a person who has a toothache? Take him to the dentist as soon as possible. If you cannot see the dentist at once, clean out the cavity* and pack the hole with cotton wet with oil of cloves. Put some oil of cloves around the gum too. But be sure that he goes to the dentist even though the tooth stops aching.

These first-aid rules must be practiced if they are to be useful when there are accidents or other special calls for help. "Be prepared." It is well to know what to do in case of accident, even though everyone you know is so careful that you need never use your knowledge.

Things to Do

1. Ask the teacher or the nurse or doctor or scout leader to show you how to treat a few of the simple common injuries. Practice each of these a good many times until you know exactly what to do.
2. Ask the nurse to tell you what to buy to make a first-aid kit for your classroom. Try to get a first-aid kit for your class or for the school.
3. Look in the medicine chest at home. Ask your mother if she has the things listed on the next page and tell her what each one is for:

A clinical thermometer* for taking the temperature of the body.

Sterilized gauze for placing over wounds.

Gauze bandages to wrap around wounds.

Adhesive tape to hold the sterilized gauze in place.

Alcohol for rubbing on sprains and bruises; for washing the skin around wounds; and for treating poison ivy.

Aromatic spirits of ammonia* to stop fainting. One puts some on cotton and holds it near the nose of the fainting person.

Boric acid* for washing skin around wounds, and for an eyewash.

Carbolated vaseline* to put on burns.

Tincture of iodine of sufficient strength for wounds.

Sirup of ipecac* to cause vomiting in case of poisoning by using 1 teaspoonful, followed by a drink of warm water.

4. Study a Scout book or a Red Cross first-aid book to learn how to do more difficult bandaging and how to treat other kinds of accidents.

5. Find out the most common causes of fires in your neighborhood and learn how to prevent them. Have a committee make a list of all the things that can be done to prevent fires in your homes. Take the list home and see whether your home has been made safe from fire. 6. If someone comes to school with a cut or bruise or hurts himself during school hours, ask the teacher to take a few minutes of the class time to show the class the best way of dealing with the injury and of applying first aid.

Practice first aid.

7. Bring to class a list of all the different kinds of accidents which you and your friends have had. Then, with your teacher, decide how they might have been prevented. Look up *safety* in the Index to get further ideas.

PREVENTING ILLNESS

Suppose you lived on a desert island. There would be nobody to help you and no one whom you could help. You would have to find your own food and cook it. If you became ill, there would be no one to take care of you. But in a city or town, the milkman brings you milk. You can buy bread at the baker's. If you are sick, someone calls the doctor. Water is brought to your house in pipes from a safe water supply. We help one another in many ways.

Keeping Well

Animals and insects help one another to keep well. There are some honeybees which stay just inside the door of the hive and keep fanning with their wings. They fan the warm air out. They fan the cool air in. They keep the hive well ventilated* (aired). There are other workers among the bees which keep the hive very clean. There are bees that look after the health of the hive in other ways. The honeybees have nurses, too.

Animals seem to know what to do to keep well without being taught. For example, there are birds which fly almost 10,000 miles in order to be in the sunshine. These birds are the arctic terns. They grow up in the far northern region in the summer when the sun shines for weeks without setting.

When the nights begin to grow long, these birds fly to the other end of the world where summer is just beginning. They are often called "birds of sunshine." There are some people who, like the arctic terns, follow the sun. They go south in January or February to escape the northern winter.

They will soon be helping one another to health. How?

Keeping the baby well. If a mother had over a thousand babies, as some fish have, she could not take much care of each one. The grasshopper mother never sees her two dozen or more babies. Wild ducklings need very little care from their mother. She takes her family of ten or fifteen children for a swim and lets them find their own food. But many birds take a great deal of care of their babies. They feed them until they are able to fly. Perhaps you have watched a family of baby birds grow up in a nest in a near-by tree or on your window sill. Baby monkeys receive care very much like the care given to human babies — that is, babies such as you were when you were little.

Human babies receive the best care for the longest time of all babies in the world. There is nothing in the world more jolly, more fun — and more work — than a healthy human baby. If you have a baby in your family, you have a large share in keeping it well.

Jim protects the family from flies. He helps to keep the manure* on the farm from piling up, because flies breed in manure. He kills all the flies he sees early in the spring. He keeps screen doors and screens in the windows closed. How does this help to keep the baby well?

Betty often takes her baby brother for an airing, and is very careful not to let anyone with a cold come near him. One day Betty's friend, Jean, came by. Although she had a bad cold, she was going to stop and talk to the baby as she usually did. But Betty stopped her and said: "Oh, Jean, please don't come near the baby. He catches cold so easily." Did Betty do a wise thing? Why?

Mary's mother learned that her baby could be protected from diphtheria.* Mary went with her mother and the baby to the doctor and the baby was given a treatment to prevent diphtheria.

Keeping the family well. People usually think that fathers and mothers take care of their children, but sometimes children take care of their parents. Just think of all the things you can do to help your father and mother keep well. You can cover your mouth and nose with a clean handkerchief when you sneeze and cough. You can stay away from them when you have a cold. You can help keep the rooms heated to about 68° F. in cold weather. Rooms that are too hot are not healthful. What are some other things you can do to help keep your father and mother well?

Keeping your schoolmates well. One important way of protecting the other boys and girls from illness is to stay at home when you are sick. Stay at home even if you have "just a cold." Stay at home after a serious illness until the doctor says you are well enough to go back to school.

Keeping yourself well. Some of the simplest, easiest, cheapest things to do are the most important for health. Washing your hands (1) before eating, (2) before touching food, and (3) after going to the toilet is a very simple thing to do. But the power of these simple habits to prevent illness is almost like magic. Keeping your hands and other objects away from your face is a simple thing to do. But it pays to do this.

Staying away from crowds and from people who have colds, scarlet fever, or similar diseases may save your mother and father the trouble and worry and expense of having you seriously ill. Taking

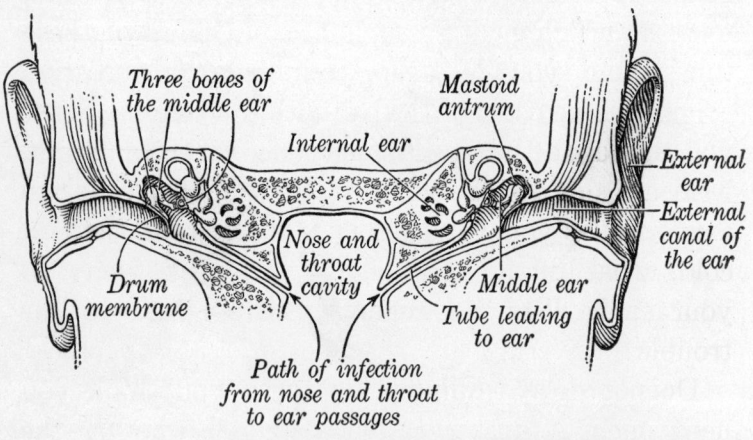

How can bacteria reach the middle ear?

care of colds and ear troubles pays. Colds may lead to ear trouble and ear trouble may lead to difficulty in hearing. Why? Study the diagram of the outer and inner ear on this page. You will notice that the outer part of the ear, which is the part of your ear which you see, leads into a tube. In this tube is ear wax, which is there for a purpose. It helps to keep insects and dirt from injuring your ears.

When you wash your ears, you should not try to dig out all the wax.

Beyond the ear wax is a thin skin stretched across the tube somewhat like the head of a drum. It is called the *eardrum*.* Leading into the head from the eardrum are three small bones. (See page 146.) Still deeper in the head are curved and winding tubes, some of which enable you to hear. Others of these tubes help you to keep your balance. Nerves connect these parts of the ear with the brain. See if you can find all the parts mentioned on the diagram. Notice also that the ear and the upper throat are connected by a passageway. When you have a cold, what might steal along this passageway to your ear? Why do colds sometimes lead to ear trouble?

Do not delay calling a doctor if you think you need one. A doctor can usually tell whether the illness is serious. He will take your temperature.* If it is higher than 98.6° F., you probably have a fever. The blood of warm-blooded animals, such as man, keeps at about the same temperature all the time. Some animals naturally have higher temperatures than others. Birds may have a temperature of 105° F. to 110° F. Cold-blooded animals like frogs and snakes have about the same temperature as the water or soil or grass in which they happen to be.

"Use your own" is a good health rule. Use your own drinking cup, your own towel and washcloth, your own hairbrush and comb, your own toothbrush. Use only your own — no one's else.

Eating the right kind and amount of food is, of course, one of the most important paths to health. You have learned a great deal about foods in the early chapters of this book.

Nature's Aids to Health

The sun not only gives to the earth color and warmth and food. It is a health giver as well. No wonder certain Indians worshiped the sun. Sitting in your bathing suit for half an hour in the middle of the day out of doors or beside an open window in the spring and fall with the warm sun shining on your bare skin is a good habit. Fifteen minutes in the morning or afternoon is long enough the first few days if the sun is bright and hot and you sunburn easily. Later the sun bath can last an hour. It is easy to get too much sunlight at one time. Severe sunburn should be avoided. Find in the Red Cross first-aid book how to treat sunburn.

Air, too, is necessary for life. The air we breathe is a mixture of gases. Aviators have shown us how necessary air is. Some aviators have flown more than nine miles above the land. Some have risen to a height of over eleven miles in balloons. At that height, the atmosphere — the mixture of gases which clings to the solid part of the earth — is thin. It is poor in oxygen. A man cannot live long in an

Good sport in the sun

atmosphere that is so poor in oxygen. When the aviator flies high, he must take enough oxygen with him in tanks for breathing. But on the land we need not think about the oxygen supply. There is plenty of oxygen in the air outdoors and in the rooms where we live. The most important thing to watch is the temperature of the air in our rooms. What should the thermometer in heated rooms read?

Both work and rest are needed for health — at least two hours of work or play outdoors every day and eleven hours of sleep at night for boys and girls of your age. And — "nothing in excess." Rest before you get "all tired out." "Take it easy." Prepare for long walks and climbs by taking short ones first. Practice a new kind of work or game you are learning a short time each day. Avoid strains of all kinds and overdoing — eating too much, exercising too hard, reading too much, and staying up late at night. Trying to lift things that are too heavy for you is a strain. Swimming too far and walking too long are strains. Name other strains and excesses which should be avoided.

OTHER CHILDREN'S QUESTIONS

If you are not sure of a right answer, look it up among the answers given.

1. Why does Jane have so many boils?
2. Why shouldn't we use towels that others use?
3. Why should we not use other people's combs?
4. How can we avoid catching colds?
5. Do wet feet cause colds?
6. Why should colds not be neglected?

Name the three rules for avoiding colds.

Answers. Boils are caused by bacteria which get into a tiny crack or pore in the skin. If the bacteria from one boil are rubbed on another part of the skin, the germs may find a place to enter there. Being out in the sunlight, keeping the skin clean, and eating few sweets and starches help to prevent boils.

Three ways of avoiding colds are: (1) staying away from people who have colds; (2) using only your own towel, washcloth, toothbrush, handkerchief, and drinking cup; (3) getting plenty of sunlight and outdoor exercise, good food, and sleep.

The nose, throat, and ears are all connected, so that bacteria from one can easily go to the other and cause trouble. (See diagram on page 146.) A cold that is not taken care of may result in an earache. Moreover, other serious illnesses are more easily caught when you have a cold. So it is very important to take care of a cold.

Germs cause colds. Wet feet may in some cases make the body less able to fight the cold germs.

People often do not wash their hands very clean. They wipe off germs on the towels. The towels are damp and warm. Harmful bacteria can live on them for some time. When you wipe your hands on these towels, you make your hands dangerously dirty instead of clean.

Diseases of the scalp may be carried from one head to another by combs. Head lice and nits may also be carried in this way.

Things to Do

1. Give a series of scenes in a play showing how illness may be prevented. All the class may take part. For example, the first scene may be "Washing the Hands before Eating," the second scene, "Washing the Hands before Preparing Food," and so on. Each scene may be worked out by a special committee of the class. This play may be practiced so that each scene is acted smoothly and well, and then given in assembly. **2.** If there is danger of scarlet fever* or measles in your school, ask a doctor or a school nurse to come into your classroom and tell the class what to do to prevent these diseases. After you have learned what to do, tell it in a simple way to other classes. Make posters about the most important things. Do not talk about the disease, but call attention to the healthful things which should be done. Write a letter to your parents telling them how they can help. Have one letter copied and sent to the parents of all the children in the school.

3. If the boys and girls in your class do not wash their hands before eating lunch in school, plan to have them all do so. Perhaps you can use one of the plans children in other schools have tried:

a. In a city school the children in charge of hand washing gave each boy and girl a colored ticket after he had washed his hands. This ticket was used in admitting children to the lunchroom.

b. In one country school, there was no running water; so the children washed their hands in this way: They used a pail as a sink. They poured clean water from a gallon measure. They used an oil can to hold liquid soap. They made the liquid soap by boiling a teaspoonful of powdered soap five minutes in a quart of water. Three children had charge of the hand washing. One poured some liquid soap from the oil can on the hands of each boy and girl as he walked by in line. A second child poured water on the hands which were held over the empty pail. A third child gave the boys and girls paper towels after they had washed their hands. In this way twenty children could wash their hands in about five minutes, and little time was lost from the noon hour.

c. In another country school one of the fathers, who was a plumber, put a small faucet near the bottom of an ordinary pail. At noon the pail was filled with warm water and placed on a table in the yard, with the faucet extending over the edge of the

Washing the hands in a school having no running water

table. One child turned the faucet while the others washed their hands in the warm water. Draw a picture of this method of washing the hands.

4. Do children in your school wash their hands before eating lunch? Do you have soap, water, and a towel of your own? Is your school ahead of or behind other schools in making it possible for children to wash their hands in school? **5.** Tell in class how you can protect other people if you have a cold. **6.** Show the class how to wash their hands and care for their nails properly and give a reason for each thing you do. Show also good ways to keep your comb, hairbrush, and nail brush clean.

7. Think of the last meal you ate. Did you wash your hands before eating? Did you have plenty of time to chew your food well? Did you talk about pleasant things? Did you read or play quiet games for a while after eating? Or did you help your mother wash the dishes? Plan to do these things at your next meal. **8.** Why do children so often get sick at Christmas time? Read pages 100–101 if you do not know. **9.** Make a list of habits which help to prevent constipation. Read the pages about constipation to see whether you have put all the important habits in your list. **10.** Make a list of the kinds of illness which, it seems to you, may be due to disobeying the rule, "Nothing in excess." Talk this question over in class with your teacher.

11. Air is made up of about one fifth oxygen and four fifths nitrogen. It contains a very little carbon dioxide and some water. We know that it is the oxygen in the air which enables things to burn. Do an experiment to show what happens when the oxygen is used up: Light a short candle. Put a glass over it. What happens to the candle flame?

12. Make a drawing showing the way in which the air over your radiator is moving.

USING — NOT ABUSING — THE EYES

THE EYE AT WORK

All through the day you are either using your eyes wisely or using them carelessly and foolishly. In this chapter you will see a little more clearly the reason for some of the good habits of using the eyes which you have already formed.

The eye and how it works. Look at your eyes in a mirror. What parts do you see? The part that has somewhat the shape of a ball and that moves up or down or sideways is the *eyeball*. Do you see a small, dark, round spot in the center? That is the *pupil** of the eye. Is the pupil always the same size? Carry the mirror with you when you face the bright light by a window or lamp and notice what happens to the pupil. Then see what happens when you go into a dark corner of the room. Look at the pupils of a cat's eyes in the light and in the twilight. What is the size of the pupils in a bright light? How do they change when the light becomes dim?

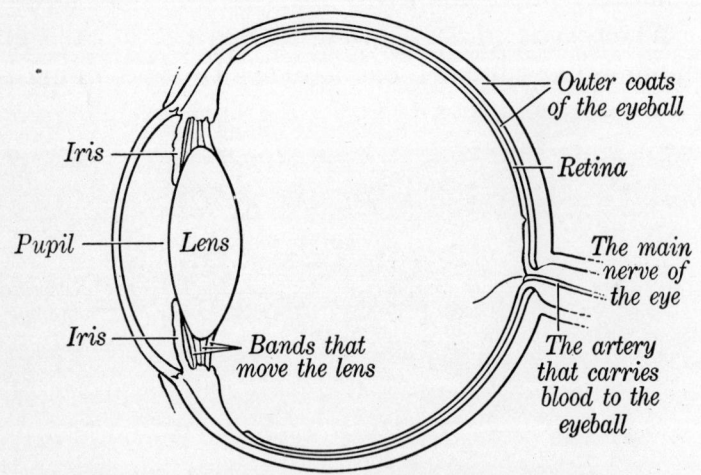

Find the parts of the eye described in this chapter.

The pupil is just a little hole in the eyeball which changes as the amount of light changes.

Across the pupil and inside the eye is the *lens.** The light must pass through the lens before it can enter the eye. The lens is clear like glass, but it is not hard. The lens can become thinner or thicker.

Look at your eyes again in the mirror. What do you see around the pupil? This colored part is

THE EYE AND HOW IT WORKS

called the *iris*.* In some people's eyes the iris is blue; in some, brown; in some, gray or other colors. What is the color of the iris of your eyes? In a dim light, the iris is drawn back and makes the pupil larger. In a bright light, it comes together and makes the pupil smaller.

When light passes through the lens, it falls on the lining at the back of the eyeball. This lining is

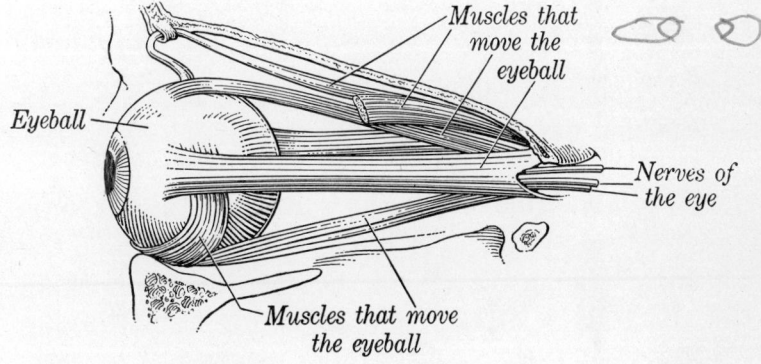

Muscles that move the eyeball

Eyeball

Nerves of the eye

Muscles that move the eyeball

How do the eye muscles work?

called the *retina*.* Everything we look at is pictured on the retina. The pictures on the retina are carried to the brain by nerves. Then we see.

Have you ever taken a picture with a camera? What do you do if an object you want in the picture is shut out because it is too large or if the object seems too far away? You move the camera nearer or farther away, right or left, or up or down, do you not? Then you can get the picture just as you want it. The eyes, too, must be moved in various ways in order to get the clearest picture.

Six muscles move the eyeball — from side to side, or up and down, or by rolling it. (See the diagram on page 159.) These muscles become tired just as other muscles do when they are used a great deal. Still other muscles make the pupil smaller or larger, and others make the lens thicker or thinner.

Now we can answer some of your questions about the eyes more easily.

Habits of Using the Eyes

Reading on moving trains. Reading on a train is very tiring to the eyes because the book and the head are being moved all the time by the shaking of the train. The eye muscles must keep working fast to make the image of the print clear in spite of the changing position of the book and of the changing distance between the book and the eye. The eye muscles have no time to rest. When you are riding on a train, it is a good plan to read a little while, look out of the window across the aisle a little while, look at objects in the car a little while, and close your eyes a little while. One should not read at all in a moving automobile because it rides even less smoothly than a train.

Why should we avoid a glaring* light? You remember that the pupil of the eye becomes small in a bright light. To close the pupil so tightly tires certain muscles. This is one reason why we should avoid a glaring light.

If you have trouble with your eyes, where shall you go? Some people go to an optician* when their eyes hurt or they have poor vision (cannot see clearly). An optician is a man who makes and sells eyeglasses. Other people go to an *optometrist** who is specially trained to test eyes and to *fit* glasses. In severe cases people go to an *oculist.** An oculist is a doctor who has studied about the eyes and the body as a whole. He will make a careful examination to discover general bodily conditions that may affect the eye. He will tell you exactly the kind of glasses you need — if you do need glasses. He will tell you when to wear them. Then you will have to go to an optician to have the glasses made. Your eyes deserve the best treatment you can give them.

Why should we not read while lying down? It is hard to hold the book in the correct position when you are lying down. Often the book is not far enough away from the eyes. Often it is not held up as it should be. Sometimes the light shines in the person's eyes instead of on the book. Sometimes people become so interested in a story which they begin to read in bed that they do not stop reading when their bedtime comes. They lose sleep as well as make their eyes work overtime.

Why should we not sit too near the motion-picture screen? Have you ever sat in a front row at a motion-picture show and felt your eyes becoming more and more tired and your head beginning to ache? A motion picture is really thousands of separate pictures. They are shown so rapidly that they look like one unbroken picture of moving objects and persons. Sitting close to the screen at a movie makes the picture harder to look at. Any rapid changing of objects before the eyes is fatiguing.* The muscles of the eye become tired trying to take so many different pictures. Similarly, looking out of a window from a moving train makes the eyes tired. If you look out of the window across the aisle of the car, your eyes do not become so tired. They do not try to see every passing object but just get the general effect.

OTHER CHILDREN'S QUESTIONS

Find the right answers to the following questions:
1. Should we read after we go to bed?
2. Why should we stay in a darkened room when we have measles?

QUESTIONS ABOUT EYES ANSWERED

3. Is pinkeye* sometimes catching? If we have pinkeye, what should we do so that we may come back to school sooner?

4. What is the cause of sties?*

5. Why do my eyes hurt if the light is too dim or too bright?

6. Why does coming suddenly from a dark to a light place hurt your eyes?

7. Why are the pupils of a cat's eyes larger at some times than at others?

Answers. The pupils of a cat's eyes grow larger in the dark in order to let more light into the eye. The pupils grow smaller as the light becomes brighter in order to shut out some of the light. Is it the same with your pupils? Why should the pupils of the eyes grow smaller in a bright light?

Pinkeye is very catching. You can catch it by using the handkerchief, towel, or other objects handled by someone who has pinkeye. Do just as the doctor tells you to do.

If the light is too dim when you are reading, certain eye muscles have to pull hard to make the print clear. They get tired pulling and pulling. That makes your eyes hurt. If the light is too bright and glaring, other eye muscles must pull hard to try to shut out some of the bright light. That makes the eyes hurt, too.

USING — NOT ABUSING — THE EYES

The eye is very sensitive to light and must be adjusted to different amounts of light. If you go suddenly from a dark to a light room, the eye cannot make the changes (adjustments*) quickly enough.

A good patient is careful not to strain his eyes.

Trying to close the pupil so tightly also may tire the muscles.

Sties are caused by germs just as boils are. The germs are carried to the eyelid on fingers, handkerchiefs, towels, or other objects. Sties may be spread easily from one eye to the other by rubbing or touching the eye that has the sty and then rubbing the

CARE OF THE EYES DURING MEASLES

other eye. Sties come more frequently when the eyes are strained or tired.

It is best to do your reading before bedtime. Then at eight o'clock go to bed and go straight to sleep.

You should have sunlight and fresh air in your room when you are getting over the measles. But the sun should not shine in your eyes. A bright light is a strain on the eyes. You should be careful not to look at a bright light until your eyes are strong again. Your bed can be moved so that the head of the bed is not facing the window. During the measles, the eyes are usually red and weak and are easily strained by close eye work. Do not try to read when you have the measles. What effect does measles or other serious illness have on your leg muscles? Do they feel strong the first time you try to walk? Do you think that illness might have a similar effect on the eye muscles?

Things to Do

1. Do you know how to draw figures like that on page 166? Draw similar pictures of children described in the following sentences.

A child holding a book in the best position

A child sitting reading in the daytime, with the book in the correct position and the light coming from above and behind

A child sitting and reading at night with the light coming from the right direction

A child writing with the light coming from the right direction

A child taking good care of his eyes when riding on a train

2. Read this chapter to your mother and father and ask them to remind you (*a*) to hold your book or other work up at least a foot from your eyes, (*b*) to have the light shine on the book from behind and above, and (*c*) to practice all the other habits which help the eyes to do their work more easily.

3. If you have never had your eyes tested, go to an oculist or find someone else who can test the eyes properly.

4. Get a writing desk for your room. Place it in the proper position. If you cannot get a desk, perhaps you can make one yourself. The following are directions for making the desk:

A homemade writing desk

Buy a large bread board. Fasten it to the wall, if that is possible in your room, with strong hinges, so that when you sit in your chair the board will be level with your elbows. Place it to the right of a window so that the light falls on the desk from the left side. Fasten a stick to it to hold it up.

5. Study the seats and desks in your classroom. Is every child's desk placed so that the light is right when he studies?   **6.** Read about the following good habits of using the eyes. How many of them have you formed? Can you say: "Yes, I always do that," to each of the habits in this list?

(*a*) Having your eyes examined once a year. (*b*) Telling your mother or teacher if your eyes hurt or are red, if they water easily, or if your head aches. (*c*) Wearing glasses if the oculist or optometrist tells you to do so. (*d*) Looking away in the distance after you have been reading or writing about fifteen minutes. (*e*) Holding your book at least a foot away from your eyes. (*f*) Choosing books having large, black print on dull paper. (*g*) Being careful that the light comes from behind and above so that there are no shadows on your work when you are reading, writing, or sewing. (*h*) Being careful that the light on your work is neither too glaring, as it is when the sun is shining brightly, nor too dull, as it is when twilight falls. (*i*) Taking care when you are recovering from measles or other similar illness: to rest your eyes as well as your body; to make objects of clay and to do other interesting things that do not require close eye work; to save your reading and sewing until you are entirely well; to be careful not to look at a bright light.

MAKING VACATIONS PLEASANT AND WORTH WHILE

Everyone looks forward to a vacation. During vacation there are many pathways to health and happiness. Some of these paths lead to country places. Some lead to cities.

VACATION IN CAMP

Even getting ready for camp is fun. And much of the fun at camp depends upon taking the right clothing with you. Usually the camp to which you are going gives you a list of all the things you should bring. All your underwear and clothing should be loose and comfortable — no tight bands anywhere. "Shorts," sleeveless shirts, and bathing suits give the sunlight and air a chance to do their healthful work. You need a warm sweater or coat to put on when you sit down after playing a game. There are rainy days in camp for which you must be prepared. You can enjoy the rain if you have a raincoat, rain hat, and rubbers or rubber boots.

Going on the train is exciting. You often meet other boys or girls who are going to the same camp. When you are on the train going to camp, and when you reach camp, you will see many boys or girls who "sit tall" and "stand tall." They just naturally carry themselves well.

One of the advantages of camp life is the friends you make. Camp is a fine place to learn to live happily with other people. It is a fine place to practice

Outdoor friends *Photo by H. Armstrong Roberts*

friendliness. On the way to camp you can find out about the interests of the other boys and girls. You are probably interested in many of the same things.

The first day at camp there are many things to learn and many things to see. It is hard to keep from doing too much the first day. But you can remember that there will be many other days to climb the hills, walk around the lake, play baseball, and go boating.

The French way of saying "How do you do" is "How do you carry yourself?" Do you carry your head high as if you were reaching up as far as you could reach with the top of your head? Do you walk with your toes pointing straight ahead? When you are sitting, do you push your hips far back in the seat and bend forward from the waist? Look at some of the pictures of children in this book and try to sit, stand, and walk like those who have the best posture. Ask your teacher to give you a posture test.

Habits of cleanliness are easy to form in camp. Seeing the other boys and girls washing their hands and faces before eating reminds you to wash yours too. A swim is the camp way of taking an allover bath every day. Swimming is one of the best kinds of cold baths. The cold water makes the blood vessels in the skin become smaller at first. Less blood is brought to the skin to be cooled. But as soon as you step out of the cold water, the little capillaries in the skin become larger. The blood rushes to the skin. It becomes red and warm. You feel "all in a glow." This is the way you should feel after a cold bath of any kind.

In your tent is a special place for your own towel, washcloth, toothbrush, drinking cup, and comb and brush. It is easy always to use your own.

Good vacation clothing

There is time every morning after breakfast to make your tent and clothing tidy. A camper soon learns to take care of himself. He does not have to be told to wash his hands and face before eating or to clean his nails, as he is sometimes told by his parents.

LEARNING AT CAMP 173

There is opportunity at camp to learn many new things. Often the morning is spent in learning to make jewelry or baskets, carve wood, or tool leather. Some boys and girls go on walks to learn the names of

A camper learns self-reliance.

birds and flowers and ferns and trees. Sometimes at night the campers go out on a hilltop and learn the names of some of the planets and of some of the thousands of stars in the sky.

Perhaps the most fun of all at camp are the games and sports — baseball in the late afternoon, walks along paths of pine needles, and swimming in the sunny morning or middle of the afternoon.

Many different kinds of games may be played at camp:

Basketball	End ball
Tennis	Fetch and carry relay
Volley ball	Leap the brook
Kick ball	Prisoner's base
Hare and hounds	Red Rover
Duck on the rock	Captain ball

Dances may be learned also. Everyone is out of doors at least three or four hours a day. Playing games suited to you out of doors every day and resting after playing (a) helps to build strong, obedient muscles, (b) develops* the body in an all-round way, (c) enlarges the chest, (d) increases the appetite, (e) encourages sound sleep, (f) improves the complexion, (g) improves your health in general. When we exercise, the heart pumps more quickly and strongly. It serves all parts of the body better. It brings blood rich with oxygen to the skin. The skin becomes pinker because of the larger amount of blood in the capillaries of the skin.

It is fun to learn games and skills you never knew before. Many boys and girls learn at camp to swim and row and paddle a canoe in the best form. They learn one new game or one new sport at a time. They do not start to learn one game and then give it up before they have learned to play it well. They prac-

Folk dancing improves posture.

tice each new exercise a short time every day at first. In this way they avoid fatigue. They spend a longer and longer time at each new exercise as they gain more skill in it.

You could spend an entire summer at a camp and never hear any quarreling on the playground. Camp boys and girls soon learn to play fair. They accept defeat in the best spirit. They are good winners and good losers. When people see boys and

The camp call to rest

girls playing at camp, they often think: "Those boys and girls play as though there were nothing in the world they would rather be doing." Do you work and play wholeheartedly, too?

RULES AND REST AT CAMP

There are not many rules at camp, but they are important. "Have a swimming buddy" is one of the rules. Why is this rule important? If you are going swimming in an unfamiliar place, find out first the depth of the water and whether it conceals any hidden rocks, strong currents, or dangerous animals. Going out in a canoe is not allowed until you have passed the swimming test. Boys and girls swimming long distances must always be accompanied by someone in a boat. What other camp rules do you know? Why are they important?

You learn to rest as well as to play at camp. Every day, after dinner, there is a quiet hour. Everyone takes a nap or writes letters or reads. On a long hike, after walking three or four miles, everyone lies down and rests for ten or fifteen minutes. No one takes a long climb until he has gone on many short ones.

At eight o'clock the bugle blows. Everyone goes to sleep. All around is the darkness and the quiet of the woods.

VACATION ON THE FARM

Summer days are busy days on the farm. They can be happy days too. Many a city child would like to spend the summer months on a farm. Some city children do so every year. Boys and girls enjoy doing worth-while things. They are proud to

Vacation on the farm

make a real contribution to the income and comfort and beauty of the farms on which they live. Their interest in doing useful work is shown by the fact that 900,000 farm boys and girls in the United States are members of the 4-H Clubs. The boys in these clubs grow an acre of cotton or corn or other farm products; or raise a pig, colt, or sheep. The girls also grow vegetables, and they can fruit and vegetables, make dresses and other clothing, paint furniture, and make the farm home and grounds beautiful. On pages 180 and 181 you will see 4-H Club members at work.

Do you know what are the four *H's* which the 4-H Clubs try to develop? They are the head, hands, heart, and health. There could be no better vacation than one in which boys and girls learn to use their minds, to become more skillful with their hands, to be friendly and helpful, and to win the best health possible for them.

Vacation in the City

People who go away for their vacations often do not know what a good time they can have at home. There are only a few things boys and girls can do at camp that they cannot do in the city. There are some things they can do in the city that they cannot do at camp — roller skating for example.

One of the best things about camp life is its regularity. There is a time for everything. Vacation in the city may be made more worth while by having a daily plan. In the morning after breakfast is a good

Courtesy U. S. Dept. of Agriculture
4-H Club boys

time to make your bed and to put your room and clothing in order.

There are many new things to learn in the city. You can take a walk in the park and learn the names of all the trees. It is fun to get a book about trees from the library and find the names of the new trees you see. You and your friends might form a tree

VACATION IN THE CITY

club or an art club. In many large cities there are art galleries and museums in which you can spend many happy mornings. Some boys and girls go to summer schools and learn many interesting things.

4-H Club girls *Courtesy U. S. Dept. of Agriculture*

If the roof of your house is flat, you can spend part of your day there. Many people in apartment houses have beach chairs which they keep on the roof. Sometimes they put on bathing suits and take a sun bath for half an hour. Sometimes they go up on the roof after supper and read or play games until dark.

Sometimes after dark they can study the stars just as the campers in the country do.

Playing three or four hours out of doors in the morning and in the afternoon is almost as easy in the

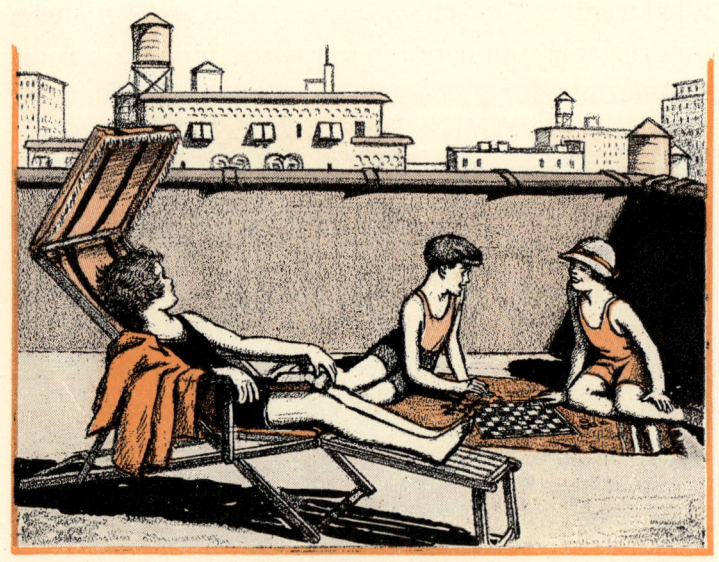

A sun bath on a city roof

city as at camp. There is always some place for play. In some of the city parks on week days there are so few people that you can easily imagine you have a big country place of your own. If there is no park near by, there is often a vacant lot. Sometimes a street is shut off from traffic for certain hours so that children can play there safely. Handball is a favorite game on city sidewalks. What other games can you play on city streets and sidewalks? More safety rules must be followed in the city than at camp.

Vacation is a good time to practice "safety first." What habits of safety can you teach younger children this summer about crossing the street, roller skating, playing games, playing with animals, using tools, going to the beach, or boating?

What do you think is the best way to keep cool in summer? When you wish to keep a room warm, you close the windows. Similarly, when your body wishes to keep warm, it makes the blood vessels in the skin smaller so that only a small amount of blood can come to the skin and be cooled. That is why a person who is thoroughly chilled looks pale. His body is trying to prevent further loss of heat from the skin.

When you wish to make a room cooler, you open the windows. Similarly, when the body is hot, the little blood vessels in the skin become larger so that more blood can come to the skin and get cooled. Heat brings the blood to the skin. That is why the skin looks red when you are hot.

One way to become cool is to sit in a breeze. Another way is to take a cool bath. In some cities in very hot weather the fire department turns on a hose in the street. Children in bathing suits flock under it. The water evaporating from their skin keeps them cool for some time. Another way to get cool is by getting hot! Hot enough to perspire! Can you explain how doing this would make you cool?

A shower bath on a city street

At eight o'clock in the evening no bugle sounds in the city, but boys and girls there are getting ready to go to bed. Fresh air comes in through the open windows. They go to sleep quickly after a happy day of work and play.

The laws of health. It pays to obey the simple laws of health in vacation time as well as during the rest of the year. No one ever became healthy except by obeying the laws of health. You may say: "Oh, it doesn't matter just this once," when you neglect to get enough rest or wash your hands before eating or keep your hands and other objects away from the face. You may think it does not matter if you buy an ice-cream soda between meals when you know orange juice or grape juice or fresh fruit would be better. But it does matter. Failing to do the healthful thing even one time makes forming the health habit harder. Try to have a long list of good habits to your credit at the end of the summer vacation.

OTHER CHILDREN'S QUESTIONS

Can you answer these questions which children have asked?

1. Why may it be harmful to sit on one's legs?
2. Is swimming better than running?
3. Is it healthful to stay up until ten o'clock every night to listen to the radio?
4. Is sleep during daylight the same as at night?
5. Why does exercising make us feel warm?
6. Why do some people go to places in Colorado, Switzerland, or Arizona for their health?

7. Why were some of the backwoodsmen so strong and healthy?

8. Why is cheerfulness in the list of good health habits?

Answers. Parts of Arizona have very dry, clean air and bright, healthful sunlight. It is so warm during the day in winter that you can be out of doors most of the time. In parts of Colorado and Switzerland the air is clear and cool and the sunlight very healthful. The scenery is so beautiful that one likes to walk, climb mountains, ride horseback, and play out of doors.

Sleep is the most complete rest for mind and body. Listening to the radio does not rest you as sleep does. If you stay up until 10 o'clock, you cannot get the sleep you need. Listening to good music on the radio (if there is good music) before going to bed at 8:00 or 8:30 is a good plan.

When we feel cold, it is because the blood in the capillaries of the skin is cooler than usual. When we feel hot, it is because the blood in the skin capillaries is hotter than usual. Except in illness, the blood is nearly the same temperature in all parts of the body. Exercise increases the heat of the body and sends more of the warm blood racing to the skin. The warm blood in the skin makes one feel warmer.

When you sit on your legs, you interfere with the flow of the blood through the blood vessels of the legs and throw your backbone into a sidewise curve. The backbone, as the drawing on this page shows, is not a single bone. It is a row of more than twenty ringlike bones. Muscles and ligaments* hold these rings together. Muscles make it possible for us to bend from side to side. If you sit on your foot or slouch in your seat for long at a time, certain muscles may become stretched and others shortened and the backbone may become fixed in this wrong position.

During daylight our sleep is not quite so sound as it is at night. The room is not so dark, and there are usually more noises. It is best for boys and girls of your age to have ten or eleven hours of sleep each night.

How may poor sitting posture affect the backbone?

The backwoodsmen led simple lives. They slept long hours; they worked out of doors; they ate simple food; they did not have the worries and hurry and noise which bother some people in cities.

Swimming is one of the best sports for the following reasons: It makes deep breathing necessary; it strengthens the muscles of the back and shoulders; it

Why not learn to swim?

trains the blood vessels of the skin to adjust to changes in temperature; it aids in getting rid of body wastes.

Cheerfulness aids health. "A merry heart doeth good like a medicine."

THINGS TO DO

1. Read this chapter to your family.
2. Tell what is the best thing to do if:

a. You are invited to go to motion pictures on sunny afternoons.

b. Company comes in when it is time to go to bed.

c. A group of boys or girls asks you to climb a

Milk and fruits have a place at picnics and parties.

mountain with them the first day you are in the country.

d. The meals at camp or at another place where you are spending your vacation consist largely of bread, meat, and sweets.

e. You have been playing hard.

3. Make a plan for your vacation days which includes all the good health habits you know and which is also the kind of day you would enjoy. Be sure to include the habits about which you have already read of caring for the eyes. Show your plan to your mother and father and ask them whether they think any changes should be made. 4. Spend part of your vacation making collections of interesting things to bring back to school, such as pressed flowers and leaves, pictures of places and people you will study next winter in geography and history, and pictures of children and adults doing healthful things. 5. Make posters of the safety rules you should follow when you are roller skating, playing baseball, in a boat, using a knife or ax, going swimming, or playing on the street if there is no other place to play.

6. Write a play about going on a camping trip:

Scene I. Getting ready to go. Taking the right kind of clothing, shoes, toilet articles, etc.

Scene II. After reaching camp. Planning meals.

Scene III. Spending the afternoon out of doors. Playing various games.

Scene IV. An accident occurs. Giving first aid. (Read the chapter on first aid again.)

Scene V. Spending the evening. Going to bed at half past eight.

Give this play for some other classes in your school.

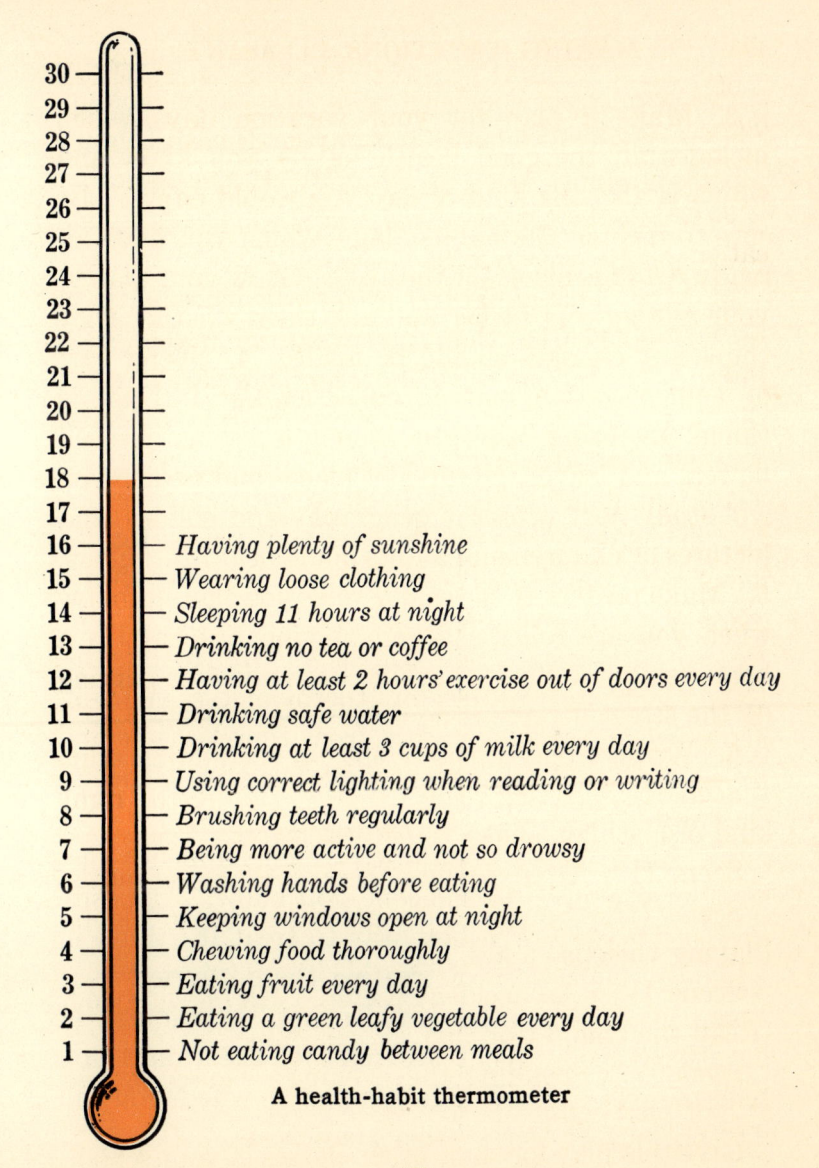

30	
29	
28	
27	
26	
25	
24	
23	
22	
21	
20	
19	
18	
17	
16	*Having plenty of sunshine*
15	*Wearing loose clothing*
14	*Sleeping 11 hours at night*
13	*Drinking no tea or coffee*
12	*Having at least 2 hours' exercise out of doors every day*
11	*Drinking safe water*
10	*Drinking at least 3 cups of milk every day*
9	*Using correct lighting when reading or writing*
8	*Brushing teeth regularly*
7	*Being more active and not so drowsy*
6	*Washing hands before eating*
5	*Keeping windows open at night*
4	*Chewing food thoroughly*
3	*Eating fruit every day*
2	*Eating a green leafy vegetable every day*
1	*Not eating candy between meals*

A health-habit thermometer

7. As a class, construct a model summer camp.

8. Ask your teacher to put in your Health Library a book of games, such as Bancroft, J. M., *Games for the Playground, Home, School, and Gymnasium*, and Pearl and Brown, *Health by Stunts*.

9. Make a list of natural sweets which are better to eat during vacation than candy and rich, sweet cake. Peaches, pears, dates, raisins, and honey are a few of the many delicious natural sweets. Make a list of summer vegetables from which to choose every day.

10. On page 191 is a habit thermometer which one girl made. The red line went up as she formed new health habits. These are the things she always does. On another page she kept a list of habits still to be formed. She said it was fun to do this. Keep such a health-habit thermometer yourself, and show it to your mother from time to time and to your teacher when you come back to school in the fall.

11. Make a list of injuries which happened last summer to you or to someone you know. Opposite each injury write the best way to treat it. Find in a first-aid book ways of treating these injuries.

12. Do you have any problems of "overdoing" in vacation time? What are some of the things you tend to do in excess? Make a plan in which you will do "nothing in excess" this summer.

PART TWO

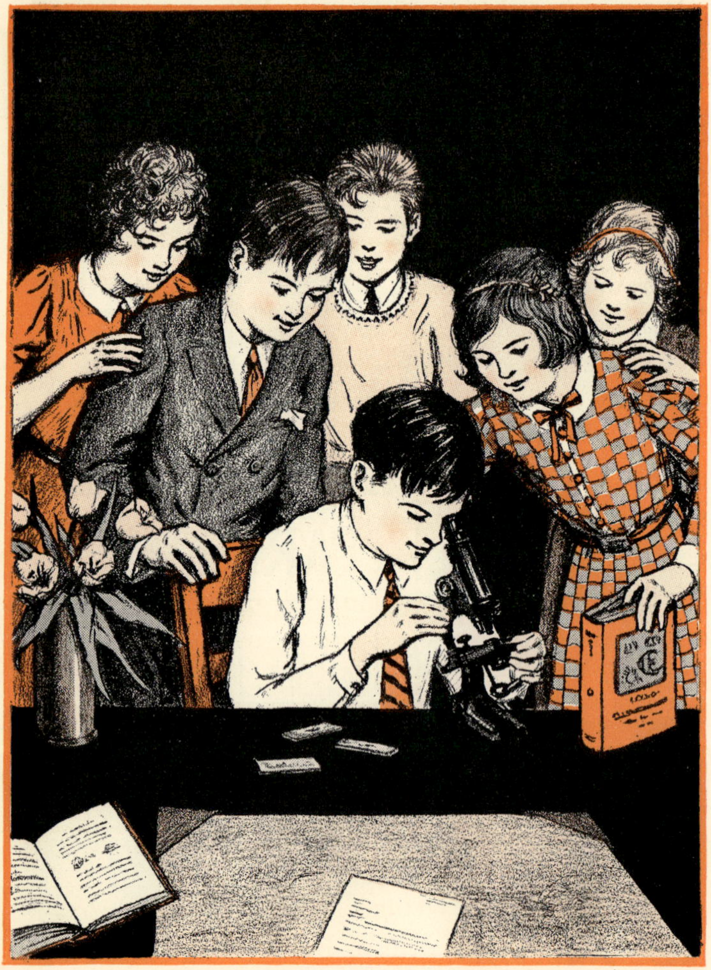

UNSEEN WORLDS

There are many worlds which you have never seen. You have never seen many of the lands which you read about in your geography books — mountains, seas, deserts, and peoples with clothing and customs different from ours. There are worlds beyond the stars, hidden from you as you look up at the sky at night. These unseen suns and planets are so far away that they are forever beyond man's reach. Some of them have never been seen clearly by anyone on this earth.

THE MICROSCOPIC WORLD

Another world which you have never seen is close at hand. This is the world of living things so small that you cannot see them with the eye alone. It is the world of things so small that they can be seen only with the microscope.* If one could look at a man under a huge microscope as powerful as that used in studying the bacteria* of the little world, he would seem to be as big as a tall mountain. Some of the bacteria seen through the same microscope look only as large as the periods and commas on this page; and there are living things so small that no one has yet been able to see them even with the most powerful microscope.

Some of the citizens of the "infinitely little world" are animals. Others are plants. There are still others which are like plants in some ways and like animals in other ways. Some of these small living things are good friends to man. Others are man's most deadly enemies.

Of the microscopic* animals, there are some eighty-five hundred known kinds. You have, perhaps, heard of one of them, the *amoeba.** It has only one cell. When it wants food, it reaches out toward it. When it comes near anything that might harm it, it moves away from it. (See drawings on page 197.) It moves by pushing part of itself out ahead and then catching up with itself. The amoeba may take many different shapes.

A few of these simple animals cause disease. One is known to cause malaria;* another is the cause of African sleeping sickness. The others, as far as

THE MICROSCOPIC WORLD 197

we know, are useful to man, or at least do no harm. They serve as food for larger animals.

The simplest of the microscopic plants is a speck

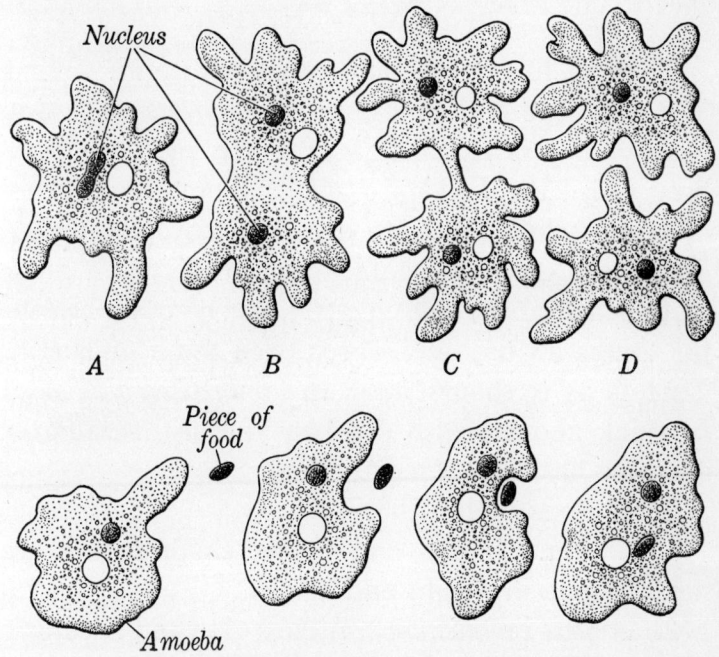

A microscopic one-celled animal, the amoeba

How does it get food?   How does it move about?   How does it increase in number?

of thin, bluish-green, jellylike substance surrounded by a cell wall that you can see through. Plants like flowers and trees are made of millions of cells and have many different parts each of which has a special use. One group of plants having a single cell is the *bacteria*. You will learn about these simple and sometimes dangerous plants in other chapters.

The Land of Health

There is, in a sense, another unseen world. What is it that one seldom thinks of if he has it? One answer to this riddle is *health*. It has sometimes been called the *Land of Health*. You seldom think of health when you have it. You may play out of doors, eat green vegetables and fruit, drink milk, go to bed at about eight o'clock, and do other healthful things all day and never once think of health. That is as it should be. The only time you need to think about health is when you are learning or choosing healthful things to do.

Some signs of health are:

1. *Growth.* Babies and young children who are healthy gain in weight and height.

2. *A good complexion.* A clear skin and naturally pink cheeks are usually signs of health.

3. *Well-developed bones and muscles.* Good development* of bones and muscles is often shown in good posture.*

4. *Joy in work and play.* The healthy boy and girl work and play happily and wholeheartedly.

In the following chapters you will find new pathways to success in games, in sports, in work, and in friendships.

Do you wish to run races, play games of many

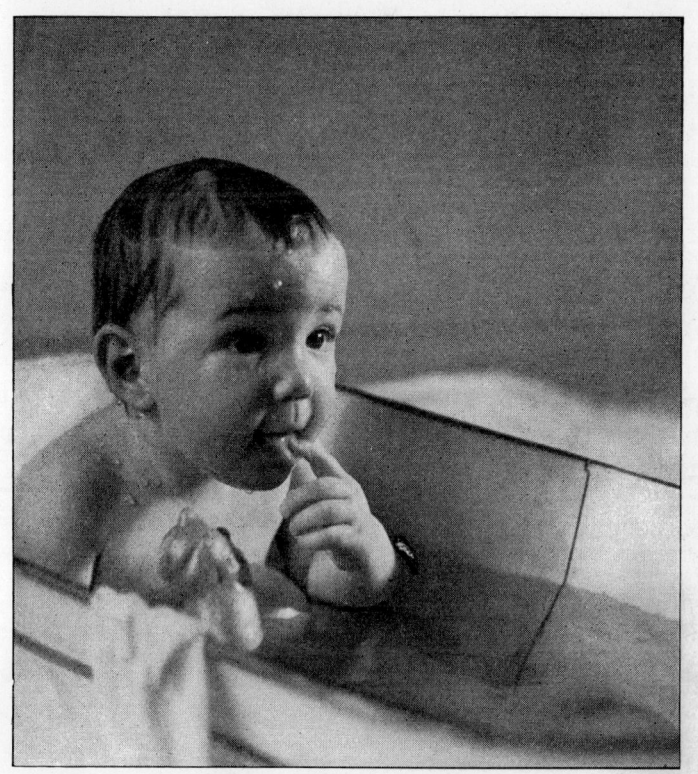

A citizen of the Land of Health

kinds, skate, and, in general, be a leader in outdoor life? Famous athletes and the best players on college teams obey training rules which are just like the health rules you have been following. They get sufficient sleep regularly every night. They eat the right kind and amount of food — *training-table food*, they call it. They do not smoke tobacco or drink alcoholic beverages They exercise regularly every day. They avoid unnecessary excesses and strains of all kinds. They do all these things in order to keep fit. Keeping fit makes it possible for them to win the race or the game.

Do you wish to do your best in school work? Arithmetic problems are not solved so easily if you are sleepy and tired. It is harder to study history and geography when you have a bad cold or headache. A serious disease, such as scarlet fever or diphtheria, makes you lose so much school work that it is hard for you to catch up with the class. Sometimes illness prevents you from passing the year's work, and you have to stay behind in the same grade while your friends go on to another class. A great deal of illness in the world is unnecessary. It can be prevented.

Do you wish to be well liked by boys and girls? In order to have friends, a person must be friendly. We often like pet cats and dogs just because they seem glad to see us and like us so much. Happiness also helps to win friends. If your health is good, you are more likely to be good-natured and jolly.

That is part of being a "good sport." Knowing how to play games which other boys and girls like and being able to swim and run and walk with them are other ways of winning friends. If for any reason you cannot do these things yourself, you can enjoy watching your friends do them. Sometimes you can teach them a new game.

Good habits of eating, sleeping, playing, and working help boys and girls to win the best health possible for them. Health and happiness are twins. They usually go together. Health is a pathway to friendships. Health attracts and holds friends.

Things to Do

1. Do you ever have to make choices regarding healthful living? Write a list of questions about health which you would like to have answered. The following are some of the questions which one class asked the first day of school. Answer them.

"Why is water necessary? How many glasses a day should we drink? When is the best time to drink it?" "What food should my family eat in order to keep warm and well in the winter? There are a baby, a sister, and a brother in my family, besides my mother and father." "How can one keep from getting colds? Is it possible to be free from colds all winter?" "What causes colds and other diseases?" "How can one keep the house really clean?" "What harm do smoking and drinking do?" "How can one avoid toothaches?" "What is the best way to take care of the baby?" "What

Reading health stories

harm do flies and mosquitoes do?" "Why do we have to be in bed by nine o'clock?"

2. Make a health magazine in your class. Put in the magazine the health news of your class. Send a boy or girl to get health news from other classes. Write health stories. Make pictures in your art period to put in the magazine. Ask your

teacher how you can make copies of the magazine for everyone in your class. Other classes might like to have copies, too, if it is very well written and interesting. One class put in their health magazine the best menus chosen in the lunchroom each month. They made riddles, too, such as: I am so small that you cannot see me with your eyes alone; I cause sickness; I cannot live in bright sunlight. What am I?

3. Make a plan for caring for your eyes and follow it all the year. The plan should include: holding your book at least twelve inches from your eyes, having the light come from behind and above, and telling the teacher or nurse if your eyes are red or sore. What other habits of caring for the eyes can you add? **4.** Do you know of someone who ate too much, or exercised too much, or did other things in excess? Tell the story. Talk in class about the relation of health to moderation in all things.

5. Write the health habits which you read about each week. Put a star (*) after the habits you have already formed. Try to form the other good habits so that by the end of the year you will have a star after every one. Bring to class pictures and paragraphs about healthful living which you find in newspapers and magazines. Use these in class whenever they help to answer questions.

HOW TO MAKE AND KEEP MILK SAFE

Milk is the best food for children. It is also one of the best foods for bacteria. Bacteria grow faster on a milk diet than children do. If milk is not kept cold, the bacteria in it will grow so rapidly during a day that there may be as many as 22,000,000 in a thimbleful of milk.

Most of the bacteria in milk are harmless. Many of them make milk sour. Some of them may cause disease. Usually, when the total number of bacteria in milk is large, there are also very many of the kind that make people sick. Our cities try to limit the number of bacteria in milk.

How Can Milk Be Made Safe?

Milk can be made safe. In fact, most of the milk that is sold today is clean and safe. Farmers are careful to keep the cows clean and the cow barn free from dust and other dirt. They keep their hands clean as well as the pails and other things they use when milking the cows. They try to get as little dirt as possible into the milk. Perhaps you have seen a farmer strain fresh milk through a piece of white cheesecloth and have seen a dark stain left on the cloth. If there is no stain or only a very faint stain on the cheesecloth, the farmer is pleased because it shows that the milking has been done carefully.

A model dairy barn

Photo by Ewing Galloway

This circular table revolves once every 12½ minutes, during which time 50 cows are washed, dried, milked, and allowed to return unguided, each to her place in the barn one eighth of a mile away.

The farmer is also careful to have all his cans sterilized.* He puts the milk into cans on which all the bacteria have been killed. He keeps the cans covered. He puts them on ice. Even with so much

Sterilizing the bottles

Photo by Ewing Galloway

care, the milk may not be safe. The person milking the cows may have been ill. Dangerous bacteria from his hands or mouth may have fallen into the milk. The cows may not be healthy. Their milk may contain bacteria which cause sickness.

PASTEURIZING MILK

But there is a simple way in which all milk, fairly clean to begin with, may be made perfectly safe. The harmful bacteria in milk, you remember, can be killed by heating it to a temperature high enough to

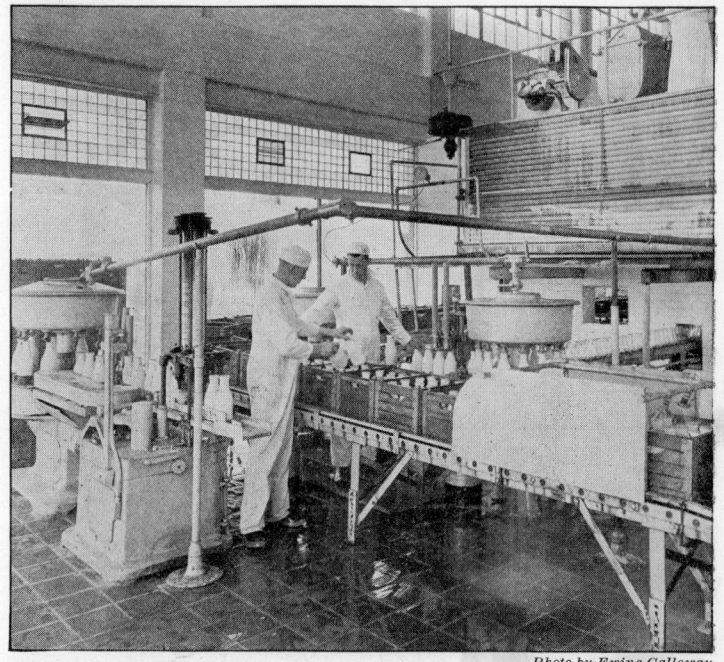

Photo by Ewing Galloway

Sealing the bottles of pasteurized milk

kill germs. Look at the top of your milk bottle. You will probably see the word *pasteurized*.* This word tells you that the milk has been heated to 145° F. for 30 minutes. Do you know how hot

145° F. is? The *F*, you remember, stands for Fahrenheit,* which is one measure of temperature.

You have, of course, read the thermometer* in your schoolroom or at home. The thermometer tells you how warm or how cold a room is. Read the thermometer in your room now. Is it about 68° F.? That is a good temperature for a room. On summer days, the thermometer may go up to 90° F. or higher. Your body's temperature is about 98.6° F. Water boils at sea level at a temperature of 212° F.

When milk is pasteurized, the thermometer goes higher than on the hottest summer day but not so high as when water is boiled. Heating milk to 145° F. for at least 30 minutes kills the dangerous bacteria. A higher temperature is not necessary and spoils the flavor. A lower temperature might not kill the germs. By being heated to 145°F. for 30 minutes and then cooled quickly, the milk has been made safe.

Take off the last three letters of the word *pasteurize*. What word do you have left? *Pasteur* is the name of a great French scientist. It was Pasteur who discovered that milk could be made safe by heating it in this way. Try to read one of the stories of the life of Pasteur.

Pasteurization* does not make dirty milk clean or poor milk rich. Pasteurization does not make milk less digestible or taste less good. Pasteurization simply kills disease germs which may be harmful. About one half of the milk used in the United States is now pasteurized. By pasteurization, milk can be made so free from bacteria that it can be sent across the ocean and back without spoiling. In the dairy the milk is pasteurized, cooled, and poured into sterilized bottles.

How Can You Keep Milk Safe?

After you buy milk that has been made safe by pasteurizing it, you must keep it safe until you can use it. Milk cannot protect itself from bacteria. Germs grow in pasteurized milk as well as in fresh milk. In how many ways may bacteria get into milk in your home? When it is left uncovered? Yes indeed. Bacteria may possibly be riding on dust particles in the air and sail into the open pitcher or bottle of milk. A person may cough or sneeze over it. A fly may come along and wash the bacteria off his feet and wings into the uncovered milk.

Before pouring out the milk, be sure to wash the mouth of the bottle. The milkman's hands have not been pasteurized! They are not free from germs. He has taken hold of the top of the bottle and left some of the bacteria from his hands there. If you pour the safe, pasteurized milk from the bottle, the bacteria may be washed off into your glass —

unless you have washed the top of the bottle before opening it and have lifted up the cap with a clean knife. (Grade *A* milk in some cities has a cap over the top of the bottle which keeps its rim clean.)

Milk should always be kept in clean glasses or dishes. Putting clean milk in dirty dishes undoes

Why wash the top of the milk bottle?

the good work done by the farmer and the dairy company in making the milk safe. When you have used part of a bottle of milk, throw the cap away and cover the bottle with a clean glass before you put it away in the icebox.

Putting the milk in a cold place promptly is most important because bacteria multiply very fast

KEEPING MILK CLEAN AND COLD

in a warm place. Therefore, milk should be kept in the coldest part of the refrigerator or icebox. Some people get up late in the morning. They leave their milk out in the sun several hours before they take it in. Other people put it in the refrigerator as soon as the milkman brings it. Others build a box to protect it from the sun and from cats and dogs. Which way do you think is best?

OTHER CHILDREN'S QUESTIONS

Find the answers to those of the following questions which you cannot answer for yourself.

The milkman's helpers in providing clean, cold milk for the family

Photo by J. C. Allen & Son

1. How can you pasteurize milk on a farm?
2. Is sour milk harmful to drink?

3. Are cheese and bread good food for the Dutch people?

Answers. Cheese and bread are the chief foods of many healthy people in Holland and in other countries. In addition to the bread and cheese, they have some fruit and vegetables. The day's meals should be built around bread and milk or milk products.

If you live on a farm, you can pasteurize milk by heating it in the top of a large double boiler to 145° F. for 30 minutes. Or you can heat it in a saucepan until the thermometer reaches 155° F. Then cool it, and keep it cold and covered. If you have no cooking thermometer, it is best to heat the milk until it reaches the boiling point. A cooking thermometer is a simple glass thermometer that has many uses. Without a thermometer, the milk is often overheated. Heating milk to near the boiling point changes its flavor so that to many people it does not have a pleasant taste.

Properly prepared sour milk and buttermilk are healthful foods. If milk sours quickly and thoroughly, harmful bacteria in it have been killed by the acid which was formed when the milk became sour. Sour milk is also easy for many people to digest. Milk just beginning to sour may be dangerous because the acid has not yet become strong enough to kill the dangerous bacteria.

MORE ABOUT MILK

THINGS TO DO

1. Add to your class health library any books or bulletins or pictures you have about milk. The story of the life of Pasteur should be a part of your class

Count your cups of milk.

library. 2. Visit a dairy, if there is one near your school, to see how the milk you get is pasteurized and bottled. 3. Make a poster telling all the ways of keeping milk free from bacteria. 4. Write a story about some harmful bacteria which, after a long journey, finally reached some baby's milk.

5. Learn the rules which the health department of your state, county, or city has made to protect people from unsafe milk. 6. How many different people handle the milk from the time it comes from the cow to the time you drink it at the table? What should each person do to keep the milk free from harmful bacteria?

7. Count the number of cups of milk you had yesterday. Did you have at least three cups in all, either to drink, in milk soups, or in puddings?

AIDING DIGESTION

You have probably already read the story about the experiment on the cat that got angry at mealtime. You have already learned that anger and even slight worry may stop the movements of the stomach and the flow of the digestive juices.

WHEN DIGESTION IS CHECKED

Does fear hinder digestion? In India a test was once used to tell whether or not a prisoner was guilty of a crime. He was given a handful of dry rice to put in his mouth. He kept the rice in his mouth a few minutes. If the rice was still dry when he took it out of his mouth, the judge said: "Guilty."

If the rice were wet with saliva, the judge said: "Not Guilty." Can you think of any reason why dry rice might be a sign that the prisoner was guilty? Fear, like anger, stops the flow of the digestive juices. The saliva in the mouth is one of the digestive juices. If the prisoner had committed a crime and was very much frightened, his saliva stopped flowing and the rice would remain dry. If he were not guilty and had no fear of being punished, his saliva would flow as usual and the rice would be wet. Of course, he might have done no wrong and still be so afraid of the test that his mouth would stay dry. Then the test would not be just.

It is interesting, however, that people in India discovered, before scientists did, that fear hinders digestion. Today people try to avoid fear and worry at and just after mealtime because these feelings interfere with digestion. It is unwise to quarrel at the dinner table.

Does haste hinder digestion? Haste may check digestion in two ways: first, by causing a feeling of worry and excitement; and second, by not giving enough time to chew the food. It is a wise plan to allow at least fifteen minutes for breakfast and a half hour for each of the other meals. If you get up early enough, you will not have to hurry through breakfast. If you do not waste time on the way home to lunch, you will not have to hurry through lunch and run back to school. If you live more than fifteen minutes' walk from school and have an hour at noon, it would be better to take your lunch to school or buy it in the school lunchroom than to run home, eat

The king's jester

quickly, and run back, worrying all the time about being late. Taking your time when eating aids digestion.

When Digestion Is Helped

How can we make our meals cheerful? In olden times kings had jesters to make their meals pleasant. The jester was dressed in a funny suit of bright, cheerful colors. He did and said things to make the king laugh. When the king laughed, the digestive juices flowed more easily. He digested his food better.

Today we have no jesters, but we can do many things to make our meals cheerful: keep calm, not argue or quarrel, talk about interesting things. Can you think of other things to do to make mealtime a happy time? "Laugh and grow fat" is an old saying. Laughter aids digestion, and a good digestion makes it easier to gain weight.

How should foods be cooked to aid digestion? Foods that are baked, boiled, steamed, or broiled digest more quickly than fried food. Frying delays the digestion of some foods, like the white of an egg, by making them very hard. They do not dissolve easily. Frying adds fat to food. Fat in large amounts delays digestion. Food that remains too long in the stomach tends to form gas and to make a person feel uncomfortable. Fat that is heated smoking hot may irritate the lining of the stomach.

How should foods be served to aid digestion? Food that looks good and tastes good makes "the mouth water." It makes the stomach water, too. In more scientific words, it increases the flow of digestive juices in the mouth and stomach. It is easy to serve a meal attractively by having a clean cloth and dishes, hot foods served hot, and cold foods served cold, and all put neatly on the plates. Meals should be served at about the same time every day. You do not keep your friends waiting to see you. You should not keep your stomach waiting past the time when it expects the next meal. Regular mealtimes aid digestion.

OTHER CHILDREN'S QUESTIONS

Answer as many as you can. Look up the answers to the others.

1. Why does a bear eat so much in the spring?
2. Why were people in Europe so anxious to have the spices of India?
3. Is the food the Spaniards eat as healthful as ours?
4. Why aren't pickles good for us?
5. Is it dangerous to bathe near mealtime?

Answers. Spanish food is likely to have more spice in it than ours and for this reason is not so healthful as our less spicy diet.

It is not dangerous to bathe before mealtime. In fact, it is very important to wash the hands and face before eating. But it is usually best not to take an allover bath immediately *after* eating a regular meal. Bathing draws some of the blood to the skin that may be needed in digesting food in the stomach and intestines.

The people in Europe did not have a very attractive and varied diet. They were glad to have spices to make the food taste better. When we have so many fruits and vegetables that have a delicious flavor of

Nature's sweets

their own, we do not need to use spices. In fact spices spoil the natural flavors of fruits and vegetables.

Most pickles are very sour and spicy. If eaten in excess, they irritate the delicate lining of the stomach and spoil the appetite for plain food.

Bears go to sleep for the winter. They live on their own fat. They cannot get food easily in the cold weather. In order to store up fat for the winter, bears eat a good deal in the fall. While they are sleeping in the winter, they are using this stored-up fat. In the spring when they come out of their caves, they are thin and hungry and begin to eat a great deal again.

Things to Do

1. Do what you can this week to make mealtime happy for everyone at the table. 2. Keep a record of all the fried foods you have at home during one week. Opposite each of the foods write how it could just as easily have been baked or broiled or steamed or boiled. Show your list to your mother and ask her if she agrees with you.

3. Make a list of concentrated* sweets, such as chocolate creams and other very sweet foods made of white sugar, which may irritate the delicate lining of the stomach. Opposite each write a natural sweet to choose in its place. 4. Tell the class about some fads* in dieting that you have read about or heard about. Are the people who follow one special kind of diet or exercise or other fad obeying the rule of "Nothing in excess"? Moderation in all things is best for most people.

A HEALTHFUL SCHOOL LUNCH

Some boys and girls bring their lunches to school. Some buy their lunches in school. Some go home for lunch. Which do you do? In every case, there is a chance to choose wisely. Here are some lunches that certain boys and girls ate one day:

1. Ham sandwich
   Cup of cocoa
   Piece of candy
2. Rolls with butter and cheese
   Cup of milk
3. Meat sandwich
   Banana
   Orange
4. Egg sandwich
   Glass of milk
   Chocolate candy
5. Lettuce sandwiches
   Cup custard
   Banana
6. Bread and jelly
   Glass of milk
7. Egg sandwiches
   Glass of milk
   Apple
8. Coffee
   Chocolate layer cake
9. Pork sandwich
   Pickles
   Pie
10. Graham crackers
    Milk
    Peaches

Which of these ten lunches do you think are good lunches? A good lunch to take to school contains "The Big Three" — cereal or bread, milk or cheese, fruit or vegetables. Your lunch box may contain some food from each of the following four groups:

Group 1. Sandwiches having any of the following kinds of filling: finely chopped boiled eggs mildly seasoned; peanut butter; dried fruit paste made by grinding raisins, dates, figs, or other fruits and nuts in

Foods for the school lunch box

the food chopper; chopped chicken liver; chopped meat; cheese of various kinds. Butter spread between date or raisin bread makes a delicious sandwich. Some children like a sandwich made by spreading one slice of bread thickly with cottage or cream cheese and the other slice thinly with jelly.

Group 2. Fruit. Fresh fruit of all kinds and ripe tomatoes are easily carried. Applesauce and other kinds of stewed fruit may be carried in small jars with screw tops.

Group 3. A sweet such as jelly sandwich, sponge cake, cookies, cup custard, dates or figs, or fruit candy.

Group 4. Something to drink. If possible, bring a pint bottle of milk or fruit juice, or a thermos bottle of hot milk soup or cocoa. At least take a drink of water.

Now let us test the lunches of these children:

Lunch No. 1 has milk in the cocoa. It has no fruit or vegetable. A few pieces of celery or some raw fresh fruit would improve this lunch.

Lunch No. 2 is very good as it is. An apple, a young carrot, or other fruit or raw vegetable would make it still better.

Lunch No. 3 has two healthful fruits. Cottage cheese instead of meat in the sandwich would improve the lunch.

If a natural sweet were used instead of the candy, lunch No. 4 would be a very good one. What natural sweet do you suggest?

It would be hard to find a better lunch than No. 5.

If some chopped raw vegetables mixed with a little salad dressing were eaten with the bread and butter instead of the jelly, lunch No. 6 would contain the "Big Three."

Lunch No. 7 is an excellent lunch which any country child might have.

Lunch No. 8 is very bad. It contains nothing but two stimulating foods, one of which is sweet and rich and both of which should be kept out of your lunch box.

Lunch No. 9 is very difficult to digest because of the sour pickles, fat meat, and pie. It includes no milk, vegetables, or fruit.

Lunch No. 10 is excellent. It includes the "Big Three."

In winter, as well as in the fall and spring, fruit and vegetables should find a place in the lunch box — chopped raw cabbage and carrots mixed with a little lemon juice or vinegar, a big stalk of celery, apples, or winter pears.

Other Children's Questions

Try to answer the following questions about foods:

1. Which foods are best for us to eat? Where can we get these foods?

2. Why do some people eat anything they want at any time they want to and still seem to be very strong?

3. Is cocoa good for us?

4. How can Eskimos live without vegetables?

5. Should children eat fried eggs?

6. Were so many potatoes good for the people of Ireland?

7. Is hominy good for children?

8. Is rye bread more healthful than white?

9. What is the reason that soup beans do not make me sick, but butter beans do?

Answers. Potatoes are an excellent vegetable. In one experiment a man and a woman lived 167 days in good health on a diet largely of potatoes. Some fats and a little fruit were added to the potatoes. Their digestion was excellent and they felt well. But although grown people can live for some time on such a diet, it is much better to balance the diet with the Big Three — fruit or vegetables, cereals or bread, and milk. If the people of Ireland had had more milk and cheese and some green vegetables or fruit to eat with their potatoes, they would have had a better-balanced diet — one which contains all the necessary foods in the right amounts.

Once in a great while there are foods which certain people cannot eat. A few people get hives when they eat strawberries. One child could not eat white of egg. But usually it is just a notion that "you can't eat this" or "you can't eat that."

The Eskimos can live without vegetables because they eat all parts of the animals they kill — not just the muscle part as we do. The other parts of the animals supply some of the same food values that vegetables do. What are these other parts?

People who eat anything they want at any time they want to may be strong for some time in spite of their bad food habits. But there is plenty of proof that food makes a difference between health and sickness, even though a person does not get sick as soon as he neglects the rules of health.

Hominy, which is made from corn, is a good cereal and is very cheap in some parts of the country.

Fried eggs are better than no eggs, but poached eggs and eggs cooked in water just below the boiling point until the yolks are mealy are more quickly and easily digested than eggs fried in very hot fat.

Rye bread contains more food values than white bread. It is good to use rye bread part of the time.

People in all parts of the world, if they have the money, can get: (1) cereals and bread; (2) dried or evaporated milk, if fresh milk cannot be obtained; (3) fresh fruit or vegetables or canned tomatoes and other canned and dried vegetables and fruits. These three kinds of foods are the foundation of a healthful diet.

Cocoa is often used to flavor milk. The cocoa itself is a stimulant, somewhat like tea and coffee. But children often drink more milk when it is flavored with a little cocoa. It is better to drink milk flavored with a little cocoa than to drink no milk at all. But the less cocoa used in flavoring the milk, the better. Light-brown cocoa is better than dark-brown cocoa.

Things to Do

1. Write the lunch you brought to school yesterday. Was it a good lunch? Could you have made it better? Then write: "A Better Lunch for Tomorrow." Show the lunch you have chosen to your mother. 2. Invite the teacher to a luncheon party some noontime. Bring a lunch like No. 5 or No. 7 on page 221. Find a pleasant spot in the school to eat your lunch. If the day is warm and sunny, have the luncheon party out of doors. Be careful to pick up all the papers and crumbs after the party is over. 3. Collect recipes for fruit candies from newspapers, magazines, and cookbooks. You will often find a page of candy recipes in the Christmas number of magazines. Some of them will tell you how to make delicious candies from nuts, figs, raisins, dates, prunes, pineapples, and other fruits.

4. If you have a garden, help to raise vegetables and fruits next spring so that you can have some to

put in your lunch box all winter. **5.** Ask your teacher if it is possible to have a hot lunch prepared at school, so that you will have at least one hot dish at noon during the cold weather.

6. Make fruit candy instead of sugar candy for

Making fruit candy

Thanksgiving, Christmas, parties, or your daily lunch box. Here are a few recipes:

Stuffed Dates

Wash the dates. Take out the pits. In place of the pits put a piece of nut or some peanut butter.

Stuffed Prunes

Wash a pound of prunes. Put them in a sieve over boiling water, or in a steamer for fifteen minutes.

When they are cool enough, cut each prune open and take out the pit. Fill each prune with nuts, dates, or a mixture of raisins, nuts, and candied pineapple which you have chopped or ground together.

Fruit Balls

Wash 1 cup of raisins; dry them; take out the stems and seeds. Add a half cup of nut meats and a few grains of salt. Add some candied pineapple if you have it. Chop all together, or better still, put all through the meat grinder. If the mixture is very dry, add a little orange juice. Make into small balls and roll in powdered sugar, coconut, or chopped nuts.

7. What are some of the difficulties boys and girls meet in having healthful breakfasts, dinners, and suppers? Talk about these difficulties in class and suggest ways in which each difficulty may be overcome. Talk this lesson over with your mother.

KEEPING HOUSE

Three or four hundred years ago keeping house was far from pleasant. The houses were overrun with flies, fleas, and lice. The floors were covered with dirty straw. There were pigpens on the main streets. People threw waste of all kinds out of the bedroom windows. There was no electricity, running water in houses, or any good way of carrying off body wastes and dirty water. Sickness spread rapidly. How different from the neat houses of today, so attractive and so easy to keep clean! How different from our orderly streets!

HEALTHFUL HOUSEKEEPING

A healthful home and neighborhood encourage healthful living. You eat good food as a matter of course when it is attractively cooked and served. You just naturally sleep soundly and comfortably in a clean, dark, cool, quiet bedroom on a well-made bed. Housework is enjoyable in a pleasant kitchen which is easy to keep clean. Keeping house well is an important pathway to health. "If anything is worth doing at all, it is worth doing well." Housework is certainly worth doing in the best way.

What is the best way to wash dishes? The best way is sometimes also the easiest and quickest way. This is the way a brother and sister who were keeping house together washed their dishes: Jean began bringing the glassware and silver from the table while Jack arranged the dishpan, dish drainer, and dishes as they are shown in the drawing on page 241 and filled the dishpan half full of warm, soapy water. Jack began at once to wash and rinse the glasses, while his sister brought out the rest of the dishes and scraped and piled them. She took the scrapings out to the covered garbage can. When Jean had done this, the glasses were ready to dry with a clean towel. She left the other dishes in the drainer and straightened up the dining room. Jack kept on

In a pleasant kitchen

washing the dishes — first the silver, then the china, then the pots and pans.

When all the dishes, except pots and pans, had been washed and placed in the wire dish drainer, Jack emptied his dishpan, placed the drainer over the dishpan, and carefully poured boiling water over all the dishes. Then he placed the wire basket of dishes back on the tray, washed the dish towels, and washed and dried the dishpan.

In the meantime, most of the dishes had become dry after having been rinsed with the boiling water. Jean lifted them out, placed them in piles, and put them away in the closet. She picked up cups by the handle and plates by the edge. She did not wish to put her fingers on the part of any dish which touched the food or the lips of the person using it. She polished the silver with a clean dish towel before putting it away. In this way the dishes were washed quickly and were very clean.

Dorothy and her little sister also had a good time washing the dishes in the same way. Dorothy washed the dishes and her little sister dried them.

An experiment was once made to see how many bacteria were left on dishes washed in different ways. When dishes were washed in cold water, many bacteria remained on them. When they were washed in warm, soapy water, there were fewer bacteria. When the dishes were washed in hot, soapy water and rinsed thoroughly in boiling water, all the germs were killed. Being kept in a temperature of 145° F. for 30 minutes will kill most of the harmful bacteria. Water, as hot as the hands can stand it, plus soap, plus a small amount of a chlorine compound, will kill

GOOD FORM IN DISHWASHING

most of the bacteria on dishes. This method of washing dishes is used in some restaurants. Rinsing the dishes by dipping them in boiling water for a few moments will kill practically all the harmful bacteria

A dishwashing plan in which little sister has a part

— a good plan that can be used at home. Let the air dry the dishes. The air has far fewer bacteria in it than most dish towels.

During the World War half of the men in one camp washed their dishes by dipping them into a large pan of warm water. The other half dipped their dishes in boiling water. The records showed that the group which washed the dishes in boiling water had only one fifth as many cases of influenza as those who washed their dishes in warm water.

A good sport does not let mother do all the housework.

What is the best way to sweep and dust? Sweeping and dusting should remove dirt — not scatter it. You have probably seen people scattering dust in all directions with a feather duster. They imagine they are cleaning the room. Do you think they are?

Many people today use a *vacuum cleaner** to clean their carpets and rugs. The vacuum cleaner pulls the dirt into the bag. It is an excellent way to get rid of dirt. If you use a broom, scatter pieces of damp newspaper or some damp sawdust on the floor. Then the dust will stick to the damp bits of paper or to the sawdust. It will not fly about the room.

When you dust, use a damp or an oiled cloth. A good way to dampen a cloth is to wet half of it, wring it, fold it together, and wring it again. This will make the cloth damp enough to catch the dust but not wet enough to hurt the furniture. The dust sticks to the cloth. It does not fly about as it does when you use a dry cloth. When you wash the cloth after dusting, all the dust is carried away in the dirty water. When you clean wooden floors, use an oiled mop which collects the dust and does not scatter it.

The best time to clean the dining room is after meals. Then there is no danger that the dust will settle on the food or dishes. Very few dangerous bacteria are found in dusty air out of doors. Direct sunlight kills most bacteria. They are more likely to live on the dust indoors where the sunlight does not reach them. Indoors you will be careful not to let the dust fly around or fall upon food or dishes.

What is the best way to care for the icebox? Some bacteria will grow in a cold refrigerator. But the colder it is, the more slowly they will grow. You should keep your icebox full of ice. You should not cover the ice with a cloth or newspaper as some people do. Covering the ice saves ice but wastes food. It is the *melting* ice which draws the heat from the refrigerator and keeps it cold. The electric and gas refrigerators keep food very cold. They are also easy to clean.

What do you see when you open *your* refrigerator? Do you see food in clean dishes — not in the paper in which it was wrapped? The paper wrappings are likely to have bacteria on them. Are the milk and butter covered? Milk and butter absorb* odors from other foods very easily. Are the green vegetables covered also? Green vegetables keep crisper and fresher if they are covered. The water does not evaporate from them so easily. Is all the food fresh? No food should remain in the refrigerator long enough to spoil.

Is your refrigerator as clean as the dishes from which you eat? It should be. Food spilled on the shelves should be wiped up at once. The refrigerator should be cleaned quickly and thoroughly at least once a week. The tube through which the water runs should be cleaned with a brush, if possible, and with washing soda and boiling water. The part where the food is kept should be cleaned with hot

A SANITARY KITCHEN

soapsuds and rinsed with clean, hot water. Shelves and ice rack should be dried in the sun, if possible.

The Healthful Home

What are the marks of a pleasant, sanitary kitchen? Take away the last two letters of the

Courtesy Good Housekeeping Institute
Why would it be pleasant and easy to work in this sanitary kitchen?

word sanitary* and add an *s*. You have the Latin word *sanitas* which means health. A sanitary kitchen is a healthful kitchen. A healthful kitchen

KEEPING HOUSE

is light and airy and easy to keep clean. How many of the following good points does your kitchen have?

1. The woodwork and furniture are plain and without grooves or cracks.

2. The floor is covered with plain brown "battleship" linoleum,* or linoleum with a simple pattern, or a floor of hardwood such as maple or beech.

3. Walls and woodwork are painted a light, warm gray, buff, or other soft, light color.

4. Furniture and the built-in closets or cabinets in which dishes and dry foods are kept are painted light, soft colors which are restful to look at.

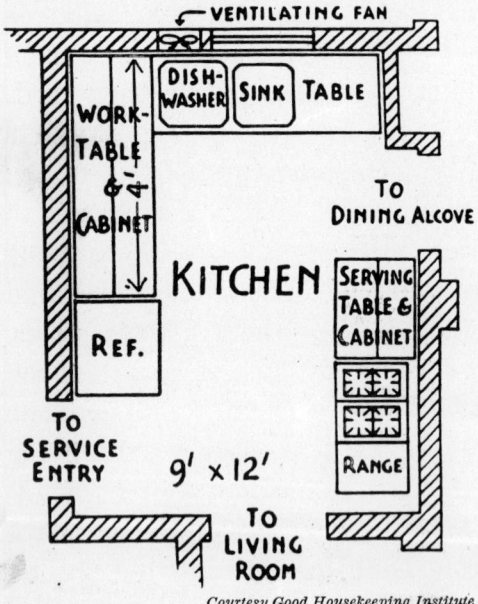

Courtesy Good Housekeeping Institute

How does this well-arranged kitchen save steps?

5. All the furniture and kitchen tools are arranged in such a way as to save steps. The drawing on

page 238 and the photograph on page 237 show good arrangements.

6. The sink measures about 32 to 35 inches from its upper edge to the floor.

The good points, you see, give the kitchen light, air, cleanliness, convenience, and cheerfulness.

How can you make the back yard and cellar or basement sanitary? This is a good task for the boys. One boy takes great pride in his back yard. He keeps it as clean as the front yard. He never lets rubbish collect there. He burns waste paper in a safe place and puts tin cans in a box or barrel to be taken away later. He never leaves cans lying around with water in them. You would never find boards with nails sticking up in them or sharp sticks, stones, or pieces of glass in his back yard. His back yard looks very much like the picture on page 240.

The cellar should be kept as clean as the living room, even though visitors do not often see it. Vegetables which have been allowed to mold or rot should never be left on the cellar floor, nor old clothes, shoes, newspapers, and dust and dirt on the shelves. The air from the cellar goes up all through the house. Some houses always seem damp and moldy because the cellars are damp and moldy. A cellar should be aired often by opening its doors and windows just as other rooms in the house are aired.

240 KEEPING HOUSE

If your cellar is full of old rubbish, choose a clear, sunny day to go exploring in its depths to see what is down there. Bring everything up into the sunlight.

What ideas does this picture give you for making your back yard attractive?

Ask your mother or father if you may sell the old clothes, rubbers, and papers to the ragman. Burn all the rubbish which is of no use to anyone; wash the glass jars and jugs; scrub the shelves and put clean paper on them; and put everything that is still useful back clean in the place where it belongs. You will have fun doing this.

Things to Do

1. Try to arrange to wash your dishes and dishpans tonight the way Jean and Jack did. Make a plan that is easiest in your kitchen. Talk it all over with your mother, who will be able to give you much good advice. **2.** Find pictures in newspapers and magazines of vacuum cleaners and other cleaning utensils. Which of these remove dust? Which merely scatter dust? **3.** Find pictures of electric and gas refrigerators and read what is said about them. **4.** Paint the kitchen furniture for your mother if she wants you to. Be sure to buy a light, soft color — not a dark color that will "*not* show the dirt."

5. Look over your back yard and cellar. Do you see any ways in which they can be made more sanitary? Spend one Saturday in making them more healthful and attractive. 6. Surprise your father and mother when they have been away for a day or two by "fixing up" the house — getting rid of rubbish, cleaning out dark corners, perhaps even repainting the kitchen furniture and closets. Get the consent of some other person first to be sure you are doing the right thing. Be careful not to throw away anything your mother or father wants to keep.

7. Help your mother to get ready for the visit of a friend or relative to your home. 8. Study all parts of your home — the porches, cellar, back yard, kitchen, living room, bedrooms, other rooms, chicken house, pigpen — to see if there are any improvements you can make. Talk over with your father and mother the changes which you think should be made and how much they will cost. One brother and sister made a great improvement in the kitchen by painting the sink, shelves, cupboard, and furniture first with cream-colored paint and then with a coat of hard, cream-colored enamel. Their mother said many times during the year: "You certainly made a big im-

provement in our kitchen. I enjoy working in it now. It is so clean and cheery."

9. Make a list of accidents which have happened in your home. Find in this textbook or in a first-aid book the best way to treat cuts and other common

Brightening dark corners

injuries. Practice these until you have learned how to treat common injuries quickly and skillfully.

10. Count the glasses of water you drink some day this week. Why do you drink more one day than another? Plan to drink one glass when you get up, another glass in the middle of the morning, and another after school.   Drink more whenever you feel thirsty.

FACTS ABOUT SMOKING

There are differences of opinion about smoking, but almost everyone agrees that young people and sick people should not smoke. Doctors say that most poisons hurt children more than they hurt adults. The chief poison in tobacco is nicotine.* The bad effects of tobacco smoking are more quickly and clearly seen in the boy or girl 13 or 14 years of age than in a person 30 or 40 years old. No one should smoke until he is past the age of 21 years. No person in poor health from any cause is doing all he can to get well unless he leaves tobacco alone.

Smoking has different effects on different people. You probably know people who have smoked for a number of years and who seem well and strong. "Smoking never hurts me," they say. Perhaps not. But the bad effects of smoking come on so slowly that the person who smokes and even his doctor may not notice them.

Smoking is not equally harmful to everyone. The sturdy adult may sometimes use large amounts of tobacco without seeming to be harmed by it. But the person who is weak or sickly might easily prevent his own recovery or hasten his death by the use of tobacco.

Adults who smoke sometimes experiment with the effects of smoking on themselves. If they are underweight, feel worn out, or are recovering from a serious illness, they stop smoking to see what happens. Many have found that they gain in weight, improve in appetite, and feel more like working or playing when they do not smoke.

Some Effects of Smoking

May smoking hurt the throat? A scientist said a short time ago: "I have given up smoking. I find that it irritates my throat." Do your own eyes and throat sometimes hurt when people are smoking close by you? Do you know people who seem to be bothered by tobacco smoke? There is something in tobacco smoke that often irritates the delicate lining of the throat — the *mucous membrane*.*

The nose passages also have a lining of mucous membrane. It is somewhat like velvet, the little hairlike parts being so small that they cannot be seen with the eye alone. But they are very active. They gently sweep, sweep, all the time and always toward the openings of the nose. Dust and bacteria are caught and moved toward the entrances to the nose and until they are removed in the mucus* when you blow your nose. Mucus is the moisture given out by the mucous membrane. What are the reasons why it is better to breathe through the nose than through the mouth?

The nose, throat, larynx,* windpipe,* and lungs are all connected. They are the organs of respiration.* The word *respiration* means breathing. The larynx is the voice box which contains the vocal cords.* These are somewhat like the strings of a violin. They make it possible for us to speak, to sing, to laugh. An irritation of the larynx sometimes causes hoarseness or loss of voice.

At the top of the windpipe is a trapdoor made of a flap of muscle. This little door opens to let the air in or out as you breathe and talk. It closes when you swallow food. Sometimes when you are laughing or talking at the table, it does not close quickly enough. A bit of food gets into the windpipe instead of into the food passageway which is so close to it. Unless the food is coughed out, air is shut out from the lungs. Choking is the result. Find the various organs of respiration on the diagram on page 247. Which is the longer journey — from the nose to the lungs or from the mouth to the lungs? Would the nose or the mouth pathway warm cold air better?

Doctors have noticed that tobacco smoke irritates the throat. The "cigarette cough" is present in a very large number of persons who use a pack or more of cigarettes a day and inhale* much of the smoke. It is true that dry tobacco gives off less nicotine and other irritating substances than does damp tobacco, but no kind of tobacco is soothing to

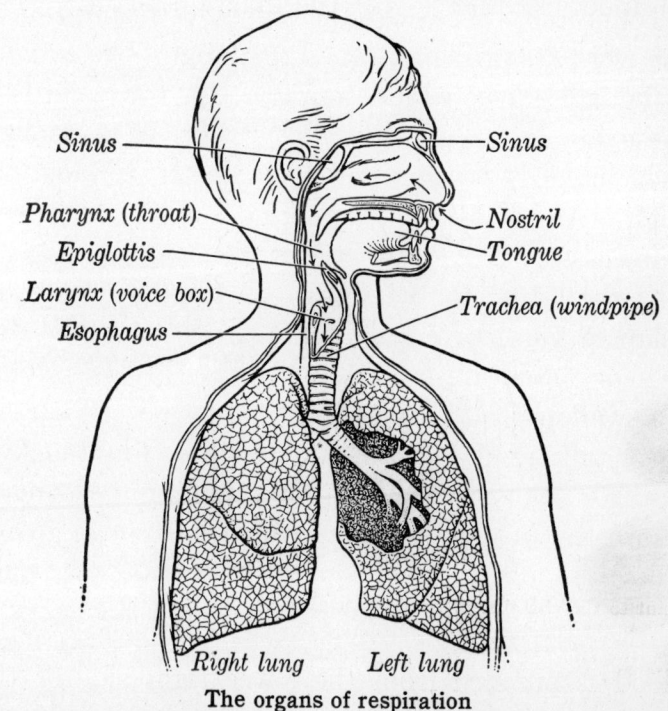

The organs of respiration
Where does inhaled tobacco smoke go?

the throat. Tobacco smoke that is inhaled is also harmful to the lungs.

May smoking tobacco hurt the heart? As you know, the blood is sent round and round the body about two to three times a minute. It circulates. The heart does this work. The heart is divided into a right and a left side. Each side has a lower and an upper chamber. (See the diagram below.) The

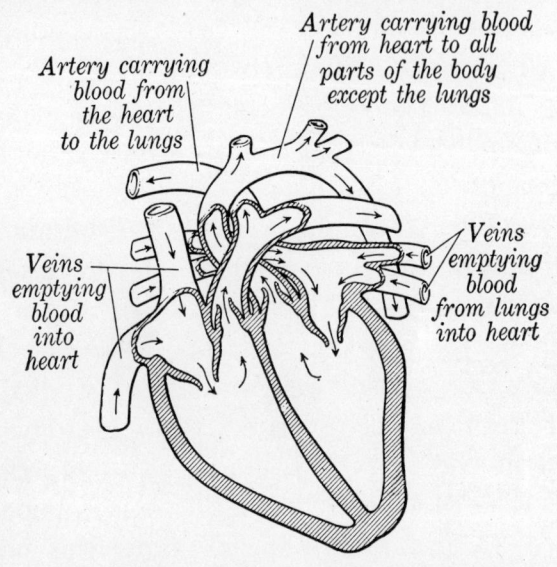

Artery carrying blood from the heart to the lungs

Artery carrying blood from heart to all parts of the body except the lungs

Veins emptying blood into heart

Veins emptying blood from lungs into heart

Point to the chamber of the heart that sends blood to the lungs. Point to the chamber that sends blood to all other parts of the body.

blood is pumped from the lower right side of the heart to the lungs. From the lower left side the blood is sent through the arteries* to all parts of the body. The arteries are elastic. Their walls stretch as blood is forced into them. They help the heart push the blood along. Sometimes they become somewhat stiff and hard. The doctors call this condition

EFFECT OF TOBACCO ON THE HEART

"hardening of the arteries." Hardening of the arteries puts a greater burden upon the heart.

There is no scientific* proof that smoking permanently injures the heart or causes hardening of the arteries. But many doctors, from their study of people who smoke, think that it does. Tobacco certainly makes the heart beat faster and makes it more apt to "race" when we are excited, nervous, or exercising.

May smoking affect the appetite? The air of a room in which many people are smoking loses its freshness very quickly. Fresh, outdoor air, as you know, helps to give one an appetite. The New York State Commission on Ventilation* studied the effect of fresh air on appetite. On some days the air in the lunchroom was fresh and at a temperature of about 68° F. On other days the room was poorly ventilated. On the "fresh air" days the people ate more than on the "stale air" days.

In what ways is the air in a room kept healthful? A well-ventilated room is one in which the warmer, used-up air passes slowly out of the room while the fresh, outdoor air comes slowly in. Opening the windows in your bedroom at top and bottom is one way of getting a circulation of air. The cooler air comes in at the bottom, rises as it becomes warmer, and goes out at the top of the window. How is your schoolroom ventilated? Look around at the walls. Do you see any openings near the top of the room through which the stale air can pass out? Where does the fresh air come in? Windows open at the bottom behind boards or glass screens send the cold air upward so that it does not blow directly on the children who are sitting near the window. Another sign of a well-regulated room is a temperature of about 68° F. What is the temperature of the room in which you are sitting? Watch the thermometers in your rooms. Keep the temperature about 68° F.

Tobacco smoke in a poorly ventilated room may decrease appetite by helping to take away the freshness of the air. This, of course, would affect the appetite of the people in the room who did not smoke as well as of the smokers.

Do boys who smoke get lower marks in school than boys who do not smoke? It has been found that in both high schools and colleges boys who smoke get lower marks and more often fail in their studies than boys who do not smoke. In a certain high school, the boys who did not smoke won A's more often than those who smoked. The 77 boys in another school who had never smoked made an average mark of 84.5 per cent, while the boys who smoked regularly made an average mark of only

76.0 per cent. The average mark of the ten highest of the boys who did not smoke was 91 per cent, while that of the ten highest of the smokers was only 79 per cent.

Now, of course, this does not necessarily mean that smoking causes failure in school work. But it does show that the boys who smoke do not do so well in their important school work as those who do not smoke. The difference in marks may have been due in part to the fact that boys of this age who smoke are often the ones who find it difficult to study. They do not prepare themselves for the future by living most fully and wisely in the present.

Disadvantages of smoking. *Does smoking make you "healthy, wealthy, and wise?"* No, quite otherwise. Experiments and common sense have shown that it may have the opposite effect. Does smoking help you to make friends? With certain people, perhaps, but are the boys of your age who smoke the ones you really want as your best friends? On the other hand, tobacco smoke is unpleasant and irritating to some people, so smoking makes you less popular with them. Does smoking make you feel more grown-up? Of course, many adults do smoke. But many other people whom you admire do not smoke. Smoking is not a sign of being grown-up.

Experiments have shown that, in general, steadiness decreases when people are smoking. The finger-tips of the person who smokes a very great deal are apt to tremble. The heavy smoker often has greater difficulty in controlling his nerves under excitement. For these reasons, football and baseball coaches say: "No smoking while you are in training."

Is smoking an expensive habit? Jack's big brother did not smoke. One day he counted up the money he saved by not smoking. "Suppose I smoked five cigarettes a day," he said. "Some people smoke many more than five. There are 365 days in a year. So I should have smoked 1,825 cigarettes. The cheaper cigarettes cost about three fourths of a cent apiece. The 1,825 cigarettes would cost $13.69."

"That's enough money to buy a baseball glove, bat, and suit; or a new pair of ice skates with shoes attached and a hockey stick; or many other things I want," said Jack. He thought his brother's plan was a good one and began to think of all the things he would like to buy with the money he would save by not smoking.

How many reasons can you give for never beginning to smoke?

Other Children's Questions

Answer as many of them as you can:

1. In what ways does tobacco injure the health?
2. Why does tobacco hinder brain work?
3. If nicotine or tobacco smoke will kill lice on plants, why isn't it just as harmful to people?
4. Is the stopping of growth in grains from lack of moisture anything like the stunting of growth of boys from cigarette smoking?
5. What is in a cigarette that makes people like it so well?
6. Can a person who smokes be healthy?
7. Does smoking do harm if one does not inhale the smoke?

Answers. At certain kinds of work where we are learning new facts and carrying out new tasks, tobacco, by its action on brain cells and fibers, has been found to slow up work. When we think, messages are sent from one nerve cell to another. Tobacco seems to interfere with sending these messages quickly and easily. In other words, smoking may make school learning more difficult.

Tobacco may injure the health by irritating the lining of the throat and lungs. It may also make the heart and blood vessels work harder than is desirable and be less able to stand strain, as in an athletic contest.

The nicotine in the cigarette usually makes the heart beat faster and makes people feel stimulated. People also like the feel of the cigarette in their mouths. But their liking is largely a habit. They like to smoke because they have the habit of smoking. But the habit can be broken.

People are so much larger than lice that the amount of tobacco smoke they breathe in is not large enough to kill them as it kills lice. But the amount of the poisonous nicotine which some smokers inhale may be harmful to people.

Yes, some people who are healthy and strong seem to keep healthy even though they do smoke.

Smoking is not so harmful when the smoke is not inhaled, but a certain amount of nicotine is always breathed in. Even people who themselves are not smoking often start coughing and lose their appetites in a room filled with tobacco smoke.

The growing boy or girl suffers from the use of tobacco, although the effects are not exactly the same as the stopping of growth in grains from lack of moisture.

Things to Do

1. Do you know someone who is on a football or baseball team? Ask him what the training rules are. Is smoking forbidden during training? Why?

TOBACCO SMOKE OR FRESH AIR? 255

2. Keep a record of the temperature of the classroom. Read the thermometer four times a day. Write the temperature on a chart each time.
3. Make a diagram showing the circulation of air in

Where good health helps

your own room. Show where the fresh air comes in, how it moves through the room, and where it goes out. 4. Weigh yourself every month. Note your gain or loss in weight. Compare your weight with the average weight of other boys or girls, which you can find in the table in the Appendix.

5. Ask the science teacher to help you perform the following experiment:

Blow into a glass of limewater through a glass tube. What happens to the limewater? Carbon dioxide turns clear limewater cloudy. Was there *carbon dioxide** in the air you breathed out? Leave a glass of limewater in the classroom all day. Is it still perfectly clear? Is there some carbon dioxide in the air you breathe in? We breathe out more carbon dioxide than we breathe in. Carbon dioxide is a waste product of the human body, given off by the lungs.

FACTS ABOUT ALCOHOL AND DRUGS

Sometimes it is hard to be independent and not to follow the crowd. This is especially true in regard to smoking and drinking. Some people find it very hard to say "No." When they "are in Rome, they do as the Romans do," even though they know it is not the best thing to do.

Everyone knows that drinks with alcohol in them do much harm. Alcoholic* beverages* have made a great many people poorer. They tend to make people less fair and just, less careful, and less obedient to laws. They often pave the way for accidents. They sometimes encourage people to do things they are very sorry for later.

Alcohol on Trial

Are alcoholic beverages ever necessary? Doctors used to give alcoholic drinks as medicine. Many doctors today say that alcohol* is not needed for this purpose. They use other drugs which are just as good or better.

Some people give another reason for using alcoholic beverages. They say: Alcohol is a *narcotic*.* A narcotic helps people to relax. In certain amounts it makes people drowsy and puts them to sleep. It has a drug action similar to that of ether, which is used to make people unconscious* while they are having an operation.* Alcohol can produce the same effect as ether but does it more slowly. A person becomes unconscious or sleepy when the higher brain centers, the parts of the brain that make thinking possible, are no longer active. Workers need relaxation.* But there are much better ways of relaxing than by reducing the activity of the brain centers with alcohol.

People can relax by listening to music at concerts or over the radio. People who work indoors can relax by working in their gardens. People find relaxation in driving or riding in their automobiles. Going to a baseball game is relaxation for many people. Some people relax when they are reading an interesting book or seeing a fine play. Just talking with pleasant people is often genuinely restful. A swim is excellent relaxation. Lying in the warm sunlight idly watching the white clouds float by and listening to the wind in the trees is perfect relaxation.

One of the best kinds of relaxation

Is the drowsiness that sometimes follows the drinking of alcoholic beverages as desirable as the relaxation that comes from healthful outdoor living? Common sense answers: "It is not." Science also says: "Relaxation from healthful outdoor living is best." Alcoholic beverages are in no way necessary for a healthy life.

Does alcohol decrease accuracy and steadiness? A group of men were given a number of tests to see how quickly they could think and move. The scores they made on each test were written on a piece of paper. Then each man was given a glass of beer, containing two to three per cent of alcohol, before he took the same tests again. The scores were lower the second time. After the men had taken the alcohol, they were less accurate and less steady. Even this small amount of alcohol, which is less than the per cent usually contained in beer and wine, decreases accuracy and steadiness. A larger amount, as in whisky, has a still more serious effect. It is the alcohol in such beverages that makes people drunk.

The amount of time a person usually requires to make a movement with his hands after a certain signal has been given is one fifth of a second. Two ounces of whisky (about one fourth of a cup) slows this time down to three fifths of a second. One fourth of a cup of whisky makes a person three times as slow as he was without it. An automobile will go about 30 feet in three fifths of a second. Suppose a man who has taken a fourth of a cup of whisky is driving an automobile and a little child runs out twenty-five feet in front of his car. What difference might the alcohol he has taken make? What relation do you see between accidents and alcohol?

Practical experience, as well as scientific experiments, shows that alcohol decreases accuracy, steadiness, and good judgment. The manufacturer of a well-known make of automobiles will not employ a man who shows any signs of having taken alcohol when he comes to work. Engineers are not permitted to run their trains if they have been drinking because so many lives depend upon the accuracy, steadiness, and good judgment of the engineer.

During the World War, when everyone tried to do as much work as possible and to save grain, most countries tried to limit and discourage the use of alcohol. Why?

Ritola, the man who beat the world's record in the 10,000 yard race in France, said: " Before I began to compete I used to smoke and sometimes took alcoholic beverages; but when I began to train as a runner, I soon saw that I would have to give up both if I wished to obtain good results. Accordingly, from the outset of my training, I gave up tobacco and alcohol, for in my opinion their use prevents one's becoming a first-class athlete."*

Examples could be multiplied to show that at any time when one has a task to do that calls for a clear head, quick thinking, keen vision, and steady muscles, there is no place for alcohol whatever.

What are the effects of long-continued use of alcoholic beverages? Life-insurance companies have found that the person who leaves alcoholic beverages alone has a better chance of living a long life than the person who uses them even, as he may say, moderately. In many cases, too, the moderate use of alcoholic beverages has led to their overuse.

The effects of long-continued overuse of alcoholic beverages are well known to all physicians.* The lining of the stomach and throat becomes inflamed,* that is, red and sore. Pimples and reddening of the skin of the face may appear, though everyone who has pimples or a red face has not necessarily been using alcohol. Later, fat tissues slowly take the place of the naturally healthy and sturdy tissues of the liver, heart, and blood vessels. Finally the nerve cells often shrink. Sometimes the nerves become inflamed and sometimes the very hard drinker has attacks of temporary insanity* in which he imagines that he sees threatening snakes, rats, dogs, or other frightful animals, so that he is sleepless, fearful, and excited. Cases of alcoholic insanity make up as high as 12 per cent of the patients who are sent to our hospitals for the insane.

Are patent medicines and drugs dangerous? If you tell someone you do not feel well, he often suggests a medicine. Sometimes it is a patent medicine* that makes you feel better for a short time but that does not cure your sickness. Patent medicines are ready-made medicines. They should be avoided for two chief reasons: first, because of the harmful drugs they may contain; and second, because they keep you from going to the doctor and finding out what is really the matter.

There are certain drugs which are called *habit-forming* drugs. People demand more and more of them, once the drug habit has taken hold of them. They make a slave of the person using them. Then it is impossible for him to follow the rule "Nothing in excess." They take away his money, his freedom, his happiness. The same thing is true of alcohol in the case of many people. They cannot use it in moderate amounts. You have probably heard of the "opium habit." Opium* contains morphine,* which is a habit-forming drug. The habit of taking it is formed very easily. Once the habit is formed, it is very difficult, usually impossible, to break.

Never take any unknown substance that may be offered to you. There are criminals who make it a business to sell drugs to young people. They want to make them slaves to the drug so that they will spend a great deal of money for it. Do not be influenced by others in doing anything you feel you should not do. No one should experiment with drugs. Once is too often to take any habit-forming drug.

Things to Do

1. What is the thing to do if:

a. An older boy says, "Come over to our club and I'll teach you to smoke"?

b. A friend of yours offers you a cigarette?

c. A person whom you do not know asks you to take a white powder?

d. Your friend tells you about a patent medicine that he thinks you should take?

e. An adult offers you a drink with alcohol in it?

Answers:

a. Probably you had planned to spend the afternoon playing ball or in some other wholesome way. Then you could say to the older boy: "I'm practicing for the baseball team this afternoon. And besides, I'm not interested in learning to smoke. There are many other things I would rather do. The best athletes do not smoke or drink."

b. You could say: "No, thanks. I've promised father that I would not smoke until I am grown up."

c. Say "No!" Then report the happening to the nearest policeman.

d. Tell him you think you had better go to the doctor first to find out what is the matter with you.

e. Say: "No, thank you. I don't like it. I'd much rather have orange juice or grape juice. I do not have to drink something I dislike, do I?"

2. Let a glass of fruit juice, such as grape juice, stand uncovered in the classroom for several days. Watch what happens to it. What are the bubbles of gas? What odor does it have? The sweet juice has fermented. Which would you rather drink — the sweet, fresh, fruit juice or the fermented juice? It is yeast floating around with the dust in the air which changes the sugar in the fresh fruit juice to alcohol and carbon dioxide. **3.** What habits are suggested to you by the facts in this chapter? List them and put stars after those you already have.

PREVENTING TOOTH DECAY

You have only two sets of teeth during a lifetime — your first set, or milk teeth, and the second set which must last the rest of your life. How can you make your teeth last a lifetime? How can you prevent tooth decay and escape toothaches? One scientist examined the teeth of two groups of children. He found that 96 per cent of the children coming to America from Italy and other southern parts of Europe had sound teeth. But 96 per cent of the American children examined had cavities in their teeth. What made the difference?

Teeth in Health and in Decay

How are teeth built? Sometimes a baby has a tooth when he is born, that is, a tooth which everyone can see. He has several other teeth hidden under the gums. Some of them are almost ready to push through the gums when the time comes.

The hard, shiny, white *enamel** which you see on the outside of the tooth is built from milk and green vegetables and other everyday foods. The yellowish white *dentine** under the enamel, which is very much like bone, is also built from these same foods. The *cement** which covers the dentine under the gums is made from food, too.

Through the dentine run tubes which carry nerves and blood. In children, new dentine is built next to the *pulp chamber** which is in the center of the tooth. The pulp chamber, as you can see in the drawings on page 266, is a space containing blood vessels, nerves, and cells which manufacture new dentine while the tooth is growing. You have a share in building your own teeth as well as in keeping them in good condition.

Sunlight also helps to build good teeth. Sunlight sometimes makes the difference between good teeth and poor teeth.

What causes toothache and abscessed teeth? What do you usually find in an aching tooth? A hole in a tooth which allows substances such as food acids* to come close to the nerves causes toothache. These substances irritate the nerves. The nerves carry a message of pain to the brain. That message of pain is the toothache. If there were no nerves in the teeth, you would never have a toothache. When Jack had a toothache, he said: "I wish there

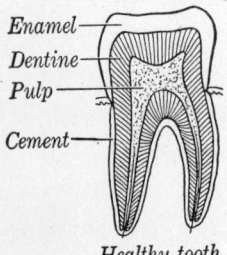

Enamel
Dentine
Pulp
Cement

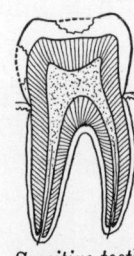

Healthy tooth | Sensitive tooth Decay down to dentine | Severe decay Decay deep into dentine | Final stage Decay has extended to pulp

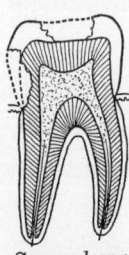

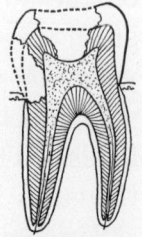

Stages in tooth decay

At which stage should the cavities have been filled? At which stage would you have a toothache? At which stage is the health of the whole body in danger?

were no nerves in my teeth." Would that be a good thing?

When a tooth decays as far as the pulp chamber, certain bacteria enter and live there. An abscess* is often formed. The nerves and blood vessels in the tooth may be destroyed. Such a tooth is said to be *ulcerated.* * An ulcerated or *abscessed* tooth is a dangerous tooth even though it does not ache. It should be treated by a dentist at once. The abscessed tooth has a pocket of pus* at the end of the root. Pus consists of dead cells, white blood corpuscles, and bacteria. Abscessed teeth may be discovered by the X-ray.

How to prevent the decay of teeth. Have you ever heard the saying: "A clean tooth never decays?" That is not strictly true, although cleaning may help to prevent decay. Soft, sticky foods, especially starches and sweets, furnish food for certain bacteria which form acid. This acid dissolves dentine easily. It eats into the tooth. Several scientists have found certain bacteria on hand wherever there is tooth decay. Other scientists have found decay in mouths free from these bacteria. More experimental work is necessary to teach us the facts about tooth decay.

If the teeth are kept very clean, there will be little food for the acid-forming bacteria, less acid in the mouth, and therefore less tooth decay. Why is it important to remove food from between the teeth as well as from the sides and biting and chewing surfaces? Why does one tooth decay and the tooth next to it remain sound? Why do some savage people who have never seen a toothbrush have better teeth than some people who clean their teeth three times a day? There must be something beside cleanliness that prevents decay. What is it?

One chief cause of tooth decay lies in the kind of food eaten. Have you ever heard people say, "Candy will make your teeth decay"? There is some truth in this statement. Candy furnishes no

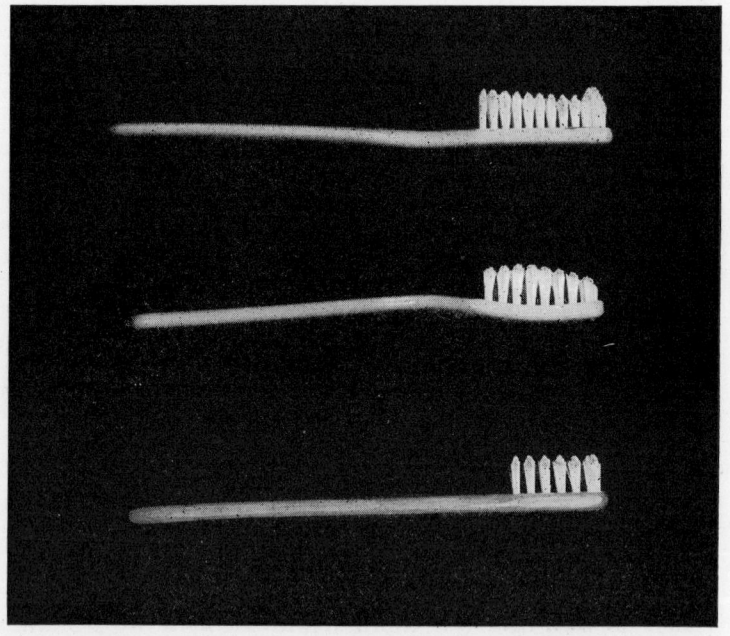

What is good about these types of toothbrushes?

building food for the teeth. It often crowds out tooth-building foods such as milk. Tough foods such as savages often ate also help to prevent decay in two ways: (1) by improving the circulation of blood through the teeth and gums, and (2) by cleaning the teeth. The fibers* in raw apples and in celery, for example, are like little brushes that help to clean the teeth while you chew. Certain other foods are more apt to cling to or between the teeth.

Certain foods are especially important in preventing tooth decay. Mrs. May Mellanby in England had for some time been interested in her husband's study of the growth of bones. The same thing that causes poor bones probably causes poor teeth, she thought. She began experimenting with some of the dogs in her husband's laboratory.* A laboratory is a place where scientific experiments are carried on. A few years ago Mrs. Mellanby had already studied 1,400 dogs. She gave puppies in the same family different diets. She found great differences in the teeth of the young dogs.

Time after time Mrs. Mellanby studied the structure of the young dogs' teeth. Time after time, she found the enamel and dentine of the teeth of puppies which ate such food as cod-liver oil and egg yolk to be hard and firm, while the enamel and dentine of the teeth of the dogs not having these foods were spongy. Sometimes it was so soft it could be cut with a knife. The teeth of young children who have had good diets are much like the teeth of the dogs who were given the best kinds of food. The teeth of children who have had poor diets are spongy and soft and irregular.* The wrong kind of food often causes children's teeth to decay.

In one home for orphans the diet was cheap but good. The children had milk, cereals, and vegetables every day. For dessert they had raw fruit. Very little sugar was included in the menus. These children had fewer cavities in their teeth than most children do.

When boys and girls on a poor diet were given orange juice and lettuce, better teeth resulted. Cod-liver oil made a difference in the case of other children who lacked milk and vegetables. If the diet is poor, these protective foods make a difference in the health of the teeth. If the diet is already good, adding more of these foods is unnecessary.

Two groups of children were also studied. One group had poor teeth. The other group had good teeth. The children with good teeth ate more fruits and vegetables than the children with poor teeth. Certain experiments have shown that children are most likely to have poor teeth when they have not had in their diets plenty of milk, orange juice, green vegetables, and cod-liver oil. Sunlight and other things help to make good use of these foods in building teeth and preventing their decay.

Small cavities become larger quickly because the dentine is softer than the enamel and decays more easily. Going to the dentist twice a year prevents little cavities from becoming big. The dentist cleans and fills the little cavity so that decay can go no farther.

Other Children's Questions

Can you answer them?

1. How many teeth do we have?
2. Why do dentists fill teeth instead of pulling them out?
3. Are first teeth ever filled?
4. How does the food you eat affect your teeth?

Answers. When permanent teeth are pulled out, the other teeth are likely to become irregular. Some teeth which are needed for chewing food properly have been lost. When teeth are filled, the decay is stopped and the tooth is saved in many cases.

The first teeth serve as guides to the second teeth. Yes, first teeth are often filled if cavities appear in them before it is time for the second teeth to come in. The first teeth should not be neglected.

Your teeth are built of calcium and other substances which are furnished by food. Milk and vegetables are the best sources of calcium. Chewing such foods as tough meat, hard, dry toast, and rolls helps to keep the teeth in a healthy condition. Raw vegetables and fruits help to keep the teeth clean and to furnish the substances which they need for growth and repair.

Twelve-year-old boys and girls usually have the teeth shown in the picture below.

Things to Do

1. Ask your teacher whether the class may send for the booklet, *Good Teeth*, from the Metropolitan Life Insurance Company, New York City. This is a simple little book that tells you very important facts about the teeth. 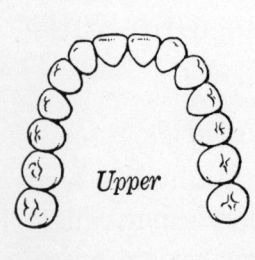
2. Make posters for the lower grades showing the children how to build good teeth and prevent decay. Make one poster about eating natural sweets instead of sweets made of white sugar.
3. Did you clean your teeth last night before you went to bed? Did you clean them after breakfast today? Do you hang your toothbrush in a sunny window or keep it in a glass by itself? If you cannot answer "yes" to all these questions today, be sure to be able to answer "yes" tomorrow.
4. Have you been to the dentist within six months? If not, it is time for a visit.

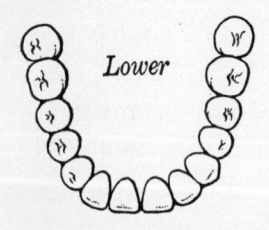

5. Add to each of the meals below one food which will help clean the teeth and make vigorous chewing necessary:

Breakfast
  Oatmeal and milk

School Lunch
  Egg Sandwiches

Dinner
  Fish, baked potato, green beans

Supper
  Milk toast

6. Answer as fully as you can the question at the bottom of page 264.

BATTLING WITH BACTERIA

All animals have enemies. Larger animals feed on smaller animals or insects. Spiders eat the little plant lice that suck the juices from certain trees. Small birds eat the spiders, and they in turn are eaten by large birds such as hawks. In the sea little fish, such as minnows, are eaten by larger fish. The larger fish are eaten by seals. Sea leopards eat birds, and they in turn are eaten by the killer whales. But many animals have weapons with which they can defend, or protect, themselves.

Our Very Small Enemies

You also have enemies — enemies which are too small to see with your eyes alone. You also have weapons with which to defend yourself.

In olden times soldiers used shields to protect themselves from darts and spears that were thrown at them. The skin is your shield against bacteria. In the skin are glands* which pour an oily substance on the skin. This gives the skin a partly waterproof coat which helps to keep out bacteria. There are always many bacteria on the skin but as long as they are not pushed into the body through a cut or scratch or other opening in the skin they do no harm. As you know, there are sweat glands as well as oil glands in the skin. Bacteria sometimes get into the openings of these glands or about the root of a hair and cause a pimple. The eyes have a special weapon. It is tears. Bacteria, as well as dust and dirt, are washed away by tears and by the moistening of the eyes that occurs all the time.

Keeping bacteria out of cuts and scratches. When you cut your finger so that it bleeds, the blood washes out some of the bacteria which may have slipped into the cut from the knife or skin. You must be careful not to let any more bacteria enter. What are some of the ways in which bacteria might get into a cut or a scratch?

The more you learn about bacteria, the more careful you will be to keep your fingers, dirty handkerchiefs, and pieces of rag away from even the smallest cut. The principal danger from small cuts is not from the wound itself but from the infection* of the wound. When bacteria get into a wound, we say the wound is *infected.*

What happens when bacteria get into a cut? Have you ever had a cut which became infected? What happened? When certain germs get into a wound, they begin to grow and multiply. As they grow, the wound becomes red, sore, and swollen. We say the wound has become inflamed, or that "inflammation* has set in." A yellowish-white, soft substance sometimes forms. Doctors call this yellowish-white substance *pus.* Some other people call it *matter.* Pus consists largely of white corpuscles which have marched up to fight the bacteria. The white corpuscles were destroyed in their fight with the bacteria.

This is exactly what happens when a wound becomes inflamed:

1. The little blood vessels near the wound become larger.

2. More blood comes to the wounded spot.

3. The white blood corpuscles in the blood begin to cling to the capillary walls. (You remember the capillaries are the very small, hairlike blood vessels that connect the arteries and the veins.)

4. The white corpuscles begin to work their way through the very thin walls of the capillaries to the

other tissues of the body. The drawing on this page shows a capillary with the round, red blood corpuscles in the center. One of the white corpuscles is clinging to the capillary wall; two are working their way through the walls and after a time will escape

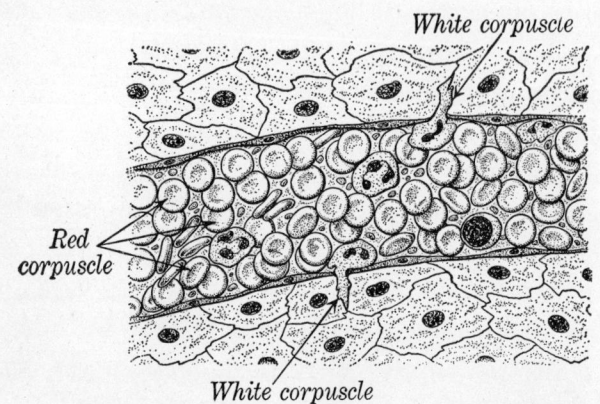

White corpuscle

Red corpuscle

White corpuscle

A small blood vessel passing through body cells

White corpuscles are going to the rescue. Where are they going? They are going to fight the bacteria shown by the dark spots outside of the blood vessel.

from the blood vessel altogether. See if you can find these things in the drawing.

5. In four or five hours all the capillaries and small veins in the neighborhood are crowded with white corpuscles ready to fight bacteria. This they do by "swallowing" the bacteria. A white corpuscle meets a bacterium, closes around it, and swallows it as shown in the drawing on page 277. One white

WHEN THE WHITE CORPUSCLES WIN

corpuscle can "eat up" as many as a dozen bacteria at one time.

6. In about forty-eight hours' time an abscess may be formed.

You know how ugly an abscess looks. Do you remember what it is? It is largely a mass of dead white blood corpuscles, dead tissue cells, and bacteria, some dead and some still living. As long as there are living bacteria in the wound, the white corpuscles continue to come to the rescue.

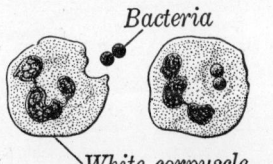

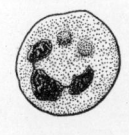

White blood corpuscle "eating" bacteria

They continue to eat up the bacteria and clear away the dead or injured body cells until they win the battle. Then the cut heals. Thus the white corpuscles prevent the spread of infection.

All this trouble was caused by allowing bacteria to get into the cut. The bacteria should have been kept out by washing the skin about the wound with sterile* water or with alcohol; painting the wound with iodine at once; and allowing nothing but a sterilized piece of cloth to touch the cut. Then the infection could have been prevented. Then the white corpuscles could have stayed in the blood stream, the abscess would not have been formed, and the wound would have healed more quickly without redness, swelling, or pain.

In what other places in the body do disease-producing bacteria gather? Bacteria which cause disease not only gather in cuts and other wounds where the skin is broken, but may also collect in other parts of the body. These places are called *foci of infection*.* (The singular of *foci* is *focus*.) The ends of the roots of teeth are common foci of infection. The tonsils* are often foci of infection. The appendix* is, at times, another focus of infection.

You already know how bacteria can get down through a cavity in the tooth to the root pulp. The same thing happens there that happens in a cut. There is inflammation — redness, swelling, pain. Sometimes the bacteria win the battle. They go through the thin capillary walls into the blood stream. Once inside the blood vessels, the bacteria or their poisons may be carried to all parts of the body. They may, it is thought, be carried to the heart and cause heart disease. A child who has heart trouble often cannot run upstairs as the other children do. He cannot race and play as hard as they do. He must follow the doctor's directions carefully. His heart trouble may have been caused by bacteria from some focus of infection which should have been removed many years ago. Bacteria or their poisons may be carried to the arms and legs and cause rheumatism.* They may be carried to the kidneys* and cause kidney disease. Foci of infection are very dangerous. Abscessed teeth should be pulled out, if the doctor advises it, before the poison can affect other teeth.

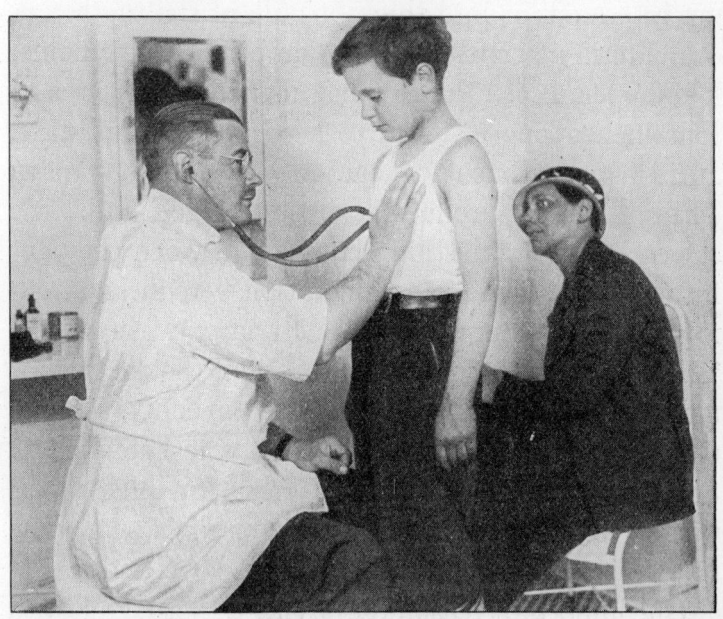

A heart examination

Bacteria often make the tonsils their home. The tonsils, you know, are two small masses of tissue on either side of the throat. You can easily see them when you look into your throat. When the tonsils are in a healthy condition, they help to catch and destroy bacteria which have found their way into the throat. But sometimes the tonsils become enlarged or diseased. Instead of destroying the bacteria, they make a home for them. When bacteria lodge in the tonsils, the same thing may happen as when they get into a cut or into the root pulp of the tooth.

Bacteria at times make the appendix their home. The appendix is a narrow bag usually from three to four inches long fastened to a part of the intestine. It is a cozy place for bacteria to gather. When certain disease-producing bacteria get into the appendix, the same thing happens as when they get into a cut. There is inflammation — redness, swelling, pain. Sometimes the bacteria win the battle. They may cause such severe pain that the doctor sees clearly that he must take out the appendix. Sometimes there is not much pain, but the bacteria are doing their bad work just the same. An infected appendix can be taken out if the doctor advises it. The appendix has no special use, so far as we know.

One important reason for having a thorough health examination every year is to discover foci of infection.

Other Children's Questions

Try to answer each question yourself.
1. What causes boils?
2. What can a person do for boils?

3. Should you keep a cloth over a sore?
4. How can we avoid getting the pinkeye?*
5. What causes blood poisoning?

Answers. Yes, it is best to cover a sore with a sterilized cloth to keep dirt and bacteria out of it and to keep the bacteria already in it from spreading to other places. Moreover, an uncovered sore is unpleasant to look at.

Blood poisoning is caused by a certain kind of bacteria getting into cuts, scratches, and especially deep wounds, and finally into the blood stream.

If a person has a boil, he should be careful not to spread the germs to other parts of the skin. He should protect the boil from bacteria in the same way that he would protect a cut.

Boils are caused by one kind of bacteria. It is very easy for the germs to be rubbed from the boil to a tiny opening in another part of the skin near by. Then another boil may begin to form there. If a person is eating too many sweets or starches, one boil frequently follows another because conditions in the body are favorable for the growth of the bacteria.

Pinkeye may be prevented in many cases by never putting your fingers or soiled handkerchief or other objects up to your eyes, and by using only your own towel and washcloth which have been properly washed and boiled.

Things to Do

1. Have you had a health examination this year? Tell your mother all the reasons why a health examination is important. 2. Find in magazines and newspapers pictures and facts about bacteria, infection, and first aid. Underline the facts you know are true. Put a question mark after those about which you are in doubt, and draw a line through statements which you know are not true. Discuss them in class.

3. Have you any problems of preventing infection in your school? Talk over this question in class. If you find ways in which bacteria might be spread from one person to another, make changes in your school which will help to prevent the spread of bacteria. 4. Practice first aid in school whenever there is need for it. In this way you will learn how to treat the common injuries. 5. Look at your hands and nails. Are they clean and well-cared-for? Did you wash your hands before eating today? Did you wash your hands after going to the toilet? Have you had a warm soap bath twice during the past week? Make a good daily program for keeping yourself clean, and carry out your program this week and the weeks following.

6. Find some other plants which, like bacteria, do not grow from seeds. Puffballs which you sometimes see in the woods do not grow from seeds. Mush-

Mushroom　　　*Puffball*　　　*Molds*

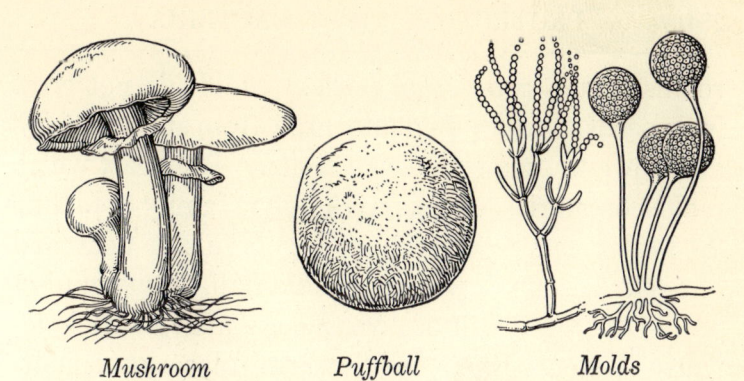

Plants that grow from spores instead of seeds

Mushrooms.　In the circle: a mold plant throwing off spores

rooms do not grow from seeds. Molds do not grow from seeds. All these plants grow from *spores** which are, however, somewhat like seeds. The yeast which makes bread rise belongs to the same family of plants.
7. Make a paste of two tablespoonfuls of flour and one-quarter cup of water. Add a half teaspoonful of molasses. Add half of a yeast cake mixed with lukewarm water. Keep in a warm place overnight. What changes do you find? What has caused the bubbles of gas? What gas is it? 8. Grow a mold garden. Put a damp piece of bread in a glass. Cover it and put it in a warm, dark place. Watch what happens. Put a dry piece of bread in a glass. Cover it and put it in the same place. What happens to it? What does mold need in order to grow? Bacteria and mold grow under the same conditions. What do bacteria need for growth?

PROTECTION FROM BACTERIA

We need not fear bacteria if we know enough about them. People in olden times thought disease was caused by evil spirits. The oldest man living today knew nothing about bacteria when he was a boy. Wonderful discoveries have been made in his lifetime. Wonderful discoveries are still being made. Scientists have discovered how smallpox* and malaria and diphtheria can be prevented.

WHAT ARE BACTERIA?

Stop reading for a minute, and write all you know about bacteria. Do not guess, but write only what you are sure is true. Perhaps you thought first of their size. A bacterium is one of the smallest living things we know. Some bacteria are about five hundred times too small to be seen with the eye alone. Because they are so small and can be seen only through a microscope, they have sometimes been called *microbes*.* Bacteria are microscopic.

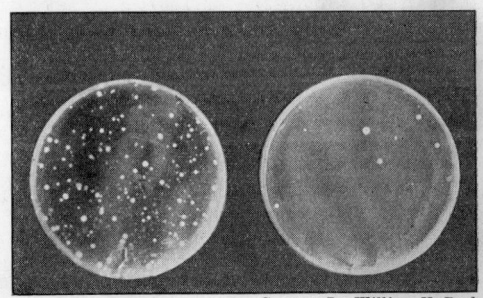

Courtesy Dr. William H. Park

Colonies of bacteria as seen with the eye alone

Each spot large enough to see is made up of millions of bacteria.

You know what a microscope is. It makes small things look larger. Have you ever looked through a microscope and seen things that you could not see with your eyes alone? Imagine the excitement of the Hollander, Van Leeuwenhoek, who invented the microscope, when he looked through the lens that showed him the living things in a drop of water. "The water is full of little beasts," he told his daughter.

Then he went about examining many different things under his wonderful new toy.

The typhoid germ is a bacterium of about average size. If you laid 12,000 of these bacteria end to end, they would form a line only one inch long. Scientists think there are germs so small that they cannot be seen under our most powerful microscopes. These are called *viruses*.*

You are right in thinking of their size first of all.

Perhaps the second thing you wrote was: "They cause disease." That is true. A large majority of the diseases of mankind are due directly or indirectly to certain bacteria. Each type of bacteria causes its own kind of disease. The bacteria that cause tuberculosis* cannot cause *typhoid fever*,* nor can the typhoid bacteria cause *chicken pox** or measles.*

But not all bacteria cause disease. There are many harmless and many helpful bacteria. Some

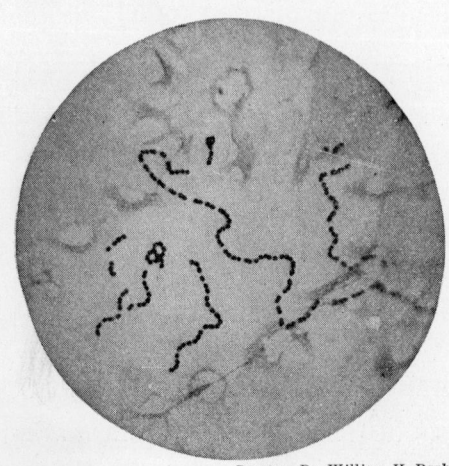

Courtesy Dr. William H. Park
Bacteria as seen through the microscope

HELPFUL AND HARMFUL BACTERIA

germs make life possible for us. Millions of bacteria in the soil are helpful. They make dead plants and animals decay and change them into good soil which furnishes food for new plants. Without these bacteria, the ground would be piled high with the dead bodies of plants and animals. Some bacteria enrich the soil by taking nitrogen,* a colorless gas, from the air and changing it into a form in which it can be used as food for plants. You have probably known farmers to plow under certain plants, such as clover, in order to increase the nitrogen in the soil. Bacteria cling to roots of clover and certain other plants and gather nitrogen for the plant. Buttermilk and cheese could not be made without the help of certain bacteria. We often forget about the good bacteria and think only of those that do us harm.

Did you think about the shape of bacteria? Some are like little short sticks. These are called *bacilli.* * (*Bacillus* is the singular form of the word.) There are more than eight hundred kinds of bacilli. Other bacteria are round like balls. These are called *cocci.* * (The singular is *coccus*.) There are more than three hundred kinds of cocci. Still other bacteria are like the letter *S* and have little hairlike arms which help them to move around very quickly. These bacteria are called *spirilla.* * (The singular is *spirillum*.) That is easy to remember because they are somewhat like a spiral or corkscrew. Nearly one hundred kinds of spirilla are known.

You will see in the drawing below pictures of these three main types of bacteria.

Did you write anything else about bacteria? Perhaps you wrote that they were animals. That is a

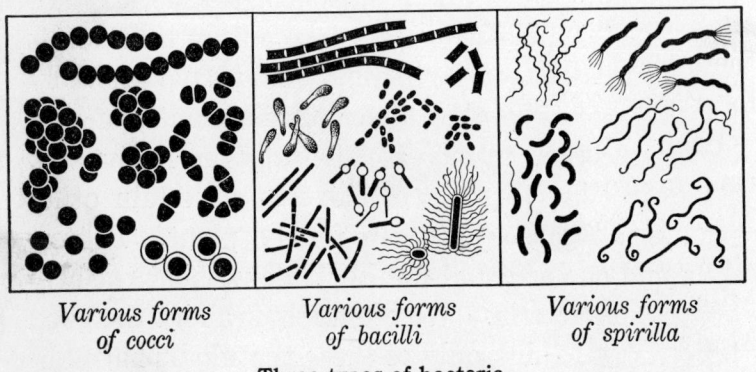

Various forms of cocci   *Various forms of bacilli*   *Various forms of spirilla*

Three types of bacteria

common mistake. Bacteria are generally believed to be plants, not animals. Some of them move about so quickly that it is no wonder that the old Dutch microbe hunter thought they were "little beasts."

How Bacteria Grow

Bacteria spring from other bacteria. They increase in number by dividing in half. One bacterium becomes two in about fifteen minutes under favorable conditions. Two become four; four become eight; eight become sixteen; sixteen become thirty-two. How many would there be in two hours' time? One germ can make a million just like itself in five hours and fifteen minutes. In a day, there would be a billion and a half, if conditions for growth were just right. In three days, there might be about seven thousand tons of bacteria, if they all lived. Of course all never *would* live because there would not be food enough for them or space for them free from their own wastes.

Bacteria need two of the same things that plants need in order to grow. They need food and water. Many of them differ from other plants in that they grow well on the same foods that make children grow. Milk, for example, helps to make children grow. Many kinds of bacteria also grow very quickly in slightly warm milk. Most bacteria die at once if they become dry. Like other living things they need water. Dried fruits and dried milk do not spoil because there is not enough water in these foods to keep alive the bacteria which make food spoil.

Most dangerous bacteria grow best in dark, warm, damp places. They are killed by direct sunlight. That is one reason why your mother lets the sunlight into the house and carries bedding and other things out into the sunlight. A very high temperature too kills bacteria. You remember that bacteria in water are killed by boiling it, and that milk is made safe by pasteurizing it. Canned foods keep because they have been boiled and sealed in airtight jars or

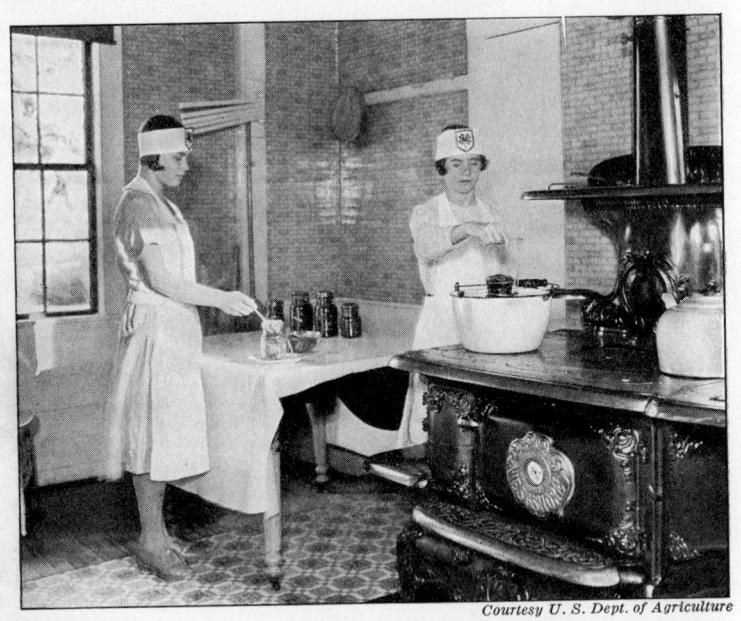

Heating food to kill bacteria

cans so that no more bacteria can reach them. It is bacteria which usually make foods spoil.

In a cold place most bacteria grow slowly or not at all. Many bacteria are killed at the freezing point. Experiments with frozen foods have shown, however, that freezing the spores of certain bacteria did not reduce the number of spores which under favorable conditions would produce living bacteria. If frozen vegetables, for example, are allowed to thaw and stand at room temperature for several days before using, they may become very dangerous.

How Do Bacteria Get into the Body?

Stop reading for a minute and write all the ways you can think of that bacteria may get into the body. You probably all put down "through a cut or scratch in the skin" because you have been reading the last chapter and have been studying first aid. That is a common way for bacteria to enter the body. As long as the skin is unbroken, bacteria cannot get in. When the skin is broken, bacteria can get into the body unless you are very careful to do the following:

Let the cut bleed freely a little while. Wash the skin around the cut with a little boiled water or with alcohol. Paint the cut with a solution of iodine or some other disinfectant. Fasten a sterile cloth over the cut. Never touch the wound with your fingers, handkerchief, or anything that is not sterile. Use a sterilized needle to take out a splinter. The needle can be sterilized by dipping it in iodine or by holding it over a flame until the point becomes red. A flame quickly kills bacteria. The needle should be used as soon as it is cooled. Can you give a reason for doing each of these things?

Another way in which bacteria can get into the body is through the mouth. You probably have that on your list. But how many ways there are in which bacteria can get into the mouth! If you put together all the ways you can think of, you will have at least twenty-five. The three principal carriers of bacteria are the three *F"s* — food, fingers, and flies. Make a list of the ways in which we can prevent bacteria from getting into the mouth by these means. Have you written all the ways mentioned in the following list?

1. To prevent bacteria from entering our bodies in food: Wash the hands and face before eating. Wash the hands before preparing food. Do not eat food picked up from the floor. Do not exchange food with another person. Keep food covered. Do not sweep the dining room or kitchen just before a meal. Wash dishes and sink in hot, soapy water and rinse with almost boiling water. Keep the icebox clean and cold. Keep cooked food covered and in a cold place. Buy clean milk that has been properly pasteurized. Boil the water you drink if you are not sure it is safe.

2. To prevent bacteria from entering our bodies on fingers and other objects: Wash hands and face before going to bed. Wash hands and face after you have been with a sick person. Wash hands after going to the toilet. Wash hands and face after you

have been in crowds. Keep your hands and other objects away from your face. Keep your fingers out of your mouth. Do not chew the end of your pencil. Do not hold any objects whatever in your mouth.

What has washing the hands to do with bacteria?

3. To keep flies from bringing bacteria to food: Take away the breeding places of flies. Kill the first flies that appear in the spring. Keep screen doors and windows shut. Keep food covered so that flies cannot reach it.

Another chief way by which bacteria get into the body is through the nose, although many bacteria are caught in the coat of mucus that covers the nose and throat. You notice the mucus especially when you have a cold. It is mucus which you catch in your handkerchief when you blow your nose or when you clear your throat. How does the mucus help to keep bacteria out of the body?

How can bacteria get into the nose? Sometimes they reach the nose on the fingers. But children to-day very seldom use their fingers to clean their noses. It is a disagreeable habit. Sometimes bacteria are breathed into the nose with dusty air. This seldom happens out of doors. A very common way by which bacteria get into the nose is by having some one sneeze or cough near you. The bacteria from his nose are carried in the little drops of spray which sprinkle your face unless you stand about six feet away from him. Even in talking and laughing, bacteria may be sprinkled on your face by a person who stands close to you. In order to prevent bacteria from going directly from one person to another:

Cover your mouth and nose when you sneeze or cough. Avoid crowds, if possible. Stay six feet away from a person who has a cold. Do not visit people who have *communicable diseases*,* that is, diseases which are catching. Do not play with children who have been with someone who has a communicable disease or with children who are themselves ill. Do not spit except on a paper or cloth that can be burned or put into a jar or can. See that persons who have tuberculosis burn all the sputum,* especially the material coughed up from the lungs. Do not hug or kiss sick people or handle things

Good form when you have a cold

they have just touched. Stay at home when you are ill until you have got entirely well. Do not use your own used handkerchief on your little brother or sister. Do not lend or borrow used handkerchiefs.

Bacteria are spread in all these and many other ways that you can think of. But all these ways of preventing the spread of bacteria are very simple. Once you have formed these habits, you need not think about them any longer.

If you wish to kill bacteria which are already in your throat or nose, it is not wise to use a nose douche* without the consent of your doctor, because it is so easy to force the bacteria farther back into the bony cavities (called *sinuses**) in your face. Yet you cannot be too careful to avoid colds and you should not neglect a cold.

Other Children's Questions

Look up the answers to the questions you cannot answer.

1. Is dirt ever clean?
2. Why do the Chinese boil the water they drink?
3. What diseases may come from milk and water which are not clean?
4. Is it true that we could not live without bacteria?
5. How are germs spread?
6. Can germs be killed by freezing?
7. Why are cultures* of children's throats sometimes taken?
8. Why do we all seem to have colds at the same time?

QUESTIONS ABOUT GERMS ANSWERED

9. How did Mary get a sore throat?
10. Why does the doctor swab your throat when you have a sore throat?
11. What is a contact?*

Answers. The Chinese have few safe, clean places to get water. The water they get often contains bacteria which cause diseases. These bacteria are killed by heat. The Chinese boil the water they drink to make it safe. We also boil the water we drink if we are not sure it is free from germs.

Dirt is never clean, but it may be harmless. Dangerous dirt carries disease germs. You cannot see bacteria on your hands or pencil, but certain of these unseen bacteria make people sick.

Many boys and girls have colds at the same time because one or two children who catch cold first play with other children. They go to school and sit near other children. By carelessly coughing or sneezing they spread the germs which are causing their colds. If the first child who caught a cold stayed at home, fewer children in the school would catch cold. At certain times of the year, as at Christmas when we often eat more sweets than usual, colds are common. At certain times in the year we go out of doors less and have less sunlight on our bare skin. That also may lower our resistance* to (our power to fight) the bacteria which cause colds.

PROTECTION FROM BACTERIA

Many diseases may come from milk and water that are not protected from bacteria. One of the most common diseases carried by milk and water used to be typhoid fever. Both milk and water can

Photo by Acme Newspictures, Inc.

A laboratory where cultures of bacteria are studied

be made perfectly safe. There is no excuse for using milk or water that carries diseases.

We could not live without bacteria. Waste materials and dead things would cover the earth. Bacteria cause dead plants and animals to decay and thus furnish food for new plants. Only a few of all the bacteria in the world cause disease.

Throat *cultures* are samples of mucus taken from the nose and throat. This mucus is studied to see whether or not a person has certain bacteria in his throat and nose.

Germs are spread in hundreds of ways — by food, water, fingers, flies, or direct contact with a sick person or a carrier.* A carrier may spread disease without being sick himself. Measles is spread, for example, by visiting people who have measles, handling things which they have just handled, and eating food that they have touched. We can catch measles from the spray scattered about by the coughing of a person who is just beginning to get sick and does not know that his running nose and eyes are the beginning of a long illness.

Mary probably caught her sore throat in the same ways that colds are usually caught. She might possibly have caught a special kind of sore throat from milk that was not pasteurized and then kept cold and covered.

Many, but not all, germs are killed by freezing.

A *contact* means being so close to a person that the germs from his mouth and nose and hands may get over to you through talking, laughing, kissing, sneezing, coughing, or handling things he has just handled.

There are disinfectants which will kill most of the bacteria on the surface of the throat without hurting the delicate mucous membrane which lines it. Since no disinfectant can go far below the upper surface of the throat, no throat disinfectants can reach all the bacteria that may be present.

Things to Do

1. Visit a bacteriology* or science laboratory. Ask the teacher to explain the use of the microscope and let you look at some bacteria through it.

2. In this chapter there are many new words. They are words which you will often see in newspapers and magazines when you read about health. Make a list of these words. Test yourself to see if you understand clearly the meaning of each one. Practice pronouncing them. Then use them whenever you can. If you do not know exactly what a word means, look it up in the Glossary at the back of this book, find the word in other books on health and bacteriology, or ask the nurse, the doctor, the teacher, or your father or mother to explain it more fully.

3. Have you any problems of preventing infection in your home? Talk over this question in class. If you find ways in which bacteria might be spread from one person to another, talk with your mother about the changes in your home which will help to prevent

the spread of bacteria. **4.** Do you have the problem of preventing eye infection in your school? Make a list of the ways bacteria may get to the eyes and the ways in which you can prevent this. **5.** Make a list of the reasons why some people you know smoke. Find a way of answering each of these reasons in your own case. Read the chapter on smoking again to find reasons for not smoking.

CHEMICAL WAR ON BACTERIA

Have you ever heard of *chemical** warfare? In battles long ago soldiers fought man to man. That was physical warfare. In the last war poison gas, acids, and other chemicals were used to kill large numbers of people. That was chemical warfare.

Our warfare with bacteria is both physical and chemical. You have read about some of the physical weapons in the last chapter — the skin, the mucus of the nose and throat, the water that washes the eyes at all times. The white blood corpuscles, too, go to the rescue of the tissue cells and surround and carry away the bacteria and the dead and injured body cells. This chapter will tell about some of the chemical weapons with which the body protects itself against bacteria.

A disinfecting* station. The healthy stomach is a disinfecting station of great value. The acid of the digestive juice is a chemical weapon which the body uses against certain bacteria. Many kinds of bacteria cannot live in an acid of a certain strength. It is the acid in sour milk that makes it safe to drink. When the milk has turned really sour, the harmful bacteria in it are usually killed.

Some of the bacteria which slip into the stomach on food meet a timely death in the acid digestive juice of the stomach before they have a chance to do any harm. There are also other digestive juices, such as the bile,* which dissolve some kinds of bacteria or prevent them from growing.

What is Antitoxin?

Diphtheria antitoxin. About forty years ago Emil August Behring saved a little girl's life with diphtheria antitoxin.* What is antitoxin? *Toxin** is a poison. *Antitoxin* means *against toxin*. Antitoxin prevents the toxins produced by bacteria from doing harm. Toxin is made by the diphtheria bacillus. Antitoxin is manufactured by the body to make toxin harmless. It was the additional antitoxin used by Behring that saved the little girl's life.

Antitoxin made by animals can be used to cure human beings of the disease when their own bodies cannot make the antitoxin fast enough. Diphtheria antitoxin is usually obtained from the blood of horses.

Only the serum* is used. The serum is the watery part of the blood left after the blood has clotted. It contains the antitoxin.

A few years ago there was a diphtheria epidemic*

Courtesy of E. R. Squibb & Sons

How does Mickey Horse protect children from diphtheria?

in a far distant part of Alaska. The only thing that could save the lives of many of those sick people was diphtheria antitoxin. The antitoxin had been obtained with great care from healthy horses. It was tested on guinea pigs to find out how well it would cure diphtheria — how much was needed to cure the disease. It takes 100 times as much antitoxin to cure a person as to cure a guinea pig. A large amount of diphtheria antitoxin was sent by steamship to Alaska. It was carried the rest of the way by a team of dogs, led by that heroic dog Balto, which fought their way through darkness and storm. They smashed all records in the long race to save the diphtheria-stricken people. The antitoxin was immediately given to the people already sick with diphtheria. The antitoxin neutralized* the diphtheria toxin already in their blood. Many of them began to get better. Nurses and others who were not yet sick but were in danger of getting diphtheria were given smaller amounts of the antitoxin to protect them from the disease.

Every physician knows that antitoxin cures diphtheria if it is given early enough. A delay of one day may make the difference between death and recovery. That is why the diphtheria antitoxin was rushed to the little town in Alaska through the night and storm. That is why diphtheria antitoxin is now often carried by airplane.

Doctors can tell if people will get diphtheria by giving them a test called the *Schick test*.* The Schick test shows whether a child is susceptible* to diphtheria, that is, whether he will catch it if he is exposed to it (has the chance of catching it). If the doctor says: "The Schick test is positive," that means that if the person is exposed to diphtheria, he will be likely to get it. Susceptible children in whom the Schick test is positive can be protected from diphtheria.

An Alaskan village

Toxoid. Discoveries are made every year in the field of health. One recent discovery is helping further to win the fight with diphtheria. A still better substance has been discovered which makes the Schick test unnecessary. This substance is called *toxoid;* * it is made from toxin by allowing it to age, by heating it, or by treating it with a certain chemical. One injection of toxoid given only twice two weeks apart will make almost 100 per cent of the babies so treated immune.*   To be immune means to be sure not to get a disease.

The majority of deaths from diphtheria occur in children under five years of age. Every day during 1928 an average of 22 children died from diphtheria. Why take a chance with the baby in your family? In one city alone diphtheria was decreased 50 per cent. No child need die from, no child need suffer from, diphtheria.

Antitoxin for other diseases.   It is not only against diphtheria that the body protects itself by making antitoxin. It makes antitoxin to neutralize the poisons of certain other bacteria. Deaths from tetanus,* as well as deaths from diphtheria, have been made unnecessary by antitoxin. The tetanus bacillus usually causes trouble only when it is pressed deep into a wound. Then it grows and makes its deadly toxin. This poison is neutralized by tetanus antitoxin. During the World War tetanus antitoxin was used a great deal and saved the lives of thousands of wounded soldiers.

In order to make harmless the toxin of the bacteria which cause scarlet fever, the body manufactures scarlet-fever antitoxin. Scientists have been trying to make an antitoxin for scarlet fever which will be as sure a cure for this disease as diphtheria antitoxin is for diphtheria.   One doctor gave an injection of the serum of a horse containing scarlet-fever antitoxin to a boy very ill with "the red sickness." In a few hours his terrible red rash began to fade. In a day his skin was as white as usual. His fever cooled. But scarlet fever is more tricky than diphtheria. It cannot yet be cured by antitoxin so surely as diphtheria can.

Warfare on Smallpox

Smallpox is another disease which the body fights by making substances which are carried in the blood. About one hundred fifty years ago, everyone expected to have smallpox sometime during his life. One person in every twelve died of it. Many kings, queens, and princes died of the disease. More than half of all the people living in England had ugly smallpox scars on their faces. Smallpox is very rare today because of the great discovery made in the time of George Washington by Edward Jenner.

People tried to protect themselves by inoculation* — that is by giving themselves a mild case of the disease so that they would not get it later. They took some of the contagious* matter (the virus) from people who had a mild case of smallpox and scratched it into the arms of people who feared they might get the disease. And often the person thus treated had a mild case of smallpox instead of the severe case he might have had if he had caught it sometime when he was tired or ill. Inoculation of this kind was better than no protection, but it was far from being the best method.

A farmer noticed that the people who worked in dairies often caught a mild disease called *cowpox*, and that people who had had cowpox did not catch smallpox. Edward Jenner got the idea that anyone could be treated with the virus of cowpox instead of the smallpox virus. He studied and experimented for a long time and finally proved clearly that smallpox could be prevented by vaccination.* (*Vaccination* comes from the Latin word, *vaccinus*, meaning *from cows*.) The thousands of people in those early days who were vaccinated did not get smallpox although they were exposed* to it. Still, many doctors did not agree with Jenner. But the King (George III), the Queen, and the Prince of Wales approved and helped in the good work of spreading vaccination throughout England. The Empress of Russia sent Jenner a ring and named the first child to be vaccinated in Russia *Vacinoff*. Napoleon in 1805 ordered all the soldiers in his army to be vaccinated. Thomas Jefferson was our first President to be vaccinated.

Vaccination for smallpox when you are well will prevent the disease. Fumigating* rooms after you have had the disease is of little or no value. Some

THE TESTING OF VACCINATION

people ask: "Why do we still have to be vaccinated when there are so few cases of smallpox nowadays?" In 1929 there were 40,000 cases of smallpox in the United States. That is not a "few cases." In 1924 there were 1,610 cases of smallpox in one city in the

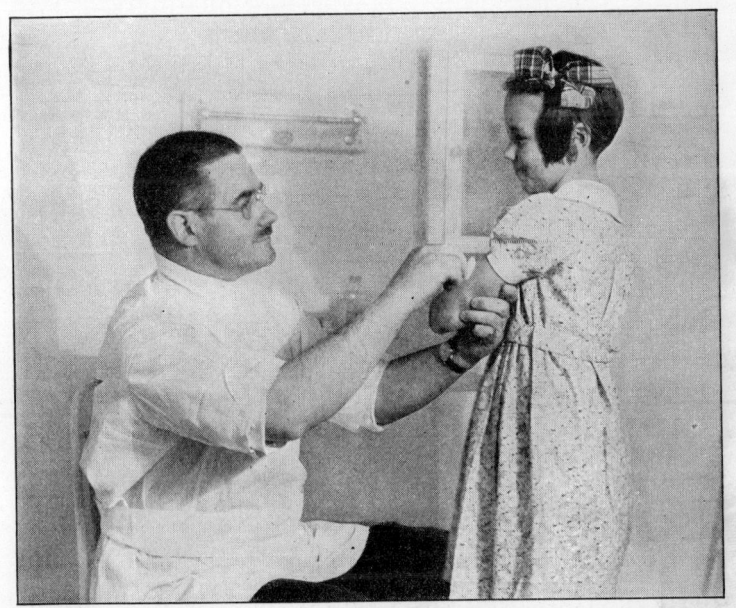

Why few people in the United States today have smallpox

United States. Of these 1,610 cases, 163 died. Among all these cases there was not one person who had been successfully vaccinated within five years. Of the 163 persons who died, 142 had never been vaccinated and nineteen had been vaccinated ten or more years previous to their infection. Do these facts answer the question: "Why do we still have to be vaccinated?" These outbreaks now and then show that vaccination is still needed.

The following figures reported in 1933 help to answer the question: Is vaccination important in preventing smallpox?

Laws Regarding Vaccination in Different States	Number of Cases of Smallpox per 100,000 People in a Year
9 states and the District of Columbia which have compulsory vaccination — that is, everyone must be vaccinated	6.6
6 states in which each neighborhood may do as it wishes	51.3
29 states which have no vaccination laws	66.7
4 states in which compulsory vaccination is forbidden	115.2

Have you been vaccinated within five years? It is a very simple thing to be vaccinated. All vaccines* in the United States are carefully tested. Your part is to do exactly what the doctor tells you to do after he has vaccinated you. Everyone should be vaccinated during the first year of life and again when he is ten or twelve years old.

VACCINATION PREVENTS SMALLPOX

Pasteur's Discovery

The same principle of having the body manufacture its own weapons to fight disease is used in preventing rabies,* or hydrophobia,* which is caused by the bite of a mad dog. For a number of years Pasteur had been studying a method of preventing hydrophobia by injecting more and more virulent* organisms. *Virulent* means poisonous. The more virulent the organisms, the more deadly they are. He had tried out his method on many animals. He was sure it would work in the case of human beings. One day a nine-year-old boy, Joseph Meister, was brought to him. He had been knocked down and terribly

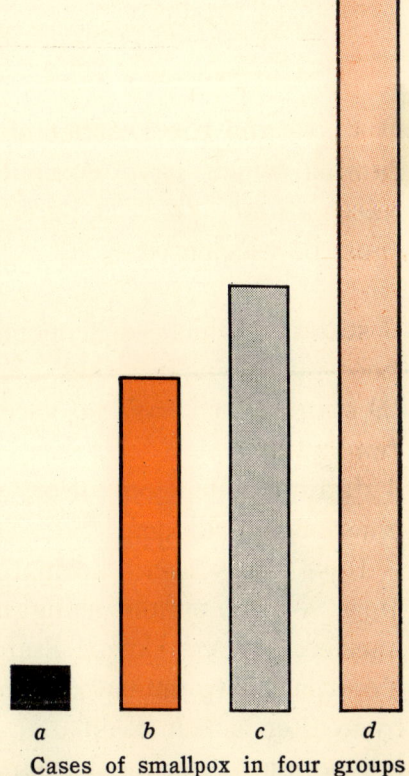

Cases of smallpox in four groups (*a*, *b*, *c*, *d*) of states. Compare with the table on page 310.

bitten by a mad dog. The boy was almost certain to get the dreaded disease.

Pasteur decided to put his cure for hydrophobia to the test and began to inject* into the little fellow small amounts of the germs, or organisms,* which cause hydrophobia. Joseph cried before the first inoculation, but when he found it was nothing but a little scratch, he lost all fear and was very happy in the laboratory playing with the animals. But Pasteur was very anxious. As he continued to inject more and more virulent organisms, he became more and more worried. He could not sleep. The last inoculation was the most virulent of all. It was sure to give hydrophobia to a rabbit in seven days, and would kill a man who had not been protected by the treatment. Joseph took this last injection* and went

Photo from Ewing Galloway
Louis Pasteur

peacefully to sleep. Pasteur stayed awake all night fearing that the boy might die. But days passed and Joseph kept well.

After many other tests, Pasteur was sure that his treatment was a success. It is used today by doctors in many lands. Although there are still more than thirty thousand people bitten by mad animals each year, less than one half of one per cent get hydrophobia. Those who get it are the ones who have waited too long before taking the Pasteur treatment; they always die. No one today need have rabies.

After a person has had certain diseases, the blood continues to make its chemical weapons. There is no danger of his getting the disease again for some time. He is immune. After having a bad cold, a person is immune for several weeks at least. After having typhoid fever, a person is usually immune for a lifetime. After being vaccinated successfully for smallpox, the person is usually immune for about five years.

Immunity* is secured also by injecting into the person a small amount of weak bacteria, or dead bacteria, or their toxins. These are not virulent enough or numerous enough to do harm, but they start the body making the substances which will protect it from further attacks.

Can you explain now how the body works in protecting itself against bacteria? Do you see more clearly that you should do the following?

1. Prevent bacteria from getting into the mouth, nose, and throat, or through a cut in the skin.

2. Prevent bacteria from the nose, mouth, and body wastes from reaching other people.

3. Protect yourselves from smallpox, diphtheria, typhoid fever, and certain other diseases by using the vaccine and inoculations which give immunity to each of these diseases.

OTHER CHILDREN'S QUESTIONS

Look up the answers to questions which you are not sure you can answer correctly:

1. What causes headache?
2. What causes *ptomaine poisioning*?*
3. What is asthma?* What causes it?
4. Are swimming pools safe places to swim?
5. Why do doctors give children the Schick test?
6. How is diphtheria carried from person to person?
7. Is antitoxin obtained from animals?
8. I had smallpox once. Do I have to get vaccinated?
9. How does one know when the vaccination is successful?

Answers. Doctors give the Schick test to find out whether or not a person is likely to catch diphtheria if he should be exposed to the disease.

Swimming pools can be made safe places to swim.

When is a swimming pool safe? *no time*

They should not be overcrowded. Everyone should wash himself with soap and water before going into the pool. The water should be kept safe and clean by frequent changing or by constant filtering and adding chlorine.

Diphtheria is carried from the throat and nose of

one person to the throat and nose of another by careless coughing, sneezing, kissing, putting fingers to the nose and mouth, and handling by a diphtheria patient of food and objects that other people will use.

If you have had smallpox a good many years ago, it is safer to be vaccinated. If you are still immune, the vaccination will not take.

If the skin becomes red, and there is some swelling and soreness around the spot where the vaccine is injected, you know that the vaccination has been successful. The reddening of the skin shows that the smallpox virus is just beginning to make trouble. But the body begins to form substances which neutralize the poisons and destroy the harmful bacteria. The tissues get the habit of producing these substances. Year after year some of them are in the blood to protect you from smallpox. Successful vaccination is almost certain to keep you from getting smallpox for several years.

Asthma is a disease which makes breathing difficult and wheezy. It is often caused by breathing in some kind of dust. One person may get asthma from the dust from hay; another person, from mold in the air of certain houses or rooms. One person got asthma from the bits of fur from a pet cat. Sometimes it is very hard for the doctor to discover exactly the substance that is causing the trouble.

THE MEANING OF IMMUNITY

The cause of headache may be in almost any part of the body. A headache is a signal that something is wrong somewhere. The trouble is often in the stomach. Sometimes the headache comes from constipation. Sometimes the headache is caused by eyestrain; sometimes, by a cold in the head. There are many causes of headache. If you have frequent headaches, you should go to the doctor to find out the cause of yours.

Antitoxin is obtained from the blood of healthy animals. Only the serum, the watery part of the blood after it has clotted, is used. It is carefully tested in laboratories before it is used.

Ptomaine is a poison formed by the action of certain bacteria on meat and certain other foods. Such food smells and tastes so badly that no one would eat it. Most so-called ptomaine poisoning is due to bacteria which might have been killed by cooking.

Things to Do

1. You will be interested in the story of vaccination as it is told in the story of the life of Edward Jenner. See whether you can get from a library some book that has this story for the class to read.
2. In this chapter also you will find many new words. Make a list of them. Be sure you understand clearly the meaning of each one.

3. Ask a doctor to show the class the different kinds of vaccines and antitoxins mentioned in this chapter and to explain how he uses them.

4. Find out the number of deaths from diphtheria in your community. Give talks and make posters telling parents how to protect their babies from

A MESSAGE TO PARENTS
HOW ANTI-TOXIN AND TOXOID HAVE CONQUERED DIPHTHERIA IN NEW YORK CITY

THIRTY YEARS AGO MORE THAN 2000 CHILDREN DIED EACH YEAR FROM DIPHTHERIA

TWENTY YEARS AGO MORE THAN 1200 CHILDREN DIED EACH YEAR FROM DIPHTHERIA

TEN YEARS AGO OVER SEVEN HUNDRED CHILDREN DIED EACH YEAR FROM DIPHTHERIA

LAST YEAR 86 CHILDREN DIED FROM DIPHTHERIA

EVEN THESE DEATHS ARE UNNECESSARY
LET US WIPE OUT DIPHTHERIA AS WE HAVE WIPED OUT SMALLPOX!
Courtesy New York City Commissioner of Health

diphtheria. 5. What are some of the other health problems in your neighborhood? Make plans in class to solve each of these problems. Look in the index of your text and in other books for information which will help you in solving each problem.

6. Why do some people drink alcoholic beverages? In what other ways could they get the relaxation they want? Find *alcohol* and *drugs* in the Index.

Read the pages referred to. 7. What are *foci of infection?* Tell how foci of infection in the teeth may be prevented. If you do not remember the facts about abscessed teeth, read the pages on this subject referred to in the Index.

PROTECTING OTHERS FROM BACTERIA

Bacteria are so small and we are so big that it seems as though we should win in the fight against them. In the last three chapters you have learned how to protect yourself from bacteria. Some of these things that protect you will also protect other people. There are still other things you can do to help fight germs.

The bacteria which do the most damage come from the bodies of people. There are three chief roads by which bacteria leave the body. They are the mouth, the nose, and the digestive tract.

TAKING CARE

How can you prevent bacteria from escaping by way of the mouth and nose? You will answer at once: "Cover your mouth and nose when you sneeze and cough." You know other ways too, but they are so important that you ought to review them and ask yourself the question: "Do I do this?"

When you have a cold or any other communicable disease:

1. Stay six feet away from other people, thus avoiding direct contact with them.

2. Do not go to motion-picture theaters or to other crowded places.

3. Observe the rules of quarantine.* Do not return to school until the doctor says there is no danger of your spreading bacteria. Quarantine is the best way of controlling a disease after a person has caught it, although the best way of preventing certain diseases is through inoculation. The rules of quarantine tell you how long you should stay away from other people if you have certain diseases. For example, the period of quarantine for scarlet fever is at least twenty-one days and until all discharges* cease. Until that time it is not safe to let the patient play with other children. The period of danger for others, if you have whooping cough, lasts about eight weeks or until one week after the last "whoop"; if you have chicken pox, at least twelve days, until all scabs disappear; if you have measles, at least seven days, or until recovery.

4. Do not kiss anyone when you have a cold.

5. Never spit on the floor. When you spit or blow your nose, use soft paper napkins or small pieces of old, clean cloths which you can burn promptly. Paper napkins and old, clean cloths, to be used a few times only, are more sanitary than hand-

kerchiefs which have to be used many times. Paper handkerchiefs can be bought very cheaply.

6. Keep your hands and other objects away from your face.

7. Use your own towel, washcloth, soap, and toothbrush; never those of anyone else.

A good bathroom arrangement

8. Use your own handkerchief and never lend it to anyone.

How can you prevent bacteria from escaping in the waste from the digestive tract? 1. Follow the doctor's orders in regard to the treatment of body wastes from sick people. Some of the most dangerous bacteria may leave the body when you go to the toilet. Epidemics of typhoid fever have occurred because a few people who had typhoid fever were careless in getting rid of body wastes. Instead of following the doctor's directions and killing all the bacteria by adding chlorinated* lime or *carbolic acid** to the waste material and letting them stand for half an hour, they poured the material just as it was into a river. In another town several miles down the river the people used the river water for drinking purposes. It looked clear and clean. They did not bother to boil it. But it contained many virulent bacteria. Many of the people became sick and some of them died because of the carelessness of the people in the town above them on the river. Bacteria are killed by certain disinfectants. Disinfecting the body wastes of sick people promptly is necessary in order to protect other people from sickness.

2. Wash your hands after going to the toilet. Bacteria can get on the hands easily. They can get to the mouth from the hands or from other objects. For example, suppose you have forgotten to wash your hands after going to the toilet. There are germs on them. You open the door, taking hold of the handle. You leave some of the bacteria on the door knob. Another person comes in. He

washes his hands carefully, but he must turn the handle of the door in order to open it. He wipes off some of the germs you have put there. Then he picks up a clean apple to eat at recess time. Some of your germs now on his hands are rubbed on the apple. He swallows them when he eats the apple. You made it hard for him to protect himself against germs. Were you playing fair?

Do only sick people carry dangerous bacteria in their bodies? It is strange but true that the same germs may be harmless to some people and deadly to others. There are people who carry typhoid bacilli in their bodies and throw out swarms of virulent bacteria in the wastes from their digestive tracts. They themselves do not show the slightest sign of illness. These people are "carriers." It is thought that one person of every twenty who have recovered from typhoid fever may be a carrier. When cases of diphtheria are frequent in a crowded section of a city, one child in ten may carry the deadly bacteria in his throat. Everyone, both sick and well, should do the simple things to avoid spreading bacteria which may be present in the throat, nose, or digestive tract.

In one city there was a cook who was later called "Typhoid Mary." She was not sick herself, but she carried the typhoid bacteria which are so deadly to many people. Typhoid Mary had never studied about health. She probably had never heard of bacteria. She took no trouble to guard the paths by which bacteria might get on to her hands, her clothes, and the food she was cooking. As the result of her ignorance, there was an epidemic of typhoid in the neighborhood. The cause was finally discovered. Typhoid Mary was no longer allowed to prepare food for people. She had to disinfect wastes from her body in exactly the same way that the trained nurse disinfects the body wastes of the patient who is sick in bed.

The bacteria which cause tuberculosis and pneumonia* are often found in active, healthy people. Everyone — not only sick people — should follow the simple everyday rules for preventing the spread of disease.

IMMUNITY

Why do some people get a communicable disease while others in the same family do not? There are three chief reasons why some people get contagious diseases while others escape:

1. Some people have acquired immunity to certain contagious diseases either by having had the disease or by having been vaccinated or inoculated. They have antitoxins and other substances in their blood which destroy bacteria and their poisons.

HOW IMMUNITY IS ACQUIRED 325

2. Some people may get a larger dose of bacteria than others in the same family. How? Whether a person catches a communicable disease depends partly upon the number of bacteria that get into his body and how virulent they are. The more bacteria

Health and happiness in outdoor play

he allows to get into his mouth or nose or through a break in the skin, and the more virulent they are, the more likely he is to get sick.

3. Some people can resist certain bacteria better than others because they are in very good health. This is especially true in the case of tuberculosis

and colds. The germs that cause tuberculosis, colds, and pneumonia are present in a person's nose and throat all the time. Whether they become dangerous or not seems to depend upon his physical condition. He is more likely to get these respiratory* diseases if he (1) is very tired; (2) has become chilled; (3) is not getting much sunlight or outdoor exercise; (4) has had little milk, green vegetables, and eggs in his diet; (5) is often worried or angry or afraid; (6) is constipated* or has other digestive disturbances; (7) has already been weakened by some disease.

These seven conditions, taken together, show why one person in a family can catch a communicable disease easily while another escapes. What things to do are suggested by the reasons why some people get sick and others do not?

Caring for the Sick

What are the most important things to do in case of sickness? Sickness sometimes happens in the most carefully protected families; we should know, therefore, exactly what to do to help the sick person to get well quickly and to prevent anyone else from catching his disease.

Of course you should do everything to build up the health of the convalescent,* the person who is beginning to get well after having been ill. Never let him get fatigued* in any way. Find ways to make him happy and contented. Give him wholesome, easily digested food at regular times and fresh air and sunlight in his room. Children

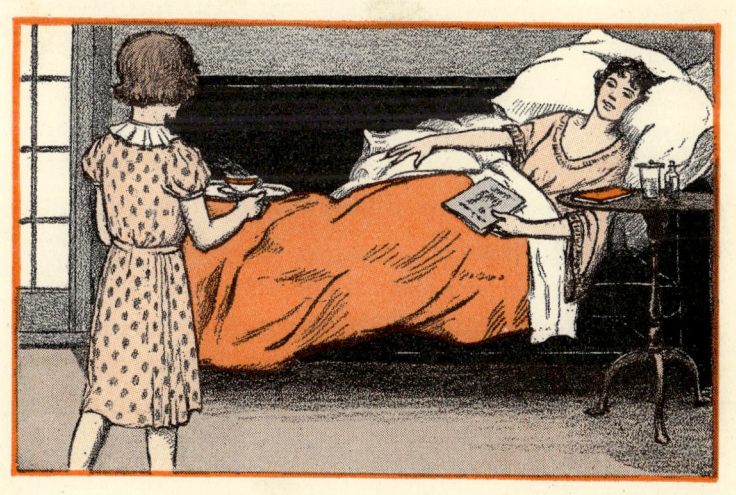

Something for the convalescing mother

convalescing from serious illness should not use their eyes for close work and should avoid glaring lights. People used to think that children recovering from measles should be kept in a dark room. But that is not wise. Children recovering from any illness need sunlight and fresh air in their rooms. Their eyes may easily be protected from the sunlight by placing the heads of their beds toward the window. Then their backs will be toward the light, and the light from the window will not shine in their eyes. If lamps or electric lights are used, they should be softly shaded so that there is no glare.

You should obey two rules which the doctor will surely give you. One is especially for the good of the convalescent; the other is especially for the protection of other people.

The first rule is: "Protect convalescents from other infections." After a person has had a serious illness, he is much more likely to catch other diseases because he is weak and has less resistance. So you should never let people with colds come to see the convalescent, and never let any visitors kiss him or come close to his bed or chair.

The second rule is to destroy all bacteria which come from the person's nose, throat, digestive tract, or other infected part. The doctor will tell you exactly how to do this and the best disinfectants to use. Follow his directions. Forgetting once may make a sad difference in the health of other people.

People used to fumigate the rooms of those who had been sick with a communicable disease. To fumigate they burned sulphur and other strong-smelling substances in the room in the hope that these substances would kill the bacteria. Now we know that the best way to protect others in the home is to kill the bacteria as soon as they come from the sick person, rather than to wait until the end of the illness.

The person who knows these facts is not afraid of sickness because he knows what to do to protect himself and others.

Other Children's Questions

Answer as many of the following questions as you can:

1. Why do bakers wear white clothes?
2. Why is Tom kept out of school when he isn't sick?
3. What shall I do with the books I had at home when I had scarlet fever?
4. The early settlers died rapidly. Why?
5. Does bathing in the Ganges River and drinking its water make the people sick?
6. Why is there more pneumonia during spring months?
7. Why were so many of the soldiers at Valley Forge ill?
8. I should think that if one person had a disease, others would get it if they used the same drinking cup. Do they?
9. What are some of the diseases that are caused by sewage?* (Sewage is waste matter carried away from houses in ditches, drains, or pipes.)

Answers. Yes, drinking water from the Ganges often makes the people of India sick. Someone has called the water in the Ganges "sacred sewage." Many Hindus drink the sacred water to gain health and often gain sickness and death instead. Drinking river water in our country too is not a safe thing to do. If river water must be used for drinking, it is usually filtered and treated with chemicals to kill disease germs.

Undoubtedly people did catch diseases by drinking from a cup other people had just used. That is why we no longer have common drinking cups. Everyone uses his own cup.

Put the books you used while you had scarlet fever out in the bright sun several hours, letting the wind turn the pages. Or put a drop of formalin* on every fourth or fifth page and leave them in a closed drawer or box for twenty-four hours.

The early settlers in America died rapidly in part because they did not have the right kind of food and enough of it. Without plenty of eggs and milk and green vegetables their resistance to certain diseases was low. In addition, they were severely exposed to cold and storms. Finally, they knew nothing about bacteria. Therefore they could not win the battle against bacteria.

Typhoid fever, cholera,* dysentery,* and other

intestinal diseases are carried by sewage which has not been properly treated and disposed of.

The soldiers at Valley Forge did not have enough food or enough clothing. They did not have a sanitary camp. They did not know how to kill germs or to prevent them from spreading. Their body resistance to colds, tuberculosis, and pneumonia must have been low and their opportunities to catch these diseases many.

Tom is probably kept out of school because his brother has a communicable disease. Tom was with his brother and so is in danger of catching the disease, too. He should stay away from school until it is certain that he has not caught the disease.

One reason why there is more pneumonia in the spring months is the fact that people's resistance is lower. During the winter they often have had less sunlight, have been out of doors less, and have eaten less green vegetables and fresh fruits. In winter they also have more colds, and colds pave the way to pneumonia and other diseases of the nose, throat, and lungs.

Bakers wear white clothes because white shows the dirt very quickly. White cotton clothes can also easily be washed and boiled and kept quite free from germs. The hands and clothing of people who prepare food should be kept very clean.

Things to Do

1. Look for advertisements of paper handkerchiefs. Send for samples if samples are offered. Ask for paper handkerchiefs in the drug store or large dry-goods store. Buy a box of them, if you can afford them, and use them, especially when you have a cold. Always cover your mouth and nose when you sneeze or cough.

2. Obtain from the doctor or nurse the names of some of the best disinfectants for each of the following purposes: to put on cuts; to gargle your throat; to mix with the body wastes from sick people; to disinfect pillows, sheets, and towels used by sick people; to use in an outdoor toilet or privy in the country or at camp. **3.** Make a list of the ways in which bacteria may be spread at mealtime. How may this be avoided? In what other ways can you make mealtimes healthful? Read pages 215–218 to see if you have remembered all the ways mentioned there. **4.** Ask a doctor or nurse to tell you why the body wastes from sick people should be treated with a disinfectant.

5. Wash your hands after going to the toilet. Form this habit and the habit of having a regular bowel movement without using laxative medicines, if you have not already formed them.

6. Raw vegetables and fruits are necessary for health. Tell in class how you make vegetables and fruits safe to eat — free from bacteria. 7. Boil the water you drink if you are not sure it is safe. Why?

8. You have met many new words in this chapter. See if you can pronounce them easily, explain their meanings clearly, and use them in sentences.

INSECTS THAT CARRY DISEASE

Germs cannot travel very far from place to place by themselves. They must be carried. Many insects carry germs and even furnish them with food. Someone has said that the two most dangerous animals in the world are the *fly* and the *mosquito*.

FIGHTING FLIES

Why should flies die, or better still, never be born? Why do you think the common house fly might be called the "typhoid fly" or the "filth fly"? Bacteria from body wastes are spread by flies. If a person leaves the toilet uncovered or unscreened, what happens? Flies gather. They walk over the material. They get germs on their feet, wings, and bodies. They buzz busily back to someone's home. When the screen door is open they sneak in. If there is any uncovered food around, they go straight to it. They wipe their feet on the bread. They shake off germs in the butter. They wash their wings in the milk. They walk over the baby's nose and lips. Everywhere they leave their load of germs.

How can the number of flies be reduced? The danger from flies can be reduced in the following ways:

1. Avoid manure* piles by throwing manure into a wagon and once or twice a week spreading it over

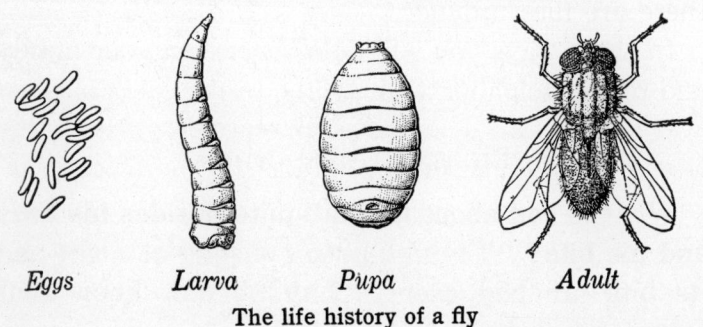

Eggs   *Larva*   *Pupa*   *Adult*
The life history of a fly

the land where it will not breed flies. If you must have manure piles, cover them and treat them with borax* or hellebore,* which destroys the eggs of flies. Flies lay their eggs in manure and grow up in it. Killing flies is good, but preventing them from being born in large numbers is still better. If there are no breeding places, there will be no flies.

2. Leave no toilets or privies uncovered, for it is there the flies pick up the most dangerous germs.

3. Kill all the flies you can in the spring. Every fly lays hundreds of eggs during the summer.

4. Screen your doors and windows and keep the screens closed so that flies cannot get into the house. Kill the stray flies that may get into the house.

5. Keep food covered so that if a fly does get into the house, it cannot reach the food.

6. Keep the sleeping baby and the baby that is less than a year old covered with a thin netting if there are flies around.

In these ways you will do a service to your family and to the neighborhood.

Fighting Mosquitoes

What is bad about the mosquito besides his buzz and his bite? The mosquito's singing at night and its bite are bad enough, but we now know that certain mosquitoes are more dangerous than many large wild animals.

Do you have malaria in your neighborhood? For many years people have had malaria, a sickness causing chills and fever. "Malaria* is due to the bad night air," people said. And they called the disease *malaria*, which means *bad air*. They noticed that epidemics of malaria and yellow fever always started in low, damp places, and that few people in high, dry parts of the same country had the diseases. They still thought it was the air that made the difference. Then someone noticed that in places where people

INSECTS THAT CARRY DISEASE

had malaria and *yellow fever** there were always mosquitoes. More important still was the fact that these diseases disappeared when the mosquitoes disappeared.

Finally, Walter Reed and other scientists, who had for some time suspected mosquitoes of being the cause of disease, began to study their habits. Dr. Jesse W. Lazear allowed a mosquito which had bitten a person sick with yellow fever to bite him. In five

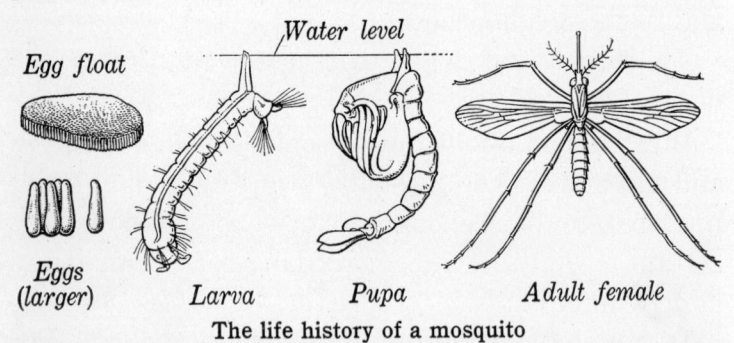

Egg float / *Water level* / *Eggs (larger)* / *Larva* / *Pupa* / *Adult female*

The life history of a mosquito

days he came down with yellow fever and died. After scientists had proved that the mosquito was guilty, they studied how to get rid of the dangerous insects.

The bite of all mosquitoes does not cause yellow fever or malaria. Only certain kinds of mosquitoes are dangerous. These mosquitoes are dangerous only when they have bitten a person who has yellow fever or malaria. The microorganisms* which cause these diseases grow in the stomach of the mosquito and are injected into the person whom the mosquito bites. What suggestions do these facts give for the prevention of the two diseases?

The *first* thing that should be done is not to let any mosquitoes bite people who are sick with either disease. Houses and hospitals should be screened.

The *second* thing is not to let the mosquito bite the well people. People's houses should be protected with wire screens and netting.

The *third* thing is to drain, that is, to dry up, the marshes and other places where water stands. Why is this done? Because the mosquito lays its eggs in still water, not in a swiftly moving stream. Mosquitoes can multiply even in tin cans partly full of water.

A *fourth* thing that is done is to pour certain oils, like petroleum,* and poisons on still water which cannot be drained. How does this prevent mosquitoes? The larvae* (the very young wingless forms of the mosquito after they have hatched from the eggs) come up to the surface of the water for air and there grow into full-sized mosquitoes. The oils form a film over the water and both poison the larvae and keep them from getting air. Substances, such as carbolic acid, which mix with the water and kill the larvae are sometimes used instead of the oil.

The mosquitoes, in either case, die before they have a chance to grow up.

By using all these methods, people have stamped

Photo by Ewing Galloway

How does digging ditches of this kind help to prevent mosquitoes?

out malaria and yellow fever in many places. America has almost conquered yellow fever by making war against mosquitoes in certain places. When the

GETTING RID OF OTHER INSECT PESTS

Panama Canal was being built, at first so many workmen died that the builders were ready to give up the task. After the yellow fever and malaria were conquered, the work went on more rapidly. The conquest of the mosquito made the building of the Panama Canal possible.

Do other insects carry disease? You have already seen that flies may carry all kinds of germs on their feet, wings, and bodies to people's food and faces. Many other insects, such as bedbugs, ants, and roaches may carry bacteria in the same way. There are other insects and animals which, like the mosquito, carry special diseases.

Cleanliness is the best weapon to use against insects. There will be no insects if there is no food for them to eat. If there are any disease-carrying insects in your neighborhood, study about them thoroughly, learn what can be done to get rid of them, and interest people in doing the things necessary to conquer them.

OTHER CHILDREN'S QUESTIONS

Find the right answer to the following questions:

1. Why do the people of Central America have more sickness of certain kinds than we have?

2. Why are the equatorial lowlands not healthful for white people? Would it be healthful to live near a swamp?

Why did the United States succeed in building the Panama Canal?

Photo from Ewing Galloway

3. Why did the French fail when they tried to dig the Panama Canal?

4. Why did people building the Panama Canal die from malaria and yellow fever?

5. What has been done to conquer the epidemics of yellow fever in the Panama Canal?

6. How can yellow fever be prevented?

7. What is a microorganism?

Answers. One reason the French failed in building the Panama Canal was the fact that they did not know how to conquer the mosquitoes before they began work on the canal.

Yellow fever can be conquered by preventing a certain kind of mosquito from breeding, from biting people who are sick with yellow fever, and from biting people who are well.

An organism is a living thing. You are an organism. A cat is an organism. A tree or a growing flower is an organism. A microorganism is a living thing so small that you can see it only by using a microscope. Bacteria are microorganisms.

There are more insects in parts of Central America that cause diseases. People there have fewer doctors and nurses than we have to tell them what to do to prevent dangerous diseases and to cure them. They are not so careful as we are to get safe water to drink and to get rid of their garbage and wastes in a safe way.

INSECTS THAT CARRY DISEASE

Lowlands and swamps are not in themselves unhealthful unless the air is so hot and moist as to be very uncomfortable. Their danger lies largely in the mosquitoes that breed there and carry the microorganisms that cause malaria and yellow fever.

Courtesy The Rockefeller Foundation
Spraying marshy places by airplane

Malaria and yellow fever have been reduced in the Panama Canal Zone by draining the low, wet places or marshes, treating still ponds of water with substances that kill the larvae of the mosquito, and screening the houses and hospitals.

People in the Panama Canal Zone used to die from

yellow fever because there were so many mosquitoes that carried the disease, the people were not protected by screens and netting, and the breeding places of mosquitoes were not destroyed. At one time it was thought the canal could not be built because so many workers died of the fever.

Things to Do

1. Are there mosquitoes in your neighborhood? See how many places you can find in which water stands — tin cans, rain barrels, ditches, ponds, etc. How many of these can you get rid of? Find out how malaria has been conquered in other places. Try to get the older people interested in helping you get rid of mosquitoes.   2. Is there any rubbish in your back yard? Take a Saturday to get it all cleaned up.   3. Are there dark, damp closets and covered corners in your kitchen? Ask your father or older brother to help clean them out and to paint them a light color after they are thoroughly cleaned.   4. If there are many flies in your neighborhood, study the best ways of getting rid of them. Make some posters about freeing the neighborhood from flies. Tell your own family ways in which they can keep flies from breeding.

5. Ask your teacher if she has the story of Walter Reed and his conquest of yellow fever. Why may

Walter Reed and the men who worked with him be called health heroes?

6. Collect some "wigglers" from a pail or pond. Put them in two jars covered with mosquito netting. Watch the "wigglers" grow into mosquitoes. Before many have become mosquitoes pour some kerosene or other oil into one jar. Put a goldfish into the other jar. What happens to the "wigglers"? 8. Make a list of all the things to do suggested in this chapter which will help to get rid of flies, mosquitoes, and other insects. How many of them do you do? 9. Think of the reasons why some children spend their money for candy and cake and sweet drinks. Write the reasons for not eating sweets between meals.

SAFETY FOR MORE AND BETTER ADVENTURES

Safety makes more and better adventures possible. A certain man and his wife go on a camping trip every year in the north woods. They go along trails which only Indians have used. They go through woods so far from civilization that the wild animals they meet show no fear of them. This trip is a great adventure. It has always had a happy ending because they climb and ride and build camp so carefully every day that accidents do not happen.

Safety should mean having good adventures instead of bad adventures. A boy who learns to play football safely has the good adventure of carrying the ball across the goal line instead of the bad adventure of breaking a bone. A girl who learns to sail a boat safely has the good adventure of sailing on over dancing water and under blue sky instead of the bad adventure of tipping over and having to wait hours, perhaps, in cold water to be rescued.

Where Safety Should Rule

Safety means good form in all kinds of work and play. Records of accidents in school show that boys and girls of your age get about as many sprains, bruises, cuts, scratches, bites, and burns as do much younger children. Should this be so? Should not children of your age have learned better form in all their work and play?

What is good form on the street? What is good form in roller skating? What is good form in coasting, in playing in the snow, in using the swings and other things on the playground? What is good form in playing with animals, in climbing trees, in playing baseball, in riding horseback?

Good form around the house and yard is about the same as good housekeeping. What are some good housekeeping habits? How may fires in the home be prevented? How do Scouts prevent forest fires?

What is good form in small boats and in canoes? How may danger on the ice be prevented? What have the Scouts and the American Red Cross found to be the best way of pulling a person out of a hole

Do these show good form in coasting?

in the ice? If you had charge of a summer camp, what rules would you make to prevent drowning?

How can special dangers to little children be avoided? More than one third of all deaths from burns are of children under five years of age. Half of

Some of the special dangers

the fatal accidents from burns happen to children under nine years of age. Falls and automobile accidents are also common among little children. What accidents have the small children in your family and neighborhood had? What are you doing to protect little children from accidents? You have already read suggestions for preventing burns. What are they? Swallowing poisonous substances is another danger. The following kind of accident sometimes happens:

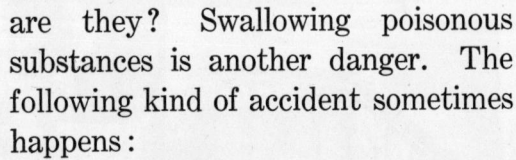

Two children are playing. One gives the other some medicine from the medicine closet. It turns out to be a poisonous disinfectant, useful to put on the skin or to disinfect body wastes from sick people but never to be swallowed. This accident could be avoided by putting all poisonous substances far out of reach of little children and by teaching them as they grow older that the word "poison" or the sign shown above means "something which they should not touch, taste, or handle."

Similarly, such small objects as buttons, marbles, and the like which little children might swallow, and sharp objects, such as knives, broken glass, and scissors, should be carefully kept out of reach. Why should a baby not have a toy that is less than an

SAFETY FOR SMALL CHILDREN

inch across? Falling downstairs could easily be prevented by a little gate at the head of the stairway.

Falling from the second story sometimes happens when the screen has not been fastened in securely. Sometimes the porch railings are so low that small

How has a possible accident been avoided here?

children could easily climb over them. In a house where there are small children, heavy objects should be fastened so securely that there is no danger of their falling on anyone. A heavy vase or lamp on a table is dangerous. An unsteady floor lamp may easily be pushed over by a small child.

How can falls be avoided? Falls are very serious, especially for grandfather and grandmother. The bones of older people are more brittle and heal more slowly than the bones of children. Sometimes an old person will break an arm or a leg or hip when falling only a short distance. Look over your house and yard and see if any of the following things might cause falls:

Slippery waxed floors with small rugs which have no pads under them to prevent them from slipping. Dark stairways with no light either at the top or at the bottom. Chairs, stools, boxes, and other things left in the path between two rooms. Chairs which are not strongly built or are coming apart. Icy steps and sidewalks, which should have ashes or sand sprinkled on them if the ice cannot be removed. Uneven or rough floors, which should be made smooth by a carpenter or covered with carpet or linoleum. Stairs without railings, which should have railings supplied. A hole in the carpet or rug, which should be mended.

What is your duty when you discover such dangers? Safety means putting the house and yard and playground in such order that accidents cannot happen. It means learning good form in work and play. It is usually the untrained, stupid, or thoughtless person who gets hurt and who hurts other people.

Safety means choosing good adventure instead of bad adventure. Safety also means knowing what to do if accidents should happen.

Who's Who in Safety

You. Boys and girls are important in making the world safe. Accidents are prevented by *you* and *you* and *you*. Safety grows out of good form in going in and out of school, in fire drills, in recess periods, in lunch periods, on trips or visits to interesting places, in work shops, and at camp.

School-boy and -girl patrols.* The duty of the patrol boys or girls is to guide and teach. They guide children in the halls and stairways. They see that everyone walks quickly, keeping to the right. They help children to cross the streets safely near the school. They do not guide traffic. They only guide the school children. At recess the patrol boys or girls make the playground safe by picking up nails, glass, wire, stones, and other things that might cause accidents. They see whether drinking fountains are clean. They look out for the smaller children, and teach them how to play together safely and happily. At lunch time the patrols help to make the lunchroom a clean and pleasant place. They permit no crowding and pushing. They see that nothing is left on the floor which might cause a child to slip and fall.

In a fire drill the patrol helps the children to leave the building quickly and in quiet, orderly lines.

Policemen. The policeman tells the automobiles, wagons, and cars when to stop and when to go. He

Photo by Underwood & Underwood

A member of the safety patrol in action

sometimes guides pedestrians* across the street. He makes drivers obey the rules of the road. He keeps a record of accidents. Ask a traffic policeman, sometime when he is not busy, about his other duties. Then tell the class about the policeman's work.

Business men. Business men are doing a great deal to make work safe. They find that safety pays. Accidents cost money as well as pain. Some companies have reduced serious accidents by sixty per cent. Their men have worked millions of hours without a single serious accident. Insurance companies have also done much for safety. It pays them to have people live longer.

The city, state, and national government. Our government makes safety laws and sees that they are obeyed. It makes safe, wide streets. It builds parks and other safe places for play. It sees that buildings are safe to live in, trains safe to ride in, water safe to drink, food safe to eat, and clothing safe to wear. Make a list of the things the town or city, state, and nation do for the safety of your family.

Safety organizations.* There are groups of people who are working for safety. These are safety organizations. They find out facts about accidents. They study these facts and teach us many ways which help to prevent accidents. They plan safety lessons for schools. They make books, posters, and motion pictures which teach people how to live safely. Learn about the work of the National Safety Council and the magazine and little books which it publishes. Have you a local safety organization in your town? Automobile clubs also help to lessen accidents.

Things to Do

1. Form a safety patrol in your school, if there is not one there already. Come a half hour before school. Teach the younger children to play in the schoolyard and to cross the street safely. 2. Keep a record of all the accidents which occur in your class — cuts, bruises, scratches, as well as more serious accidents. Ask each boy or girl to tell exactly how the accident happened and how it might have been prevented. Give first-aid treatment when necessary.

3. In the oral-English period describe some good adventure you have had. 4. Give each boy or girl in your class one of the safety rules in this chapter. Ask him to write a short play about the rule. Let each pupil act his play before the class. Choose the best ones to give before the other classes.

5. Look over your house and yard. See how many things you can find which may harm little children. See how many of these things you can remove. Teach the little children how to treat dangerous objects which cannot be removed. 6. Ask one of your town or city policemen to tell your class the most important ways to avoid accidents on the street. 7. Find out and report to the class what has been done to make your neighborhood safer.

8. Form a first-aid club to learn what to do in case of accident. A doctor, nurse, or teacher will show

you the best method of treating common injuries, and you can practice each one in the club meetings. **9.** Make a list of things to do to prevent injury to the eyes. **10.** If someone you know is beginning to smoke, try to persuade him to spend his money and

Photo Acme Newspictures, Inc.

What safety rule is Policeman Nixon teaching these children?

his time in other ways. You can find more facts about smoking in this and other health books by looking up the word *tobacco* in the Index.

11. In class talk about the relation of accidents to the drinking of alcoholic beverages. **12.** Apply the rule "Nothing in excess" to the prevention of accidents. Tell in class how moderation in speed helps to prevent accidents.

BUYING YOUR OWN CLOTHES AND SHOES

Do you often buy your own clothes and shoes? Do you think about their healthfulness and comfort as well as their style and color? Jack usually buys the first thing he sees in order to finish shopping as soon as possible so that he can go out to play. The next week when he is wearing his new suit or shoes he finds they are too tight in places and altogether uncomfortable. Spending a little time buying the right kind of clothes and shoes will make your play happier for many days.

RULES FOR CLOTHING

What rules do you think are the most important for both boys and girls? Did you think of all of the following?

1. Buy clothing that is comfortable and that gives freedom to every part of the body. See that none of your clothing feels tight anywhere. Loose clothing gives the air a better chance to bathe the body. Loose clothing does not cramp the lungs or pull the bones into wrong positions.

EFFECT OF CLOTHING ON THE BODY

Bones are made of two kinds of substances — a living substance that bends easily and another substance that keeps the bones from bending. It is calcium which makes the bones hard and firm. Milk and green leafy vegetables are the best foods to furnish calcium in a form which the body can use. Babies' and children's bones are softer than the bones of older people because they have less calcium in them. Since children's bones are softer, they are more easily bent in the wrong way. Do you see how a waist that is too narrow in front across the chest might pull your shoulders forward and make you round shouldered?

Turn again to pages 246–247 for facts about the respiratory system. Knowing something about the way you breathe will show you how blouses and belts that are too tight may interfere with breathing. The bony cage made of the ribs and the breastbone incloses the chest. You can feel the ribs if you put your hand on your side above your waist. The lungs lie in the chest. They move with the ribs. Anything that makes the chest space larger helps the lungs to grow larger, too.

As you breathe in, the ribs rise and extend outward a little. You can feel them moving up and down as you breathe. As the ribs rise, the lung space becomes larger. Air rushes in. You inhale. As the ribs are lowered, the lung space becomes smaller. Air is forced out. You exhale.

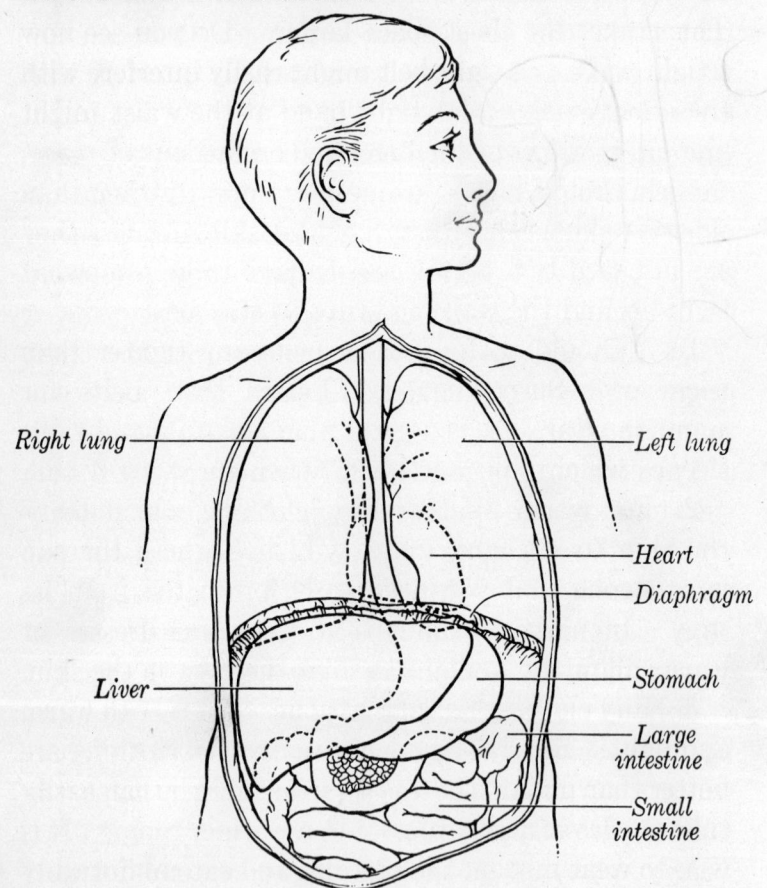

The cavity of the chest and abdomen

At the bottom of the lung cage is a large muscle. It is shaped somewhat like a big saucer upside down.

This sheet of muscle is called the diaphragm.* It is pulled down as you breathe in until it is almost flat. This makes the chest space larger. Do you see how a tight waist or a tight belt might easily interfere with these movements? A tight band at the waist might also crowd some of the digestive organs out of place.

Girls should choose a one-piece dress rather than separate skirts and waists, because skirts, unless they are fastened to a cotton waist, have to be somewhat tight around the waist in order to stay on.

Boys should not pull their belts any tighter than necessary. Suspenders are better than belts for common wear. It is a good plan also to avoid tight sleeves which bind one's arm when throwing a ball.

2. For warm weather buy clothing which bares the skin to sunlight, unless you live where the sun is so strong that you need to be protected from its rays. In northern lands thin, sleeveless dresses or waists allow the sunlight to shine directly on the skin.

3. Buy clothing for cold weather that is both warm and light. Several layers of thin woolen clothing are better than one thick, heavy garment. You can easily take one layer off if you go into a warmer room. It is wise to wear just enough clothing to keep comfortably warm.

4. Simple, washable clothing is good for school all the year round, because you can always keep it

clean. If your play clothes are strong and washable, you need not worry about spoiling them.

Daily care of clothing. The following are good habits of caring for your clothing. How many have you formed?

(1) Keeping your clothing clean, mended, and pressed. (2) Wearing a big apron in the kitchen. (3) Changing underwear at least once a week and after a bath. (4) Taking off all your clothes at night, and putting the clothing worn during the day to air. It is more comfortable to sleep in clean night clothes while your daytime clothing is given a chance to lose its body odors. (5) Putting clothing worn at night to air during the day.

These are habits which help you to make good friends wherever you go. It is such things as neat, clean clothing which is free from body odor, on a clean boy or girl, that sometimes help one very much.

Shoes and the feet. There is no one best type of shoe for all. A shoe has to be bought to fit the foot that wears it. If the shoe does not fit the foot, it either changes the shape of the foot for the worse, or the foot slowly forces the shoe to fit it. In either case it is an uncomfortable, painful process. So it is best in the beginning to buy a shoe that fits the foot. As soon as you put on a new shoe you can tell whether it belongs to your foot.

Signs of a Good Shoe

1. The shoe should be about three fourths of an inch longer than your foot. As you walk, your foot spreads out and becomes longer than it seems to

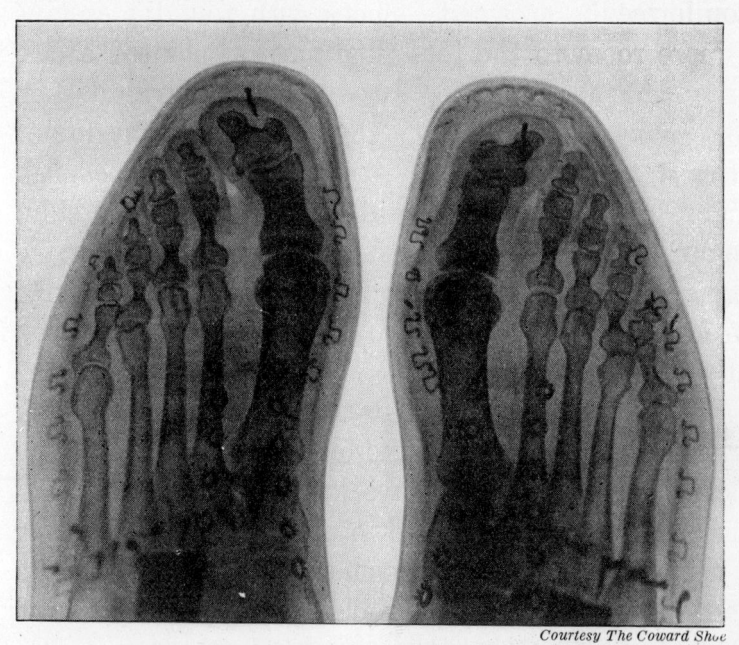

Courtesy The Coward Shoe

X-ray picture of feet in poorly fitting shoes

be when you are sitting in the shoe store. That is why it is a good plan to stand up and walk in a new pair of shoes to see if they fit when you are walking as well as when you are sitting. Bunions* are caused by shoes that are too short or are pointed in such a way that the joints of the big toes are forced out of line and there is a painful bulging at the base of the big toes.

2. The shoe should be wide enough so that the toes will not be crowded. Shoes with round toes give more room to the toes than narrow, pointed shoes. Corns result when shoes that do not fit press or rub against the skin.

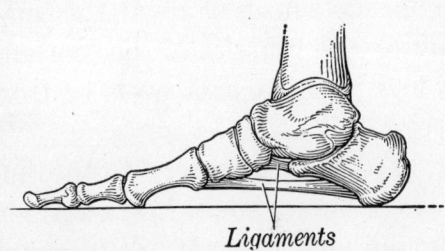

Ligaments
The lengthwise arch of the foot

3. The narrow part of the sole of the shoe between the heel and the ball of the foot is called the *shank*.* The shank should fit the arch* of the foot like a glove. If the muscles of the feet are weak, the arches tend to fall when the weight is thrown upon them in the wrong way. Then the feet become painful. High-heeled, stiff shoes give little exercise to the muscles of the foot. Indians who wore very soft leather shoes were not known to have flatfoot or other foot troubles. The Indians, however, did not walk on hard city pavements. Strong arches are essential to foot comfort. If the arches become weak or break down, flatfoot or fallen arches result. They cause much pain.

4. The heel should be broad and not too high. A broad heel prevents the ankle from rocking from side to side. It helps to make the foot steady. If the heel is too high, it causes the body to tip forward too far and may result in poor posture. It puts too much weight on the front of the foot. All the shoes for the same person should have heels of about the same height. It is a strain on the muscles of the foot and leg to change from low heels to high heels or from high heels to low heels.

5. Look at your bare foot tonight. Is the line from the outer edge of the big toe to the heel a straight line? Your shoe should have an inner line to match your foot.

6. Buy stockings also that fit the foot and are about a half inch longer than the foot. Although stockings seem so soft, they can push the toes out of place just as do shoes that are too tight.

Can you remember these six points when you go to buy shoes and stockings?

Daily care of the feet. Soldiers in the army are advised to wash their feet daily in cool or cold water and to dry them thoroughly. That is a good rule for everyone to follow. Be especially careful to wash and dry the skin between the toes very thoroughly. The toenails should be as well cared for as the nails of the fingers. "Ingrowing" toenails are thought to be caused by shoes which pinch at the toes. Cut the toenails so that they are square across and but very slightly beyond the tips of the toes. The stockings should either be changed every day or two, or washed, if possible, just as often. Shoes should be kept in the best repair possible.

Be an Indian walker: Walk with the toes pointing straight ahead. Put more weight on the outer than on the inner edge of the foot in both walking and standing. Practice exercises which strengthen the muscles of the feet. Picking up corks with the toes, scooping up sand with the outside edges of the feet, and walking on tiptoe in bare feet are all good exercises.

OTHER CHILDREN'S QUESTIONS

Questions asked by other children. Answer as many as you can. Look up the answers to the others.

1. Do the Chinese women still bind their feet?
2. Are corns caused by tight shoes?
3. What kind of shoes should I wear?
4. Do high heels hurt the spine?*
5. What height of heels is the best for children?
6. If the Colonists had worn heavy clothing and kept their feet dry, would they have fallen sick in the winter?

Answers. Corns may result from shoes which are too tight or too loose so that they press or rub against the skin. They are best prevented by buying shoes which fit your feet.

Wearing warm clothing and changing their shoes promptly, if they got them wet, might have helped the Colonists to resist certain diseases, but clothing alone would not have kept them well. They needed also the right kind and amount of food and protection from bacteria.

Most Chinese women have given up the practice of binding their feet. In fact many of them are more sensible than the women in some countries who wear high heels and tight shoes that are too short.

The best kinds of shoes are those which (1) are of the shape of your foot; (2) have a straight inner line; (3) are about three-fourths inch longer than your foot; (4) have a sole that is easily bent, not stiff; (5) have broad rather than narrow toes; (6) have broad heels, one to one and one-fourth inches high.

High heels may hurt the spine (the backbone) by throwing the weight of the body forward in an unnatural way. This causes the person to straighten back in order to keep his balance, and produces a bad forward curving of the spine and a "kangaroo posture."

A heel about an inch high is best for children as well as for grown-ups.

THINGS TO DO

1. Have a shoe exhibit. Put the well-made shoes in one place and the poorly made shoes in another

What does this shoe exhibit teach?

place. Make cards telling why certain shoes are good and why other shoes are poor. **2.** Make or get posters showing how to prevent painful feet. **3.** Study the picture of the bones of the feet (page 362). The place where one bone joins another is

STUDIES OF THE FEET AND OF CLOTHING

called a joint. Find a joint in the picture. Explain how a stocking or shoe that is too small would enlarge the joint of the great toe and form a painful bunion. **4.** Draw a large picture of a healthy foot. How many parts of it can you name correctly?

5. Teach your younger brothers and sisters how to take proper care of their clothing. You will find on page 360 a list of good habits they should form.
6. Ask some of your classmates if they would like to have you take pictures of them when they are not looking, so that they may see how they stand and sit. The pictures may help them to improve their posture.
7. Take foot exercises in your bare feet to strengthen the arches. Several good exercises are suggested on page 364.

8. Find pictures of the clothes people wore about fifty years ago. In how many ways is our modern clothing more healthful than the clothing our grandparents wore? In what ways is the clothing of today more healthful than the clothing of fifty years ago?

BUYING AND COOKING FOOD

At the Market

When you go to the store for your mother, does she tell you exactly what to buy? Or does she sometimes let you decide what to buy? There are many things to think of when you are buying food for the family.

Buying food. The small storekeeper gets food in large quantities from the farm or the factory. He puts some of it in packages and sells you the amount you need. He should try to have his food *clean,* to avoid germs; *fresh,* so that it will taste good and have the most food value; *pure,* that is, free from harmful substances; and as *cheap* as is possible. More and more, manufacturers are putting their products in germ-proof packages. They seal food in cellophane,* which keeps it clean and fresh. You go to the store to get food that is clean, fresh, pure, and suited to your pocketbook and taste.

Is the store clean? First of all, you should choose a clean store. Did you ever think of a store having to pass a test? You can test stores by asking yourself such questions as the following:

1. Is the food in the store kept covered? Are the covers always put back on the milk cans? Are the sugar bins kept closed? Are the crackers kept in tightly closed boxes? Is the cheese put back under cover as soon as a piece is cut from it? No flies or dust should be allowed to reach the food. 2. Is the storekeeper clean? Does he have clean hands and a clean apron? 3. Does he weigh and measure food, such as butter, cheese, and other ready-to-eat

MARKETING HINTS

foods, without touching it with his hands? 4. Does he measure the foods into clean bags, wrapping paper, or boxes, and not into the metal dish that is a part of the scales? Give a reason for each test.

What makes this store sanitary?

These are some of the things to notice when you choose the stores at which you will buy food for the family:

Is the food fresh? You will soon learn which stores have the freshest food. You will not go back to a store in which the lettuce which looked fresh on the outside was rotted at the heart. You will not buy from a storekeeper who gives you fruit that is beginning to decay. You will buy eggs at another store if the yolks of the ones you bought last broke easily and mixed with the whites. The yolk of a fresh egg is plump and does not break easily. Another test of fresh eggs is to drop them into a bowl of water. Fresh eggs sink to the bottom. Stale (old) eggs stand end up in the water as if they were going to float. Some of the water has evaporated from eggs that have been kept a long time. There is a large air space in one end of them. This makes them lighter than fresh eggs.

If you have more eggs in the spring and summer than you can use, you can store them for winter. Eggs may be kept by putting them in water glass.* Ask your teacher how to keep eggs fresh for the winter.

How much money should you spend for the different kinds of food? Buy milk first. If there are five in the family — your mother, father, big brother, little sister, and yourself — you should buy at least three quarts of milk a day. How much will three quarts of milk cost in your neighborhood? Buy plenty of milk before you spend your money for meat.

Buy fruit and green vegetables next. Try to buy one green leafy vegetable and some kind of fresh fruit every day. If you have plenty of money, you can buy oranges, other fresh fruit, lettuce, spinach, celery, and other fresh vegetables every weekday.

If you have little money to spend, you can buy canned tomatoes, instead of oranges or other fresh fruit, and the cheapest green leafy vegetable that is for sale. You will buy potatoes enough for every day. Every week you will buy some of the dried fruits and vegetables — prunes, peaches, apricots, raisins, split peas, and beans. A careful study of food needs showed that adults should have about two pounds of fruit and vegetables a day. Country people are fortunate because they can raise their own vegetables and fruit.

Enough butter and other fats should be bought to supply every member of the family, except the baby, with about one half of a pound of fat a week.

Bread and cereals are the cheapest foods. Cereals in boxes cost more than cereals bought by the pound. Bread that is a day old costs less than fresh bread and is really more healthful. If you have very little money to spend for food, you will have to spend most of it on cereals and bread and milk. In this case, it is important to buy the brown cereals and brown bread part of the time.

One well-known scientist, Dr. Henry C. Sherman, says that each dollar spent for food should be divided

Fresh eggs reduce the meat bill.

in the following way: one fifth or more for milk and cheese; one fifth, more or less, for fruit and vegetables; one fifth or more for cereals and breads; one fifth or less for meats, fish, and eggs; one fifth or less for fats, sugars, and flavorings.

The following table shows the amounts of food a family of three or four should have during one week. Use the "Liberal Plan" if you have plenty of money. Use the "Thrift Plan" if you do not have much money. You will see that more fruits and vegetables and eggs and less bread and cereals are included if you have money enough for the "Liberal Plan."

Weekly Grocery Order for a Family of Three or Four [1]

Multiply by 2 for 5, 6, 7; by 3 for 8, 9, and 10 people. The number of people that may be fed on the foods listed below will depend on their ages.

Liberal Plan *Quantity*		Thrift Plan *Quantity*
14 to 21 qt.	MILK	10 to 14 qt.
Part or all evaporated milk may be used.		
6 to 18	EGGS	3 to 6
8 to 15 lb.	BREAD, CEREALS	17 to 24 lb.
5 to 10 loaves	Bread	14 to 18 loaves
3 to 5 lb.	Cereal, flour, rice, macaroni	3 to 6 lb.

[1] Lucy H. Gillett, *Food at Low Cost.* American Child Health Association, 1931, 450 Seventh Avenue, New York City.

BUYING AND COOKING FOOD

The smaller the amount of money, the more essential are whole-grain bread and cereals.

17 to 27 lb.	VEGETABLES	20 to 29 lb.
6 to 10 lb.	Potatoes	15 to 20 lb.
1 to 2 lb.	Dried beans and peas	1 to 2 lb.
10 to 15 lb.	Other vegetables	4 to 7 lb.
7 to 11 lb.	FRUIT	3 to 5 lb.
1 to 3 lb.	Fresh or canned tomatoes (in place of oranges)	2 to 3 lb.
8 to 12	Oranges	
8 to 12 pieces	Other fresh fruit	
2 lb.	Prunes and other dried fruit	1 lb. to 2 lb.
$4\frac{1}{4}$ to $6\frac{1}{2}$ lb.	MEAT, FISH, ETC.	$\frac{3}{4}$ to $4\frac{1}{2}$ lb.
4 to 6 lb.	Meat, fish	$\frac{1}{2}$ to 4 lb.
$\frac{1}{4}$ to $\frac{1}{2}$ lb.	Cheese or peanut butter	$\frac{1}{4}$ to $\frac{1}{2}$ lb.

Reduce meat, fish, and fats before cutting down on milk or vegetables.

$2\frac{1}{2}$ to 4 lb.	FATS	$1\frac{1}{2}$ to 3 lb.
2 to 3 lb.	Butter	1 lb.
$\frac{1}{2}$ to 1 lb.	Lard or oil	$\frac{1}{2}$ to 2 lb.
2 to 3 lb.	SUGAR, SWEETS	1 to 2 lb.
25 to 35¢	Seasoning, cocoa, and the like	15 to 25¢

COOKING

Baking, broiling, boiling, and steaming are, in general, better ways of cooking food than frying. You can bake potatoes and other vegetables whenever you are using the oven. Meat and fish broiled over the coals have a flavor that reminds one of camp life.

Most people boil their vegetables in a large amount of water. It is better to steam the vegetables or cook them in a small amount of water and use the water in which they are cooked for soup. Adding milk and butter to the water in which spinach has been cooked makes a delicious spinach soup. Adding small pieces of carrots, onions, parsley, or celery to the water in which vegetables have been cooked makes a good vegetable soup. Many people cook vegetables too long. Spinach and other green vegetables should look fresh and green when they are served. They should be taken from the fire as soon as they are tender.

Eggs are easy to cook, and the way they are cooked makes little difference in their food value. Poached eggs are good. Soft-boiled eggs are good. Eggs cooked in water just below the boiling point until the yolk is crumbly are good. Hard-boiled eggs take a little longer to digest than eggs cooked in these other ways. Fried eggs take the longest time of all to digest.

Things to Do

1. Find out how much your mother spends for milk, and how much she spends for meat, fish, and eggs. Does she spend as much for milk as for meat, fish, and eggs together? If she does not, should she

buy more milk or less meat? 2. When your mother is sick or away on a visit, do you have to cook the meals for the family? If your mother is away at noon, do you get lunch for the younger children? Do you ever help your mother cook the meals?

A poached egg — one of the best ways to cook eggs

Both boys and girls should know about home cooking as well as camp cooking. How many of the following rules for cooking foods do you practice?

a. Wash very carefully such foods as lettuce, celery, and tomatoes which are served raw.

b. Cook vegetables just long enough to make them tender. Spinach, cabbage, and other vegetables are spoiled by cooking them too long.

c. Bake potatoes whenever the oven is lighted.

d. Bake, boil, broil, or steam foods rather than fry them.

e. Keep foods covered to protect them from dust and flies.

f. Clean the top of the milk bottle before pouring out the milk.

g. Keep cooked food in a cold place.

3. Each of the foods in the following list yields the same amount of power to work or to play. You get as much energy from a quart of milk, for example, as from nine eggs. In other food values these foods are not equal. Find the price in your neighborhood of each of the foods in the list.

Foods	Amounts
Milk	1 qt.
Fowl	About $\frac{7}{8}$ lb.
Codfish	$3\frac{1}{5}$ lb.
Round Steak	1 lb. $\frac{3}{5}$ oz.
Eggs	9 eggs
Bread	A little over $\frac{1}{2}$ loaf

Which is cheaper in your neighborhood, as a source of energy — meat or fish?

4. Using the foods in the weekly grocery order on pages 373–374, plan the meals for a day. Judge your meals by the standards for a good breakfast, dinner, and supper given in the first chapter.

PLANNING YOUR DAY

"Early to bed and early to rise." The best way to begin a new day is to go to bed early the night before. If you go to bed at eight or half past eight, you will feel like getting up early enough so that you will not have to hurry through breakfast and run off to school while you are still chewing the last mouthful. If you have been working and playing wholeheartedly all day, you are ready for bed.

Sleep is the most complete rest of mind and body. During the day many messages are sent to and from the brain — messages of taste, messages of touch, messages of sound, messages of pain. These sensations are sent to the brain, and some of them command the muscles to make certain movements. The brain is the thought center in which messages come and go. It is connected with other parts of the body by *nerves*.* These are made up of the long, hairlike ends of nerve cells. Along these nerves messages pass from the brain when you bend your finger or write the answer to an arithmetic problem. Most of our movements are not made

THE PRECIOUS GIFT OF SLEEP

by a single muscle. Walking, for example, requires many muscles all working together in just the right way. The *nervous system** makes it possible for muscles in many different parts of the body to work together for a common purpose. All the time,

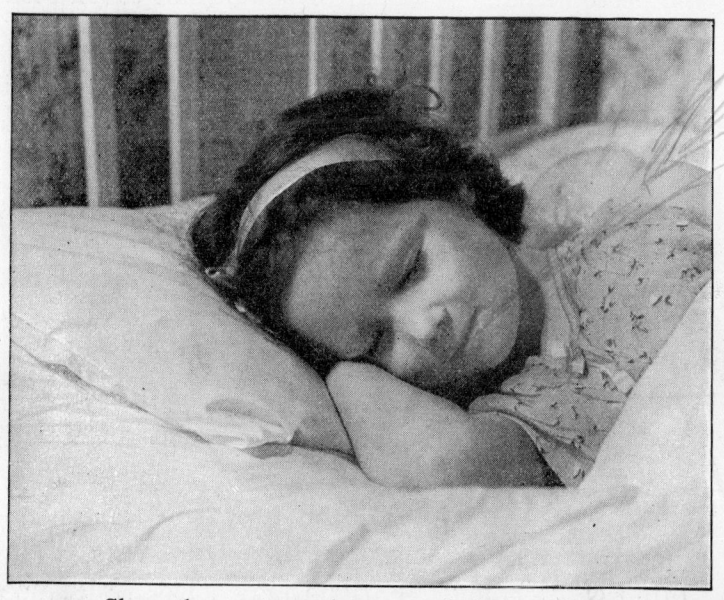

Sleep, the most complete rest of mind and body

whether you think about it or not, messages are passing back and forth along the nerves. But there are fewer messages sent to and from the brain when you are asleep than when you are awake. Sleep rests the brain and the nervous system. Sleep rests every part of the body and helps it to get ready for the next day's work and play. During sleep the body has a better chance to grow. It can make repairs more easily than when it is more active.

Fatigue is like a red light which means *danger*. One person said: "I'm sure I should not catch cold

Plenty of time to get to school

so easily if I rested more. When I am very tired, I often catch cold." Fatigue may lower resistance to colds, tuberculosis, and other respiratory diseases. Poor posture is often the result of fatigue.

A cool, quiet, dark room and a well-made bed make sleep sounder and more restful. Ask your mother or a nurse to show you the best way to make the bed with the sheets stretched smooth without wrinkles and the covers firmly fastened at the foot. Then make your own bed this way every day. It does not take much longer, and it is much more comfortable.

"Get up when you wake up" is a good rule. You will wake up regularly at a certain time, once you have formed the habit. Getting up early gives plenty of time for bathing; dressing; cleaning your teeth; eating a good breakfast of fruit, cereal, and milk; collecting your schoolbooks; and enjoying your walk to school without hurry or worry. This plan is much more pleasant than hurrying and worrying for fear you will be late.

During the day. There are many habits you are forming all during the day:

Good Habits	*Bad Habits*
Sitting well	Sitting badly
Standing well	Standing badly
Holding your book in an upright position at least a foot from the eyes	Laying the book on the desk and bending close over it
Working or playing as if there were nothing else in the world you would rather be doing at the time	Working or playing in a "don't-care" way

Good Habits	Bad Habits
Continuing with a task until it is completed	"Giving up" when the first difficulty arises
Facing facts and saying, for example, when you have done something wrong: "Yes, that was my own fault."	Blaming someone else or something else for a difficulty which is really your own fault, or just worrying about the problem
Attending to the work at hand	Daydreaming too much
Controlling your anger and meeting disappointment bravely	Getting angry and sulking if things do not go as you wish them to go
Forgetting grudges quickly	Brooding over wrongs, real or imagined
Playing fair in games	Cheating in games

Which of these habits are you building? You are forming one kind or the other all the time in everything that you do. You learn readily the things that you do over and over again with satisfaction. Good rules are: Plan for the future. Do your best in the present. Forget the past except as it helps you to do better in the present.

A purpose for each day. Days go more smoothly and happily if they are planned. Make a plan for this afternoon and evening. Plan to do something to help your mother and father. Plan to play or work outdoors two or three hours while the sun is shining. Get tanned slowly. Never expose the bare

Photo by J. C. Allen & Son

"Stop worrying and saw wood." What do you think this saying means?

skin to the hot sun for more than half an hour at a time if your skin is not used to direct sunlight. Outdoor work and play of the right kind and amount make you feel more alive. During exercise you breathe more quickly. The heart beats more rapidly.

The blood circulates faster. A larger amount of oxygen is carried to all parts of the body. Waste products are carried away more quickly. Certain exercises such as swimming and running fill the lungs more completely with air than when you are quiet. The lung capacity* often becomes greater as a result of these exercises. Plan to study an hour before supper or an hour after supper, if you have home work to do. Plan to make mealtime a happy time.

Make a plan for the coming Saturday. Include in your Saturday program three or four hours of outdoor work and play, but do not plan an entire day of heavy exercise if you are not used to it. Do not stay in the hot sun on the beach in your bathing suit an entire morning or afternoon. You can have too much of even such a good thing as sunlight. Show the plan to your parents to see if they think it is all right.

Living heathfully. As boys and girls grow older, they like to take command of their own health habits. They do not need parents and teachers to keep telling them what to do. They have learned how to live healthfully. They can read more about health in books, papers, and magazines. They need to ask their parents and teachers only about new and difficult health problems. They like to be independent and to do healthful things of their own accord.

They like to *live* healthfully — not merely *talk* about health. They want the success which health makes possible. And they are entirely right.

If they do not feel well, they go to the doctor, nurse, dentist, or other specialist in health, who will tell them exactly what to do. It is interesting to know what good care successful people take of their health. Most of the actors and actresses whom you see are very careful about their exercise, food, and rest. Some take special exercises, such as fencing and dancing. Famous John Drew and some of his fellow actors played baseball every morning. He said it was good fun and helped to keep them all in good physical condition. Other successful people pay especial attention to eating plenty of fresh fruits and drinking four glasses of water a day.

Others believe that moderation in all things — "nothing in excess" — is the secret of health. Many successful people avoid fatigue by not staying up late at night. They find that they cannot go to parties and do their work also without getting overtired.

Helping the younger children to be healthy. Sometimes you may have to take care of a baby or small child and wish that you did not have to do it. Of course, just wheeling a baby back and forth is dull. But when you think of all the things

Suitable playthings make taking care of small children easy.

you can do to keep the baby well, it becomes an interesting game.

What should you say or do: If someone comes along and offers to give the baby something to eat? If someone with a cold comes up to the baby? If someone wants to kiss the baby? If there are flies and mosquitoes around? If a friend tells you to give a soothing sirup to the baby to keep him from crying? If the baby wants to crawl on dirty floors or sidewalks? If the baby is getting the habit of sucking his thumb or a pacifier?* If friends of yours want to play with the baby during his nap? If the baby has nothing to amuse him when he is awake? If the baby has a physical defect? Some defects grow worse more quickly, the younger the child is. If the milk you get for the baby is not safe milk?

Suppose the baby cries just to get your attention. What should you do after you have made sure he has no pin sticking into him or is not sick? Suppose the two- or three-year-old child teases for something he should not have. What should you do? Should you give it to him so that he will stop fussing? Should you pay no attention to him? Should you give him something else in its place?

Choosing your life work. Perhaps at the end of this school year it seems necessary for you to leave school and go to work. If you are able to do school work, three reasons why you should not leave school and go to work are: (1) You may be able to get a better position when you have had more education.

Photo by J. C. Allen & Son

In what ways is farm work better for boys and girls than most factory work?

(2) You will have more time to play out of doors while you are attending school. One reason why factory, store, or office work is bad for children is that it keeps them indoors when they ought to be

out of doors in the sunlight playing and developing. (3) It is very difficult to continue your studies at the same time that you are working.

But whenever you have to begin work, you should think not only of the wages, but also whether it is a kind of work which you can do well — not too hard nor too easy for you — and whether the position may lead to better positions. You should think also of the healthfulness of the work — whether you have a clean, sunny, airy place in which to work; whether you can get a good lunch near by; whether the hours are short enough to give you some time for outdoor play every day; whether you have to work with harmful materials such as finely ground stone or poisonous* substances which may be breathed in or absorbed through the skin; and whether you can be happy with the people with whom you work.

Other Children's Questions

If you do not know the answer to a question, look it up among the answers given. Do not guess.

1. When is the best time to exercise?
2. Is dancing the Highland Fling good exercise?
3. Why should one not lie on the back when sleeping? Why should one lie on the side?
4. Is it more healthful to sleep with a pillow or without one?

5. Do children who work in factories grow strong?

6. Why did the Indians of South America, whom the Spaniards forced to work in the mines, die rapidly?

Answers. The best times for exercise are at recess, immediately after school in the afternoon, and in the mornings and afternoons of the days you do not go to school. It is best not to exercise just after you have finished eating. It is best to stop exercising when you feel tired.

The Indians died more quickly in the mines probably because they missed the sunlight and free life of the woods and did not know how to protect themselves from disease.

Lying on the back is not unhealthful, but seems to favor snoring and sleeping with the mouth open. It is, however, easy to relax when lying on the back.

A small pillow is all right, especially if you sleep on your side. A high pillow tends to throw the head and shoulders forward, if you lie on your back, but so far as we know it is not harmful if you sleep on your side.

Children who work in most factories do not get enough sunlight and outdoor play. Sunlight and outdoor play should be in every child's life.

Performing the Highland Fling and other dances uses muscles that you do not usually use in walking and running and helps you to gain control over your

Dancing helps to develop grace and ease of movement.

body so that you will move more gracefully and easily.

Things to Do

1. If you were going to get a new mattress for your bed, which would you choose, a soft one that you would sink into all huddled together, or a firm mattress that you would lie comfortably *on*, not *in?*

2. Practice making your bed in the same way that a nurse makes a bed for a sick person. Test how comfortable a well-made bed feels.

3. Does "early to bed and early to rise make a man healthy, wealthy, and wise"? Talk about this in class.

4. Look for summer menus in magazines or newspapers. Write three of the most healthful menus. Make a plan for each of these meals which will include: (*a*) washing the hands before eating, (*b*) talking of pleasant things, (*c*) avoiding hurry and worry, (*d*) resting a while after eating.

5. Make a plan for preventing constipation during the summer.

6. Visit someone working in a trade or other occupation in which you are interested. Ask about the health habits necessary for success in this occupation.

7. Make a clock for your vacation days and compare it with the one on page 393.

8. Stop reading for a minute. How are you sitting? Are your feet — heel and toe — resting on

A WELL-PLANNED SUMMER DAY

the floor? Is your head held high? Is your book held in an upright position about a foot from your

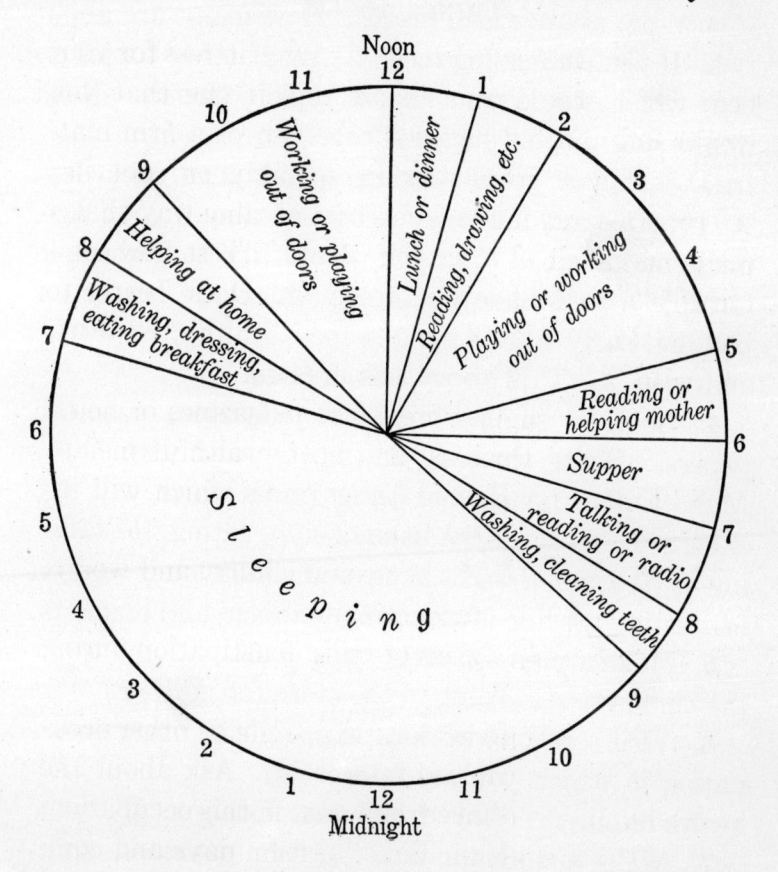

Clock diagram showing a 24-hour day divided into activities: Working or playing out of doors; Lunch or dinner; Reading, drawing, etc.; Playing or working out of doors; Reading or helping mother; Supper; Talking or reading or radio; Washing, cleaning teeth; Sleeping; Washing, dressing, eating breakfast; Helping at home.

eyes? If so, very good. 9. Collect clippings about health from newspapers and magazines. See how many you can find in one week. Divide your clippings into groups. How many are about food? How many are about fresh air and exercise? How many are about cleanliness? How many are about health contests or "drives"? What other topics do you find? 10. Plan a healthful picnic lunch. Read pages 222–224 for suggestions.

11. Plan a good way to spend next Saturday. Here is a plan made by a boy of about your age. Copy as much of it as you would like to include in your plan. Add other things which are better for you to do.

7 : 45	Got up and dressed.
8 : 00	Ate breakfast — berries, oatmeal, toast and butter, and milk.
8 : 15	Helped father on the farm.
10 : 00	Went fishing.
12 : 00	Went home and had lunch — egg on toast, cream cheese and crackers, glass of milk, fruit.
12 : 30	Went to the store for mother.
1 : 00	Read a popular-science magazine.
3 : 00	Helped father.
5 : 00	Played ball out of doors.
6 : 30	Had dinner — fish, potatoes, spinach, rice pudding.
7 : 30	Talked and listened to the radio.
9 : 00	Went to bed.

APPENDIX: WEIGHT IN RELATION TO AGE, HEIGHT, AND TYPE

(Based upon the tables of BIRD T. BALDWIN, PH.D.)

INSTRUCTIONS FOR USE OF CHART

1. Before the pupil is measured, it should be determined by careful observation to which physical type he belongs. In case of doubt it may be helpful to note that the Nordic races (central and northwestern Europe) are usually of the tall, slender type; the southern European or Mediterranean races are usually of the short, stocky type.

2. The pupil's height in inches should be taken against the scale of the type to which he belongs. A right-angled triangle or square placed against the wall and on top the pupil's head should be used to secure accuracy.

3. The following illustrations will serve to interpret the scale:

A 14-year-old boy of the tall slender type, 67 inches tall. He is of normal weight if he weighs 128 pounds; he would be considered underweight if he weighed under 115 pounds; and overweight if he weighed over 153 pounds.

A 15-year-old girl of the average type, 63 inches tall. She is of normal weight if she weighs 116 pounds; she would be considered underweight if she weighed under 104 pounds; and overweight if she weighed over 139 pounds.

(Courtesy Board of Education, Division of Physical and Health Education, The Board of Public Education, Philadelphia, Pa.)

TALL, SLENDER TYPE								AVERAGE TYPE								SHORT, STOCKY TYPE							
BOYS				GIRLS				BOYS				GIRLS				BOYS				GIRLS			
Weight (Lbs.)					Weight (Lbs.)			Weight (Lbs.)					Weight (Lbs.)			Weight (Lbs.)					Weight (Lbs.)		
Underweight Under	Overweight Over	Normal Weight	Age (Years)	Height (Inches)	Age (Years)	Normal Weight	Overweight Over	Underweight Under	Underweight Under	Overweight Over	Normal Weight	Age (Years)	Height (Inches)	Age (Years)	Normal Weight	Overweight Over	Underweight Under	Underweight Under	Overweight Over	Normal Weight	Age (Years)	Height (Inches)	Age (Years)	Normal Weight	Overweight Over	Underweight Under
147	195	163	19	72									72									72				
142	189	158	18																							
140	187	156	17																							
140	187	155	16																							
138	183	153	15																							
137	182	152	17	71					143	191	159	19	71									71				
136	181	151	16						139	185	154	18														
135	180	150	15																							
133	177	148	17	70					140	187	155	19	70									70				
130	174	145	16						135	180	150	18														
130	173	144	15																							
129	172	143	14																							
125	167	139	15	69	18	142	170	128	137	182	152	19	69									69				
125	167	139	14		17	140	168	126	134	179	149	18														
					16	138	166	124	131	175	146	17														
									129	172	143	16														
121	161	134	15	68	18	138	166	124	132	176	147	19	68									68				
121	161	134	14		17	138	166	124	129	172	143	18														
					16	136	163	122	127	169	141	17														
					15	135	162	121	123	164	137	16														
					14	133	160	120																		

APPENDIX: WEIGHT IN RELATION TO AGE, HEIGHT, AND TYPE (*Cont.*)

TALL, SLENDER TYPE							AVERAGE TYPE							SHORT, STOCKY TYPE						
BOYS				GIRLS			BOYS				GIRLS			BOYS				GIRLS		
Weight (Lbs.)				Weight (Lbs.)			Weight (Lbs.)				Weight (Lbs.)			Weight (Lbs.)				Weight (Lbs.)		
Underweight	Overweight	Normal Weight	Age (Years)	Height (Inches)	Age (Years)	Normal Weight	Overweight	Underweight	Underweight	Overweight	Normal Weight	Age (Years)	Height (Inches)	Age (Years)	Normal Weight	Overweight	Underweight	Underweight	Overweight	Normal Weight	Age (Years)	Height (Inches)	Age (Years)	Normal Weight	Overweight	Underweight
115	153	128	14	67	{18 17 16 15 14}	{135 133 133 131 130}	{162 160 160 157 156}	{121 120 120 118 117}	122 121 117	163 161 156	136 134 130	{17 16 15}	67					128 125	170 167	142 139	{19 18}	67				
110 107 107	146 143 143	122 119 119	{14 13 12}	66	{18 17 16 15 14 13}	{130 129 128 125 124 124}	{156 155 153 150 149 149}	{117 116 115 112 112 112}	119 115 112	158 153 150	132 128 125	{17 16 15}	66					125 122	167 163	139 136	{19 18}	66				
105	140	117	13	65	{15 14 13}	{122 121 120}	{146 145 144}	{110 109 108}	110 108 106	146 144 142	122 120 118	{16 15 14}	65	{18 17 16}	{126 125 123}	{151 150 148}	{113 112 111}	121 118 115	161 157 152	134 131 127	{19 18 17}	65				
100 98	133 131	111 109	{13 12}	64	{13 12}	{115 114}	{138 137}	{103 103}	103 102	138 136	115 113	{15 14}	64	{18 17 16 15 14}	{123 122 120 119 117}	{148 146 144 143 140}	{111 110 108 107 105}	117 113 109 105	156 151 145 140	130 126 121 117	{19 18 17 16}	64				
96 95	128 127	107 106	{13 12}	63	{13 12}	{110 110}	{132 132}	{99 99}	99 97	132 130	110 108	{15 14}	63	{18 17 16 15 14}	{120 119 117 116 112}	{144 143 140 139 134}	{108 107 105 104 101}	115 111 106 102	152 148 142 136	127 123 118 113	{19 18 17 16}	63				
91	121	101	12	62	12	105	126	94	93 92	123 122	103 102	{14 13}	62	{15 14 13}	{113 109 108}	{136 131 127}	{102 98 95}	100 96 94	133 128 125	111 107 104	{17 16 15}	62	{18 17 16}	{118 117 115}	{142 140 138}	{106 105 103}
86 85	115 114	96 95	{12 11}	61	{12 11}	{100 99}	{120 119}	{90 89}	89 87	119 116	99 97	{14 13}	61	{14 13}	{105 101}	{126 121}	{94 91}	93 90	123 120	103 100	{16 15}	61	{18 17 16 15}	{116 113 112 108}	{139 136 134 130}	{104 102 101 97}
83 83	110 110	92 92	{12 11}	60	{12 11}	{95 95}	{114 114}	{85 85}	84	112	93	13	60	13	97	116	87	86 85 85	115 114 113	96 95 94	{16 15 14}	60	{18 17 16 15 14}	{111 109 108 105 101}	{133 131 130 126 121}	{100 98 97 94 91}
79 78	106 104	88 87	{11 10}	59	{11 10}	{90 87}	{108 104}	{81 78}	80 80	107 107	89 89	{13 12}	59	{13 12}	{92 90}	{110 108}	{83 81}	81 81	108 108	90 90	{15 14}	59	{16 15 14}	{103 100 96}	{123 120 115}	{93 90 86}

APPENDIX: WEIGHT IN RELATION TO AGE, HEIGHT, AND TYPE (*Cont.*)

TALL, SLENDER TYPE							AVERAGE TYPE									SHORT, STOCKY TYPE								
BOYS					GIRLS			BOYS						GIRLS				BOYS					GIRLS			
Weight (Lbs.)					Weight (Lbs.)			Weight (Lbs.)						Weight (Lbs.)				Weight (Lbs.)					Weight (Lbs.)		
Under Underweight	Over Overweight	Normal Weight	Age (Years)	Height (Inches)	Age (Years)	Normal Weight	Over Overweight	Under Underweight	Under Underweight	Over Overweight	Normal Weight	Age (Years)	Height (Inches)	Age (Years)	Normal Weight	Over Overweight	Under Underweight	Under Underweight	Over Overweight	Normal Weight	Age (Years)	Height (Inches)	Age (Years)	Normal Weight	Over Overweight	Under Underweight
76 76	101 101	84 84	11 10 }	58	{ 11 10	86 84	103 101	77 76	76	102	85	12	58	12	86	103	77	78 77 76	103 103 102	87 86 85	15 14 13 }	58	{ 15 14 13	96 93 88	115 112 106	86 84 79
72	96	80	10	57	10	82	98	74	73 73	97 97	81 81	12 11 }	57	{ 12 11	82 82	98 98	74 74	75 74	100 98	83 82	14 13 }	57	{ 14 13	88 84	106 101	79 76
69 68	92 91	77 76	10 9 }	56	{ 10 9	78 76	94 91	70 68	69 69	92 92	77 77	12 11 }	56	{ 12 11	79 78	95 94	71 70	70 70	94 94	78 78	14 13 }	56	{ 14 13	83 81	100 97	75 73
65	86	72	9	55	{ 9 8	74 72	89 86	67 65	66 66	88 88	73 73	11 10 }	55	{ 11 10	74 74	89 89	67 67	67 67	89 89	74 74	13 12 }	55	{ 13 12	77 75	92 90	69 67
63 63	84 84	70 70	9 8 }	54	{ 9 8	70 69	84 83	63 62	63	84	70	10	54	{ 11 10	71 70	85 84	64 63	64 64 63	85 85 84	71 71 70	13 12 11 }	54	{ 13 12	73 71	88 85	66 64
60	80	67	8	53	8	67	80	60	60 60	80 80	67 67	10 9 }	53	{ 10 9	68 67	82 80	61 60	61 60	82 80	68 67	12 11 }	53	{ 12 11	69 68	83 82	62 61
58 57	77 76	64 63	8 7 }	52	{ 8 7	64 63	77 76	58 57	58	77	64	9	52	{ 10 9	64 64	77 77	58 58	58 58	77 77	64 64	11 10 }	52	{ 12 11	67 65	80 78	60 58
55	73	61	7	51	7	59	71	53	55 55	73 73	61 61	9 8 }	51	{ 9 8	61 60	73 72	55 54	55 55	73 73	61 61	11 10 }	51	{ 12 11 10	65 63 61	78 76 73	58 57 55
52 51	70 68	58 57	7 6 }	50	{ 7 6	56 56	67 67	50 50	52	70	58	8	50	8	57	68	51	52 52	70 70	58 58	10 9 }	50	{ 11 10 9	61 59 58	73 71 70	55 53 52
49	66	55	6	49	{ 7 6	54 54	65 65	49 49	49 49	66 66	55 55	8 7 }	49	8	55	66	49	49 49	66 66	55 55	10 9 }	49	{ 10 9	56 55	67 66	50 49
47	62	52	6	48	6	52	62	47	48	64	53	7	48	7	52	62	47	48 48	64 64	53 53	9 8 }	48	{ 10 9 8	53 52 52	64 62 62	48 47 47
44	59	49	5	47	{ 6 5	50 49	60 59	45 44	45 45	60 60	50 50	7 6 }	47	7	50	60	45	45 45	60 60	50 50	9 8 }	47	{ 9 8	50 50	60 60	45 45

397

GLOSSARY

This glossary explains less common words and expressions as they are used in this book. You will find in the glossary the words in the text that have a star (*) after them.

KEY TO SOUNDS

ā *as in* āte
å *as in* car′bon-åte
â *as in* câre
ă *as in* ăm
ă *as in* fin′ăl
ä *as in* ärm
à *as in* àsk
a *as in* so′fa
ē *as in* ēve
ė *as in* ė-vent′
ĕ *as in* ĕnd

ẽ *as in* move′mẽnt
ē *as in* moth′ēr
ī *as in* īce
ĭ *as in* ĭll
ō *as in* ōld
ȯ *as in* ȯ-bey′
ô *as in* ôr′der
ŏ *as in* ŏdd
ǒ *as in* cǒr-rect′
oi *as in* oil
o͞o *as in* fo͞od
o͝o *as in* fo͝ot

ou *as in* out
ū *as in* ūse
ụ *as in* ụ-nite′
û *as in* bûrn
ŭ *as in* ŭp
ŭ *as in* cir′cŭs
ŋ *as in* iŋk
th *as in* bathe
zh *like the* s *in* treas′ure

abdomen (ăb-dō′mĕn). The front part of the trunk just below the chest.

abscess (ăb′sĕs). A place in the body where pus has formed.

absorb (ăb-sôrb′). To swallow up; to soak up.

acid (ăs′ĭd). A substance that is sour, sharp, or biting to the taste.

adhesive tape (ăd-hē′sĭv). A narrow strip of cloth which has a gluelike substance on one side.

adjustment (ă-jŭst′mĕnt). A fitting or making suitable.

alcohol (ăl′kŏ-hŏl). The part of beer, wine, and whisky which makes people drunk.

alcoholic (ăl′kŏ-hŏl′ĭk). Of, or relating to, alcohol.

ammonia (ă-mō′nĭ-a). A chemical compound of hydrogen and nitrogen.

amoeba (a-mē′ba). An animal consisting of a single cell.

antitoxin (ăn′tĭ-tŏk′sĭn). A chemical substance made by the body which can change the poisons of bacteria so that they become harmless.

appendix (a-pĕn′dĭks). A small, narrow tube near the beginning of the large intestine on the lower right side of the abdomen.

appetite (ăp′ĕ-tīt). A desire for food or drink.

application (ăp′lĭ-kā′shun). A laying on; something put on a cut or bruise.

arch (ärch). Any curve in the form of an arch, as the bottom of the foot.

aromatic spirits of ammonia (ăr′ŏ-măt′ĭk). A medicine used to treat fainting.

arteries (är′tēr-ĭz). Blood vessels carrying blood away from the heart.

asthma (ăz′ma). A disease which seems somewhat like a cold in the chest and makes breathing difficult.

athlete (ăth′lēt). One trained and fit to take part in exercises requiring great physical skill or strength.

bacillus (ba-sĭl′us). Any rod-shaped bacterium. The plural is bacilli.

bacteria (băk-tē′rĭ-a). Very small living things belonging to the plant kingdom. The singular is bacterium.

bacteriology (băk-tē′rĭ-ŏl′ŏ-jĭ). The science of living

things too small to be seen with the eye alone.

balance (băl′ăns). Equality of things.

bandage. A strip of cloth used in dressing wounds.

beverage (běv′ēr-ĭj). A drink.

bile. A juice secreted by the liver which helps to digest fats.

blood vessels. Tubes through which the blood flows.

borax (bō′răks). A white powder which has many protective uses.

boric acid (bō′rĭk). A liquid used in washing wounds and as an eyewash.

bowel movement. A movement of the large intestine to throw off body waste.

broccoli (brŏk′ō-lĭ). A green vegetable of the cauliflower family.

bruise. An injury to the flesh in which the skin is not broken. The flesh feels sore and sometimes turns black and blue.

bunion (bŭn′yŭn). A painful swelling, usually at the joint of the great toe.

caffeine (kăf′ĕ-ĭn). A stimulant found in coffee, tea, and some other drinks.

calcium (kăl′sĭ-ŭm). A substance needed in building bones and teeth.

capacity (kȧ-păs′ĭ-tĭ). Room, space, or power to receive, or power to do.

capillaries (kăp′ĭ-lĕr′ĭz). Very small tubes which join the arteries to the veins.

carbolated vaseline (kär′bō-lāt′ĕd văs′ĕ-lēn). A jellylike substance to aid the healing of bruises and the like.

carbolic acid (kär-bŏl′ĭk). A substance valuable for killing germs.

carbon dioxide (kär′bŏn dī-ŏk′sīd). A gas having no

color, no odor, no taste, formed in the body or in a flame.

carrier. A person who carries the germs of a communicable disease in his body but is not himself sick with the disease.

cathartic (kă-thär′tĭk). A medicine used to cause a bowel movement, as castor oil.

cavity (kăv′ĭ-tĭ). A hollow.

cellophane (sĕl′ŏ-făn). A transparent material used to wrap many kinds of articles to protect them from dust, dirt, and moisture.

cells. The tiny living parts of which the body is built.

cement (sĕ-mĕnt′). A substance which covers the root of the tooth.

cereal (sē′rĕ-ăl). Any grain used for food.

chemical (kĕm′ĭ-kăl). Of or relating to chemistry.

chicken pox. A catching disease of childhood in which white-headed pimples appear.

chlorinated lime (klō′rĭ-nāt′ĕd). An excellent disinfectant for outdoor toilets.

chlorine (klō′rĭn). A chemical element, usually in the form of a poisonous, greenish-yellow gas, which kills bacteria quickly.

cholera (kŏl′ẽr-ă). A bacterial disease common in Asia, which comes on quickly and often causes death.

clinical thermometer (klĭn′-ĭ-kăl thẽr-mŏm′ĕ-tẽr). An instrument used in taking the temperature of the body.

coccus (kŏk′ŭs). A ball-shaped bacterium. The plural is cocci (kŏk′sī).

communicable disease (kŏ-mū′nĭ-kă-b'l). A disease caused by germs which may be spread from one person to another.

concentrated (kŏn'sĕn-trāt'ĕd). Made less watery; increased in strength.

condensed (kŏn-dĕnst'). Made less watery, more concentrated.

consciousness (kŏn'shŭs-nĕs). State of being awake.

constipated (kŏn'stĭ-pāt'ĕd). Having few or difficult movements of the bowels.

constipation (kŏn'stĭ-pā'-shŭn). A state in which there is a lack of regular and easy movement of the bowels.

contact (kŏn'tăkt). A touching or meeting which spreads bacteria from one thing or person to another.

contagious (kŏn-tā'jŭs). Carried from one individual to another by contact.

contaminate (kŏn-tăm'ĭ-nāt). To make unclean.

contract (kŏn-trăkt'). To shorten or draw together.

contraction (kŏn-trăk'shŭn). Act of drawing together or shortening.

convalescent (kŏn'vă-lĕs'-ĕnt). A person who is getting well from an illness.

convulsions (kŏn-vŭl'-shŭnz). Sudden contractions of the muscles, when the person has not willed them. Also called *fits*.

corpuscles (kôr'pŭs-'lz). Very small cells floating in the blood.

cramp. A painful contraction of a muscle or muscles against the person's will.

culture (kŭl'tŭr). A growing of microorganisms for scientific study or medical use.

curd (kûrd). The cheese-like substance formed from sour milk.

custard. A pudding made of eggs, milk, and sugar.

decay. To rot.

dental (děn′tăl). Relating to the teeth or to the work of the dentist.

dentine (děn′tēn). The bonelike material of which the main part of the teeth is built.

dermis (dûr′mĭs). The layer of the skin underneath the top layer or epidermis.

develop (dĕ-vĕl′ŏp). To grow in size, power, or skill.

development (dĕ-vĕl′ŏp-mĕnt). Growth. Growing bigger and better in many ways.

diaphragm (dī′*a*-frăm). A broad dome-shaped muscle which forms the floor of the chest cavity and the roof of the abdominal cavity.

diet (dī′ĕt). The food and drink a person takes.

digest (dĭ-jĕst′). To change food into forms which can be used by the body.

digestion (dĭ-jĕs′chŭn). The act of digesting.

digestive system or **digestive tract.** The mouth, stomach, intestines, and other parts of the body which help to digest food.

diphtheria (dĭf-thē′rĭ-*a*). A contagious disease in which the person has a fever and a special kind of sore throat.

discharges (dĭs-chärj′ĕz). Waste materials sent out from the body.

disinfect (dĭs′ĭn-fĕkt′). To free from disease-producing organisms.

disinfectant (dĭs′ĭn-fĕk′-tănt). Something like heat or carbolic acid or chlorated lime used to destroy disease-producing organisms.

dissolve (dĭ-zŏlv′). To dis-

GLOSSARY

appear in water or other liquid.

douche (dōōsh). A spray or stream of water or vapor applied to any part of the body.

dysentery (dĭs′ĕn-tĕr-ĭ). A disease in which there is inflammation of the large intestine.

eardrum. The skin, or membrane, stretched across the canal that leads into the ear.

enamel (ĕn-ăm′ĕl). The hard, shiny outer coat of the teeth above the gums.

energy (ĕn′ēr-jĭ). Strength; power.

epidemic (ĕp′ĭ-dĕm′ĭk). A disease common to many people in a community at the same time.

epidermis (ĕp′ĭ-dûr′mĭs). The outer layer of the skin.

essential (ĕ-sĕn′shăl). Something so important that one cannot get along without it.

excess (ĕk-sĕs′). That which is beyond the limit of what is needed.

excite (ĕk-sīt′). To stir up; to make restless or lively.

exhausted (ĕg-zôs′tĕd). Worn out; tired out; used up.

experiment (ĕks-pĕr′ĭ-mĕnt). A kind of test; a trial made to find out the truth about something.

exposed (ĕks-pōzd′). Laid open to; unprotected.

fad. A custom followed to excess.

Fahrenheit (fä′rĕn-hīt). A thermometer scale for measuring degrees of temperature; 32° on this scale is the freezing point of water, and water boils at 212° at sea level.

fatigue (fȧ-tēg′). Weariness or loss of power from work or exertion.

fatiguing (fȧ-tē'gĭng). Tiring; causing weariness.

ferment (fẽr-mĕnt'). To undergo a chemical change in which gases and acids or alcohol are formed.

fever. A sign of sickness in which the body is hotter than usual, the face is flushed, and one is restless.

fiber (fī'bẽr). A thread or threadlike structure.

field of vision (vĭzh'ŭn). The scene which can be taken in by the eyes in a fixed position.

filter (fĭl'tẽr). To pass a liquid through material which will strain and clean it.

first aid. Treatment given an injury or sudden illness at or near the place where it occurs.

foci of infection (fō'sī). Places in the body where bacteria gather and multiply in large numbers.

food value. The amount of healthful substances contained in the food.

formalin (for'mȧ-lĭn). A useful disinfectant.

fumigate (fū'mĭ-gāt). To apply smoke or vapor to any thing or place for the purpose of killing bacteria.

gastric (găs'trĭk). Of, or relating to, the stomach.

gauze (gôz). A very thin, soft cloth.

gelatine (jĕl'ȧ-tĭn). A jelly obtained from animal tissues.

germ (jûrm). A very small living thing; any microorganism.

gland. A part of the body that secretes useful fluid.

glare. A dazzling light.

goiter (goi'tẽr). A disease in which the thyroid gland becomes enlarged.

Graham (grā'ăm). A man's name. He advised people to eat whole-wheat bread, or graham bread.

gruel (grōō'ĕl). A thin food made by boiling cereal in water.

health examination. A thorough going-over of different parts of the body to see if there is ill health or defects.

hellebore (hĕl'ė-bōr). The powdered root of the white hellebore plant.

hydrogen peroxide (hī'drŏ-jĕn pēr-ŏks'īd). A disinfectant.

hydrophobia (hī'drŏ-fō'bĭ-à). An acute infectious disease occurring chiefly among dogs and wolves.

immune (ĭ-mūn'). Free from or resisting disease.

immunity (ĭm-ū'nĭ-tĭ). Freedom from and resistance to a certain disease.

infected (ĭn-fĕkt'ĕd). Contaminated with any disease-producing thing.

infection (ĭn-fĕk'shŭn). The state due to germs growing in the body and producing poisons.

inflamed (ĭn-flāmd'). Red, swollen, feverish, and painful.

inflammation (ĭn'flă-mā'shŭn). A condition in which there is redness, fever, swelling, and pain.

inhale (ĭn-hāl'). To breathe in.

inject (ĭn-jĕkt'). To put or force in.

injection (ĭn-jĕk'shŭn). A liquid medicine forced into the body.

inoculation (ĭn-ŏk'ŭ-lā'shŭn). Preventing certain diseases by injecting substances to help the body fight infection.

insanity (ĭn-săn'ĭ-tĭ). Madness; the state of having an unsound mind.

intestine (ĭn-tĕs′tĭn). The tubelike part of the digestive tract below the stomach; the *bowels*.

invisible perspiration (pûr′-spĭ-rā′shŭn). Perspiration, or sweat, which cannot be seen.

iodine (ī′ŏ-dīn). A chemical substance often used on cuts in the form of tincture to kill germs.

iris (ī′rĭs). The colored part of the eye.

irregular (ĭ-rĕg′ū-lȧr). Not even.

irritate (ĭr′ĭ-tāt). To make unusually sensitive.

junket (jŭŋ′kĕt). A pudding made of milk and sugar.

kidneys. A pair of organs, located in the abdomen near the spinal column, which remove poisonous and waste substances from the blood.

laboratory (lăb′ŏ-rȧ-tŏ-rĭ). The workroom of a scientist.

larva (lär′vȧ). The second or worm stage in the development of insects. The plural is larvae.

larynx (lăr′ĭŋks). The air passage between the throat and the windpipe; the organ of voice.

laxative (lăk′sȧ-tĭv). A medicine given to cause a bowel movement.

lens. A clear, oval body in the eye, curved outward on both sides. Also a glass part of a microscope or eyeglasses.

ligament (lĭg′ȧ-mĕnt). A tough membrane that fastens bones together.

linoleum (lĭ-nō′lĕ-ŭm). A floor covering with a hard, smooth surface.

macaroni (măk′ȧ-rō′nĭ). A starchy paste of wheat flour, dried in thin tubes.

magnify (măg′nĭ-fī). To make appear larger.

malaria (m*a*-lā′rĭ-*a*). A germ disease in which the patient has attacks of fever at regular times.

manure (m*a*-nūr′). The body waste from horses, cows, and other animals.

measles (mē′z'lz). A contagious disease in which the person has a fever and the skin breaks out with red spots.

membrane (měm′brān). Any very thin, soft layer of animal or vegetable tissue.

menu (měn′ů). A bill of fare; a list of foods served in a meal.

microbes (mī′krōbz). Very small plants or animals usually having only one cell, as bacteria.

microorganism (mī′krȯ-ôr′-găn-ĭz′m). A plant or animal so small that it can be seen only under a microscope.

microscope (mīk′rȯ-skōp). An instrument which makes an object under its lens look many times larger than it really is.

microscopic (mī′krȯ-skŏp′-ĭk). So small as to be seen only under the microscope.

morphine (môr′fēn). A bitter, white substance in opium which produces narcotic effects.

mucous membrane (mū′k*u*s měm′brān). The thin layer of tissue lining certain cavities such as the mouth and stomach.

mucus (mū′k*u*s). A slippery, watery secretion of the mucous membranes which keeps them moist and helps to lubricate them.

muscle (mŭs″l). A part of the body that makes it possible to move.

muscular (mŭs′kŭ-lȧr). Of, relating to, or consisting of, muscles.

narcotic (när-kŏt′ĭk). A drug which depresses or dulls bodily and mental activity.

nerve. One of the white threadlike bands that carry messages back and forth in the body.

nervous system. The system of nerve cells, nerves, and brain which help to keep all parts of the body alert and able to adjust to changing conditions.

neutralize (nū′trăl-īz). To destroy the peculiar properties of; to take away the effects of.

nicotine (nĭk′ō-tĭn). A poisonous substance contained in tobacco.

nitrogen (nī′trō-jĕn). A colorless, odorless gas; an important chemical element in proteins.

nourish (nŭr′ĭsh). To supply with material needed for growth and health.

oculist (ŏk′ŭ-lĭst). A doctor who is especially prepared to treat the eyes and to fit them with glasses when needed.

operation (ŏp′ēr-ā′shŭn). A surgical act on the living body to improve or restore health.

opium (ō′pĭ-ŭm). A powerful, habit-forming drug, obtained from the juice of the poppy.

optician (ŏp-tĭsh′ăn). A person who makes and sells eyeglasses and other things for the eyes.

optometrist (ŏp-tŏm′ĕ-trĭst). One who is skilled in testing eyesight and in fitting eyes with eyeglasses when needed; not a doctor.

organism (ôr′găn-ĭz′m). Any living thing.

organization (ôr'găn-ĭ-zā'-shŭn). A group of people working for a common purpose.

overdevelop (dĕ-vĕl'ŏp). To develop too much.

overstimulating (stĭm'ū-lāt'ĭng). Too stimulating or exciting.

oxygen (ŏk'sĭ-jĕn). A gas which is a part of the air we breathe and which is necessary to life. It has no color, odor, or taste.

pacifier (păs'ĭ-fī'ẽr). An object sometimes given to a baby to put in his mouth to keep him quiet.

pancreas (păn'krẽ ăs). A gland which pours a digestive juice into the small intestine and a secretion into the blood.

pasteurization (păs'tẽr-ĭ-zā'shŭn). A process invented by the great French scientist, Pasteur, for preventing or checking the growth of bacteria in liquids.

pasteurize (păs'tẽr-īz). To kill or check the growth of bacteria in milk and other liquids by heating them to about 145° F. for thirty minutes.

patent medicine (păt'ĕnt mĕd'ĭ-sĭn). Ready-made medicines which are sold in the stores with the permission of the government.

patrol (pa-trōl'). A body of guards who go the rounds to prevent accidents or wrongdoing.

pedestrians (pĕ-dĕs'trĭ-ănz). People who walk or go on foot.

permanent (pûr'ma-nĕnt). Lasting.

perspiration (pûr'spĭ-rā'-shŭn). Sweat; salty water, plus a very small amount of waste substances, poured out by the skin.

petroleum (pĕ-trō'lĕ-ŭm). A mineral oil.

physician (fĭ-zĭsh'ăn). A doctor of medicine.

pinkeye. An acute, contagious disease of the mucous membrane of the eye.

pneumonia (nŭ-mō'nĭ-a). A disease in which there is a serious inflammation of the lungs.

poisonous (poi'z'n-ŭs). Containing substances which will cause sickness or possibly death if taken into or brought in contact with the body.

pores. Small openings in the skin, leading out from the sweat glands.

posture (pŏs'tŭr). The position in which a person sits, stands, or walks.

pressure (presh'ŭr). Steady force acting on a body to change its position or shape. *Blood pressure* is the pressure of the blood against the walls of the blood vessels.

ptomaine (tō'mān). A substance, sometimes poisonous, formed when meat and other proteins decay.

pulp chamber. The hollow space in the center of a tooth filled largely with blood vessels and nerves.

pulse (pŭls). The swelling or throb which is felt in the arteries each time that the heart beats and sends out blood.

pupil. The opening surrounded by the colored part of the eye.

pus (pŭs). A whitish mass of white corpuscles, bacteria, living and dead, and injured tissue, formed at a point where bacteria are located.

quarantine (kwŏr'ăn-tēn). Keeping people who have been sick with, or exposed to, communicable disease from moving from place to place, so as to prevent the spread of their disease to others.

rabies (rā′bĭ-ēz). A disease caused by the bite of a mad dog; hydrophobia.

refrigerator (rĕ-frĭj′ẽr-ā′-tẽr). A box or room for keeping food cold.

relaxation (rē′lăk-sā′shŭn). A letting down or a lessening of activity.

resistance (rĕ-zĭs′tăns). Ability to withstand or bear.

respiration (rĕs′pĭ-rā′shŭn). The act or process of breathing.

respiratory (rĕ-spīr′a-tō′-rĭ). Of or pertaining to the act of breathing.

retina (rĕt′ĭ-na). The inner lining or coat at the back of the eyeball which receives the images of objects.

rheumatism (rōō′ma-tĭz′m). A disease in which there are pains of various kinds, especially in the joints and muscles.

rickets (rĭk′-ĕts). A children's disease, caused by a poor diet, which affects bone development.

saliva (sa-lī′va). The watery fluid which is secreted in the mouth and begins the digestion of starchy food.

sanitary (săn′ĭ-tĕ′-rĭ). Of or pertaining to health.

scalp. The skin and hair that cover the head.

scarlet fever. A contagious disease in which the throat is sore, the skin of the mouth is red and rough, and there is fever.

Schick test (shĭk). A test by inoculation to find out whether a person is likely to catch diphtheria.

scientific (sī′ĕn-tĭf′ĭk). Agreeing with the rules or principles of science.

scientist (sī′ĕn-tĭst). A person who knows a great deal about science and makes science his special work.

scurvy (skûr′vĭ). A disease in which the gums often become sore and bleeding, there is usually loss in weight, and communicable diseases are caught more easily.

secretion (sė-krē′shŭn). A useful liquid given off by certain parts of the body.

sensitive (sĕn′sĭ-tĭv). Quick to feel; easily affected.

serum (sē′rŭm). The watery part which separates from clotted blood.

sewage (sū′ĭj). Watery wastes from houses and other buildings.

shank. The part of a shoe which supports the instep of the foot.

sinus (sī′nŭs). A hollow space in certain bones of the face.

sirup of ipecac (ĭp′ė-kăk). A medicine used to make a person vomit, or throw up.

skeleton (skĕl′ė-tŭn). All the bones of a human being or animal. The skeleton is the framework of the body.

skull. The bony covering of the brain.

smallpox. A very contagious disease which may leave ugly marks on the skin.

spine. The backbone; spinal column.

spirillum (spī-rĭl′ŭm). A corkscrew-shaped bacterium, which moves about in a lively way. The plural is spirilla.

splint. A piece of wood or other stiff material used to hold or protect an injured part.

spore (spōr). A cell which,

like a seed, has power to make a new plant.

sprain. To injure a joint by a sudden and severe strain.

sputum (spū'tŭm). Mucus from the throat, lungs, or nose mixed with saliva and coughed out.

sterile (stĕr'ĭl). Free from germs.

sterilize (stĕr'ĭ-līz). To make free from disease-causing bacteria.

stimulant (stĭm'ū-lănt). Something that excites or makes a person more active.

stimulating (stĭm'ū-lā'tĭng). Having the effect of stirring up or arousing the nerves.

structure (strŭk'tŭr). Arrangement of parts or tissues in a body.

sty (stī). A sore, red swelling on the edge of the eyelid.

suction (sŭk'shŭn). The act of drawing liquids into a tube or jar by the withdrawal of air.

susceptible (sŭ-sĕp'tĭ-b'l). Capable of catching a certain disease.

sweat glands. Glands of the skin that secrete sweat, or perspiration.

Swiss chard (chärd). A green leafy vegetable somewhat like spinach.

symptom (sĭmp'tŭm). A sign of disease.

tense (tĕns). Not relaxed.

temperature (tĕm'pēr-*a*-tŭr). Degree of heat or cold.

tetanus (tĕt'*a*-nŭs). A painful, often fatal, disease caused by a certain kind of bacteria and marked by continuous, uncontrolled contractions of voluntary muscles; also called lockjaw.

thermometer (thēr-mŏm'ĕ-tēr). An instrument for

measuring the degrees of heat or cold.

tincture (tĭŋk′tŭr). A solution of a medical substance in alcohol.

tissue (tĭsh′ů). A collection or mass of cells which forms some part of the body.

tonsil (tŏn′sĭl). One of the masses of tissue at the back of the mouth.

tourniquet (toŏr′nĭ-kĕt). A device or instrument for stopping bleeding by pressure.

toxins (tŏk′sĭnz). Poisons produced by bacteria.

toxoid (tŏk′soid). A substance used with very young babies to protect them from diphtheria.

tuberculosis (tŭ-bûr′kŭ-lō′sĭs). A communicable disease, commonly affecting the lungs, caused by the tubercle bacilli.

typhoid fever (tī′foid fē′vẽr). A very serious disease caused by a certain kind of bacterium (the typhoid bacillus) usually carried in food or drink.

ulcerated (ŭl′ser-āt′ĕd). Affected with a sore which is near the surface and which discharges pus.

unconscious (ŭn-kŏn′shŭs). Not conscious; not aware of what is going on.

vaccination (văk′sĭ-nā′-shŭn). Art, act, or practice of preventing smallpox by injecting a small amount of the smallpox virus.

vaccine (văk′sēn). Weakened germs, extracts of germs, or killed germs of a certain kind which can be put into the body to protect it against smallpox.

vacuum cleaner (văk′ů-ŭm). A machine for cleaning carpets, rugs, hangings, and the like by drawing the dirt out of the carpets by suction without scattering dust.

vegetarian (věj′ê-tâ′rĭ-ăn). One who believes that plants are the only proper food for man.

vein (vān). A blood vessel which carries blood back toward the heart.

venom (věn′ŭm). The poisonous substance which certain animals secrete and inject into people by biting or stinging.

venomous (věn′ŭm-ŭs). Full of venom; poisonous.

ventilate (věn′tĭ-lāt). To cause fresh air to circulate through a room.

ventilation (věn′tĭ-lā′shŭn). Act of ventilating or state of being ventilated.

virulent (vĭr′ů-lěnt). Extremely poisonous.

virus (vī′rŭs). The poison which causes a communicable disease.

vision (vĭzh′ŭn). Sight.

vocal cords. Either of two pairs of folds of mucous membrane which extend into the cavity of the larynx.

water glass. A substance used to keep eggs fresh.

whey (hwā). The watery part of sour milk separated from the curd.

whisky (hwĭs′kĭ). A drink containing 40 to 54 per cent of alcohol.

windpipe. The tube which carries the air you breathe down to the lungs.

X-rays (ěks′-rāz′). Rays which show certain inner parts of the body.

yellow fever. A germ disease caused by the bite of a certain kind of mosquito.

INDEX

abscess, 277
accidents, in school, 345; protecting others from, 348–350; to small children, 346–349
adhesive tape, 124, 140
air, composition of, 157, 169; effect on appetite, 249; necessary for life, 148–149
alcohol, 140, 256–262; effects of long use of, 261; harmful effects of, 259–260; used for wounds, 277, 291
alcoholic drinks, 32, 36, 45, 200, 202, 256–258, 263, 355; not necessary for health, 258
amoeba, 196, 197
antitoxin, 302–307, 317; diphtheria, 302–306
appendix, 278, 280
appetite, effect of air and smoking on, 249–250
arch of the foot, 362
aromatic spirits of ammonia, 140
artery, 127, 130, 131, 248
asparagus, iron in, 114
asthma, 316
automobile accidents, 348

baby, taking care of, 385–387
bacilli, 287, 288
backbone, 187
bacteria, 46, 50–51, 56, 62, 64, 68, 125, 129, 152, 196, 198, 232, 324, 341; cause disease, 286, 298; chemical war on, 301–318; helpful, 286–287, 298; how they get into the body, 291–296; how they grow, 288–291; in milk, 204–212; protecting oneself from, 274–281, 284–301, 330; protecting others from, 319–324; types of, 287–288
bath, cold, 171
bathing, 218
beer, 32, 259
Behring, Emil August, 302
beverages, 32
bile, 302
blood, 61, 171, 186, 247–248
blood poisoning, 281
blood vessels, 129–132, 183, 186, 276; effect of smoking on, 253
body, food needed by, 8; temperature of, 147; wastes, 9
boils, 152, 164, 281
bones, 76, 78; composition of, 76, 198, 357; first aid for broken, 132
boric acid, 140
bowel movement, 38, 46, 53, 107
bran, 45
bread, 12, 17, 22, 212, 226, 371; starch in, 43
breakfast, foods for, 10–15; menus, 11–12

420 INDEX

bunions, 361-362
burns, fatal accidents from, 346-348; first aid for, 134
butter, 11, 22, 371
buttermilk, 212, 287

caffeine, effects of, 33
cake, 100
calcium, in milk, 76, 84, 271, 357; needed by body, 8-9, 84
camp life, advantages of, 170-177
candy, 97, 98, 100; and teeth, 268; when bad for us, 32; when to eat, 101
Cannon, Walter B., 51
capillaries, 130, 132, 171, 275, 276
carbon dioxide, 256; in air, 157
carrier of disease, 299, 323
castor oil, 53
cathartics, 53-54
cavities, 139, 270, 278
cellar, care of, 239-241
cells, of the body, 6-7
cement, 265
cereals, 10, 11, 12, 15, 17, 22, 32, 106, 226, 371
cheese, 16, 20, 72, 83, 212, 287; calcium in, 76
Chicago water supply, 69
chicken pox, 286, 320
chlorine, 66, 69
city, vacation in the, 179-184
cleanliness, 50, 59-60; and health, 145; in care of food, 206, 368; learned at camp, 171; of swimming pools, 315; protects against insects, 339
clinical thermometer, 140

clothing, daily care of, 360; rules for choosing, 356-360
cocci, 287, 288
cocoa, 227
cod-liver oil, 269, 270
coffee, 11, 12, 32, 33, 34-35, 37, 227; harmful effects of, 34-35; why people drink it, 34
colds, 294, 296, 317, 331; how to avoid, 152; how spread, 297; preventing the spread of, 320
constipation, 46, 52, 53, 115, 326
convalescent, care of the, 326-329
cooking, 374-375
corns, 362, 365
corpuscles, red, 129, 276; white, 275, 276, 277, 301
coughing, precautions when, 294, 295, 319
cramps while swimming, 52
cream, 11
curds, 71

dancing, 175, 390
dates, iron in, 103
dentine, 265, 269
dermis, 125
diaphragm, 359
diet, 74
digestion, 41-46, 51-52, 61; affected by worry and haste, 214-215; aiding, 214-218
digestive juices, 45, 50, 61, 215, 217; fight bacteria, 302
digestive organs, 359
digestive system, 41-46, 49
dinner menus, 22, 25-27

INDEX

diphtheria, 145; antitoxin used to prevent, 302–306; how carried, 316

disease, carried by insects, 333–339, 341; caused by bacteria, 286; communicable, 294, 324–325, 331; preventing spread of, 337; resistance to, 380

dishes, bacteria on, 232; washing, 230–234

disinfectants, 300, 322

dogs, experiments with, 269

drinking. *See* alcohol, alcoholic drinks

drugs, 36, 53, 256; habit-forming, 261–263

ear, 146–147
eardrum, 147
eating habits, 46–54
education, importance of, 388–389
eggs, 11, 12, 15, 16, 20, 93–94, 330; fresh, 370; value of, 89–90; ways of cooking, 226, 375; yolks of, 269
enamel, 265, 269
energy, food needed for, 7–8, 34
epidermis, 125
ether, 257
evaporated milk, 84
exercise, 200; best times for, 390
eyeball, 157
eyes, 157–168; care of, 160–165, 168, 203, 327; how they work, 157–160; muscles of, 159, 160, 162, 163
eyestrain, 317

fainting, treatment for, 135, 136
falls, 349, 350
farm, vacation on, 177–179
fatigue, 380
feet, daily care of, 363–364; importance of right shoes, 360–363
fibers, in foods, 269
first aid, for broken bones, 132–134; for burns, 134; for cuts and scratches, 125–126; for miscellaneous mishaps, 134–139; for serious bleeding, 127–129; for wounds, 122–124, 127
fish, 94; iodine in, 90; ways of cooking, 93
flies, carry germs, 292, 333–334; reducing the number of, 293, 334–335
food, and energy, 7–8, 34, 377; and growth, 4–7, 82, 85; and health, 8–9, 148, 365; and resistance to disease, 330; and teeth, 47, 269–270; at recess, 31; buying, 368–374; canned, 290; cooking, 374–375; digestion of, 41–46, 51–52; effect on height, 85; frozen, 290; habits, 36–39; how much to spend for different kinds of, 370–374; need for, 3–10; spicy, 44; starch in, 43; ways of cooking, 217, 220
foot, arch, 362
formalin, 330
4-H Clubs, 179
fresh air, 327
frostbite, treatment for, 137

INDEX

fruits and vegetables, 226, 330, 331, 370–371; advantages of, 107; as regular part of diet, 107–108; build good teeth, 270, 271–272; canning, 110–111; for everyone, 107–110; necessary for health, 9, 47, 105–106; why we should eat, 114; wrong uses of, 106. *See also* vegetables
fumigation, 328

games, at camp, 174
gauze, sterilized, 124, 140
germs, 152, 164; how spread, 299; in milk, 204; tuberculosis, 326. *See also* bacteria
glands, 274; sweat, 125
goiter, 90
graham bread, 32, 37
growth, affected by food, 4–7
gums, 54

habits, eating, 46–54; good and bad, 201, 381–382
headache, 46; causes of, 317; treatment for, 138
health, aids to, 148–150; examination, 280; food and, 8–9, 148; laws of, 185; preservation of, 142–153; vacation as aid to, 169–192
heart, 8, 174; effect of smoking on, 247–249, 253–254
home, a healthful, 237–240
housekeeping, 230–243; caring for icebox, 235–237; sweeping and dusting, 234–235; washing dishes, 230–234
hydrogen peroxide, 127

icebox, care of, 235–237
illness, 200; prevention of, 142–148
immunity from disease, 306, 313, 324–326
infection, 275; foci of, 278–280; prevention of, 274–281
inoculation, 307–308
insects, carry germs, 333–339, 341
intestine, in fish, 90; large, 46, 52; small, 45
iodine, 90, 277, 291; tincture of, 124, 126, 140
ipecac, sirup of, 140
iris of the eye, 159
iron, in dates, 103; in liver, 90; in other foods, 92, 112, 114; needed by body cells, 8

Jenner, Edward, 307–310

kitchen, a sanitary, 237–239

larynx, 246
laxatives, 53–54
Lazear, Dr. Jesse W., 336
lemon juice, 36
lens of the eye, 158
life work, choosing, 387–389
ligaments, 187
liver, iron in, 90
living healthfully, 384–385
Los Angeles water supply, 67
lunch, foods for, 16–20
lungs, 246, 357–358, 384

malaria, caused by mosquitoes, 335–336; reduced in Panama Canal Zone, 342

INDEX

meals, camp, 30; number per day, 31; regular time for, 218; summer, 28–30; time allowed for, 33; wholesome, 10–28. *See also* menus

measles, 165, 286, 299, 320

meat, advantages and disadvantages of, 90–92; and health, 88–89; in our meals, 87–94; iron in, 90

medicine chest, contents of, 139–140

medicines, patent, 261–262

menus, 115; breakfast, 10–15, 39; dinner, 22–28, 39; lunch or supper, 16–20, 39; school lunch, 221–224. *See also* meals

microbes, 285

microorganism, 341

microscope, 196, 285

milk, 10, 12, 14, 15, 22, 37, 89, 92–93, 204–212, 268, 330; and weight, 6, 74–75, 82; bacteria in, 204, 209, 212; calcium in, 8–9, 76, 84, 271, 357; dry or evaporated, 84, 226; goat's, 83; how it can be made safe, 204–212; in our meals, 71–85; most important food, 370; needed for health and growth, 47, 72–78; pasteurizing, 207–208, 290; sour, 212, 302; why good, 32

milk chocolate, 102–103

morphine, 262

mosquitoes, carry germs, 333, 335–339, 342; cause malaria and yellow fever, 335–336; reducing number of, 337–338

mucous membrane, 245, 300

mucus, 245, 294, 295, 299, 301

muscles, 34, 187, 198, 358, 379, 390; of the eyes, 159, 160, 162, 163, 186; of the feet, 362

narcotics, 257. *See also* drugs

natural sweets, 97, 98, 103, 192

nerve cells, 7

nerves, 378; in the teeth, 265, 266

nervous system, 379

New York City water supply, 65

nicotine, 244, 247, 254

nitrogen, 157, 287

nose, 246

nosebleed, treatment for, 138–139

oculist, 161

opium, 262

optician, 161

optometrist, 161

orange juice, 36, 270

oranges, 12, 13, 47

organism, 341

outdoor play, 255, 317, 325, 383, 390

overeating, 106

oxygen, 129, 149, 157

Pasteur, Louis, 311–313

pasteurization, 207–208, 212, 290

patent medicines, 261–262

patrols, duties of boy and girl, 351–352

perspiration, 59, 125

pickles, 219

pinkeye, 163, 281

planning your days, 382–384, 394
play, outdoor, 255, 317, 325, 383, 390
pneumonia, 331
policemen, insure safety, 352
pores, 125
posture, 171, 198, 380
potatoes, 225
ptomaine, 317
pulp chamber, 265
pupil of the eye, 157, 158, 163
pus, 275; in abscessed teeth, 267; in wounds, 275

quarantine, 320

rabies, inoculation against, 311–313
raisins, 12
rats, experiments with, 75–76, 78, 88
raw vegetables, 9, 22
reading, correct position for, 166; importance of good light for, 163; lying down, 161–162; on moving trains, 160
Reed, Walter, 336, 343
refrigerator. *See* icebox
relaxation, 257–258
respiration, effect of smoking upon, 247, 260; organs of, 246, 247
respiratory diseases, 326
respiratory system, 357
rest, 378–380
retina, 159
rheumatism, 279
ribs, 357
rickets, 99

safety, first, 183; where it should rule, 345–351; who helps to secure, 351–353
saliva, 43, 45, 61, 215
San Francisco water supply, 67
scalp, 76; diseases of, 153
scarlet fever, 200, 306, 320
Schick test, 304, 315
scurvy, 33, 35–36, 105
serum, 303, 317
sewage and disease, 331
shoes, best kind, 365; rules for choosing, 360–363
sick, caring for the, 326–329
sickness caused by spoiled food, 29. *See also* illness
sinuses, 296
skeleton, 77, 78
skin, 274; tissues of, 7
skull, 78
sleep, 186, 187; importance of, 378–380; position in, 390
smallpox, 307; vaccination against, 308–310
smoking, disadvantages of, 251–252; some effects of, 245–251, 253, 263. *See also* tobacco
snakebite, treatment for, 137–138
sneezing, precautions when, 294, 295, 319
"soft" drinks, 32
spices, 218, 219
spinach, iron in, 114
spirilla, 287–288
spores, 283, 284
sprained ankle, first aid for, 137
sputum, 295
starch in foods, 17, 43

INDEX

sterilizing, a needle, 291; milk bottles, 206
sties, 164–165
stimulant, 33, 227
stockings, choice of, 363
stomach, 43–44; lining of, 44, 101
sugar, advantages and disadvantages of, 99–101; and health, 96–102
summer meals, 28
sunlight, 78, 152, 169, 327, 330, 331, 384; and health, 148; helps build teeth, 265, 270; importance of, 148, 390; kills bacteria, 289
supper, foods for, 16–20
sweat glands, 125, 274
sweeping and dusting, 234–235
sweets, 220; effect on teeth, 97–98; in your daily food, 96–104; natural, 97, 98, 103, 192; sugar, 99–101
swimming, 150, 171, 188, 315; after eating, 52; at camp, 171, 177

tea, 32, 37, 227
teeth, 41, 57; abscessed, 266–267, 278, 279; care of, 47–48, 54, 56, 100; cavities in, 270, 278; effect of food on, 269–270; effect of sweets on, 97–98, 100; how built, 265; permanent, 47; preventing decay of, 267–271
temperature, of body, 147; of rooms, 145, 250
thermometer, 208

throat, 146, 246; sore, 299
tissues, of the skin, 7
toast, 11, 12, 15
tobacco, 200, 202, 247; effect on work and health, 253–254. *See also* smoking
tonsils, 278, 279–280
toothache, 56; causes of, 265; temporary treatment for, 139
toothbrush, types of, 268
tourniquet, 129, 137
toxin, 302
toxoid, 305
typhoid fever, 62, 286, 298, 313, 322

vacation, 169–192; at camp, 169–177; days planned, 394; in the city, 179–185; on the farm, 177–179
vaccination, 308–310, 316
vacuum cleaner, 235
Van Leeuwenhoek, Anton, 285
vaseline, carbolated, 140
vegetables, 108, 113, 114; canned, 114; cooking, 375, 377; dried, 111–112; iron in, 114; leafy, 9, 22; raw, 9, 22; ways of preparing, 108. *See also* fruits and vegetables
vegetarians, 88
veins, 130, 132
ventilation, 249–250
virus, 286, 307
vocal cords, 246

walking, 364
water, amount one should drink, 61–62, 68, 243; danger from polluted, 62, 64; diseases

carried by, 297; in foods, 61, 62; our need of, 58–62, 69; safe, 65–68, 69; supply, 62–68; when unfit to drink, 330
whey, 71
whiskey, 259
windpipe, 246
wine, 32, 259

work, choosing, 387–389
wounds, first aid for, 122–124, 127; infected, 275

X-ray machine, 51

yellow fever, 341; caused by mosquitoes, 336; reduced in Panama Canal Zone, 342

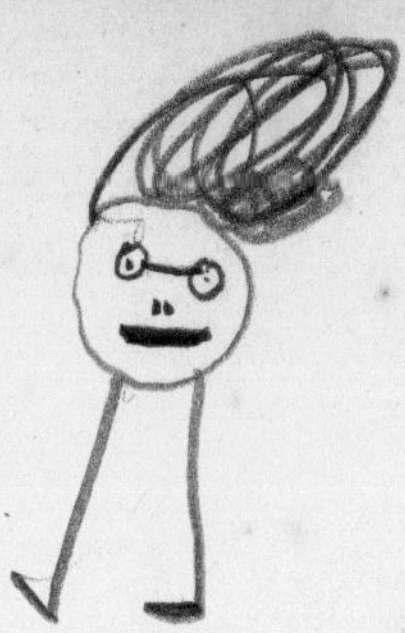

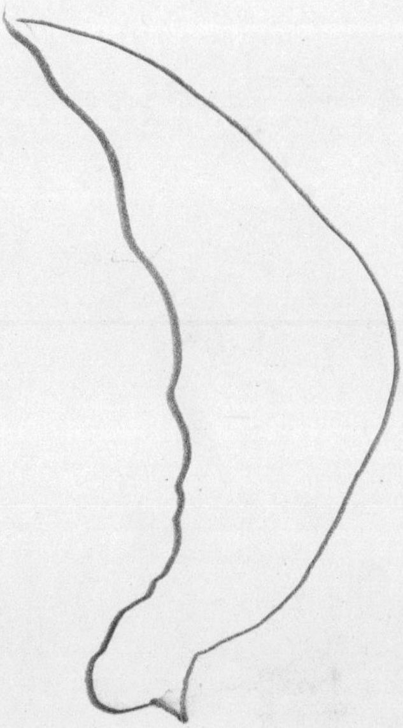

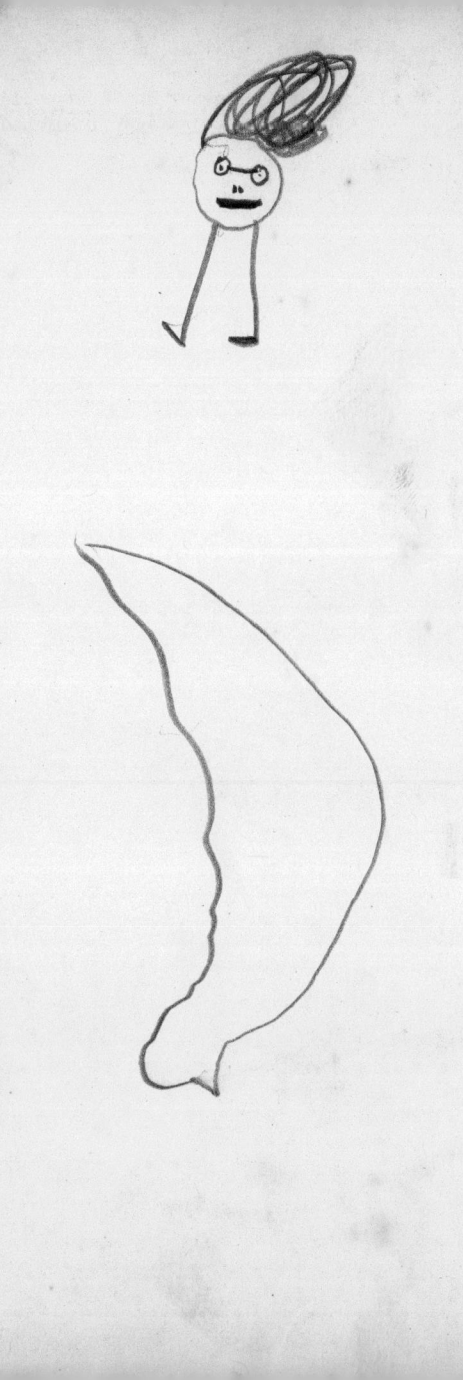

thirty one

HAPPY

you can't make me shirt
up + be her
shut up or ill rock ya

same to you

same to you